HIP AND TRIVIAL

HIP AND

Robert Wright

T R I V I A L

Youth Culture,
Book Publishing
and the Greying
of Canadian
Nationalism

Canadian Scholars' Press

Hip and trivial : youth culture, book publishing
and the greying of Canadian nationalism
by Robert A. Wright

First published in 2001 by
Canadian Scholars' Press Inc.
180 Bloor Street West, Suite 1202
Toronto, Ontario
M5S 2V6

CSPI acknowledges the financial support of the Government of Canada
through the Book Publishing Industry Development Programme for
our publishing activities.

Canadian Cataloguing in Publication Data

Wright, Robert A. (Robert Anthony), 1960 –
    Hip and trivial : youth culture, book publishing and the greying
    of Canadian nationalism

ISBN 1-55130-188-1

1. Youth – Books and reading – Canada.
2. Publishers and publishing – Canada.
3. Canadian literature – History and criticism.
4. Nationalism and literature – Canada.   I. Title.

Z1037.A1W73 2001   028.5'5'0971   C00-932959-5

Managing Editor: Ruth Bradley-St-Cyr
Marketing Manager: Susan Cuk
Cover model: Kate Zieman
Cover photo: Baudouin St-Cyr
Cover and text design: Gordon Robertson

00 01 02 03 04 05 06   6 5 4 3 2 1

Printed and bound in Canada by AGMV Marquis

For Laura and Helena,
who were reading *Pride and Prejudice*
aloud together as I was writing this. . . .

CONTENTS

Acknowledgements

It is a great pleasure for me to acknowledge those persons without whom this book would never have seen the light of day.

I am greatly indebted to my friends Patrick Tobin and William Fizet of the federal Book Publishing Industry Development Program (BPIDP), not only for commissioning this research but for providing their expertise and support at every stage in its preparation. I would also like to thank those in the Department of Heritage who offered me their comments and suggestions at a seminar I presented at Hull in February 2000, and especially Gordon Platt of the Canada Council for his valuable correspondence in the early stages of my research. I owe a special vote of gratitude to the many Canadian publishers who took the time to correspond with me, especially Jean Baird, Beth Fowler, Tim Inkster, Mike O'Connor, Andy Brown, Judith Isherwood, Darren Wershler-Henry and Joe Blades. My thanks go out as well to the many writers who contributed to this study, but especially to Andrew Pyper, Hal Niedzviecki and Russell Smith, whose extensive correspondence with me greatly informed its "generational" emphasis. Ka Yan Ng transcribed what must have seemed like miles of micro-cassette tape for me, for which I am indebted.

Lynda Allison, Ruth Bradley-St-Cyr and Keith Walden read a draft version of this book in its entirety, providing invaluable commentary and rescuing me from pitfalls large and small. Other friends and colleagues whose ideas about culture and citizenship have helped to shape my own include Jody Berland, Reginald Bibby, Molly Blyth, James Laxer, Ian McLachlan, Alan O'Connor, Joan Sangster and Jim Struthers. I am grateful to Lari Langford and her staff at Robarts Library, for providing me with a private sanctuary in which to work, and to the many anonymous Toronto Public Library workers, especially at the Sanderson branch, without whose extraordinary efficiency this project would no doubt still be in the start-up phase.

I would like to make a special point of thanking my undergraduate students, especially those in my first- and second-year Durham University Centre courses in 1999-2000. Writing about youth can be a tricky business for the not-so-young, thus I am deeply in the debt of those students who have so generously indulged my obsession with youth culture in their tutorials and seminars, and who have contributed so profoundly to my sense of what it is like to be young and powerless in a time of great social and cultural upheaval. As it happened, my students also played an important role—entirely on their own initiative—in disseminating my online reading questionnaire among their friends and peers, vastly enlarging my pool of respondents (John Neundorf was especially helpful in this respect). I do not exaggerate when I say that they have significantly deepened my faith in the liberal arts tradition, according to which professors and students learn from each other.

My deepest debts are, of course, personal. The influence of my academic mentor, the late George Rawlyk, always great, seems only to have deepened in the years since his death. By his own admission a "morbidly introspective" scholar, George never missed an opportunity to remind me that all writing is autobiography, an aphorism that seems especially germane to the study of youth culture. That he imparted to me the kind of wisdom that reveals itself even in his absence is a most extraordinary legacy; that I miss him greatly goes without saying.

I would also like to thank my father, Robert Kenneth Wright, for his unwavering support over forty years, though I am struck by how inadequate this language is to express such an enormous debt. My father has been a model of honesty, generosity and fealty to his sons, as well as source of indomitable strength— something I have come to appreciate all the more acutely since becoming a father myself. I am also greatly indebted to my brother, Daniel Wright, who is himself a writer, though here too the language of gratitude pales. Dan is perhaps my greatest ally, both personally and intellectually, and hence my most exacting critic. He read the entirely of this book in manuscript form and, as he so often does, took me to task on its broadest philosophical implications. My thanks go out as well my oldest friend, Craig Walker, now a professor of drama at Queen's but, back in the day, someone with whom I shared the many tumults and triumphs of my own youth.

My greatest debt of all is to my wife, Laura. Our first child, Helena, was born in the fall of 1999, thus I ended up writing this book through the entirety of Laura's maternity leave, while simultaneously teaching full-time in a distant city. For her extraordinary willingness to take up the domestic slack—and for making my job as a father so easy—I can hardly begin to thank her. As for Helena, words alone cannot express the wondrous effect that she has had in every facet of my existence. I lead a charmed life, and it is entirely due to the love of these two beautiful souls.

INTRODUCTION

T HIS BOOK began as a commissioned study for the Book
Publishing Industry Development Program (BPIDP) of
the federal Department of Heritage.[1] Its original mandate
was to:

> examine the current relationship between Canadian youth
> and Canadian literature. The study will consider the reasons,
> if any, for an evident retreat from reading Canadian literature
> among young Canadians. Elements such as technological
> change, differing set of values, inefficient marketing by pub-
> lishers and the collapse of traditional windows onto Cana-
> dian literature for youth will be examined in this regard. If
> possible, the disconnect of Canadian youth from Canadian
> literature may be situated in a larger social and economic
> context of youth disaffection. The author will also examine
> those cases where youth respond positively to Canadian liter-
> ature. In such instances, the study will identify what actors
> have contributed to the success of Canadian publishers in
> penetrating the youth market. The study will conclude with
> recommendations as to how public policy might be shaped,

at the federal level, to support Canadian publishers in attracting the youth franchise.

Having agreed to undertake what I thought would be a relatively modest project examining the relationship of youth and the Canadian publishing industry, I quickly discovered that very little serious research had been done in the area, and that, indeed, most of what passes for insight on the question could be summarized in a single sentence: *Youth don't read.* This powerful generalization, which I encountered practically daily as I was conducting my research, has two essential components: either young people *cannot* read, because their literacy skills are so abominable, or they *do not* read, because they have been weaned on television, video games and the Internet, and hence, they have lost both the habit of, and the capacity for, sustained concentration. They are, in a word, the "television-addicted kids with gnatlike attention spans" identified by Ray Conlogue of *The Globe and Mail,* and they represent nothing less than a standing threat to the publishing industry.[2] In essence, this book is my response to the far broader socio-cultural context within which Canadian youth have been stigmatized as illiterate and culturally benighted; and though it includes analysis of concrete issues such as publishing succession and book marketing, it is framed by a much broader contemplation of what it means to be young and to occupy such a condescended and stigmatized cultural space.

Needless to say, contemporary youth suffer under far worse stereotypes than the one claiming that they are illiterate or too lazy to read. Variously identified as "slackers," "whiners" and, of course, "Gen Xers"—a term that now signifies a dizzying array of intellectual, emotional and social defects—Canadians who came of age in the late 1980s and the 1990s live in a socio-cultural space popularly circumscribed by two extraordinary generalizations: on the one hand, youth are believed to be violent, apathetic, depoliticized, suicidal, deviant, criminal—in a word, *alien*; on the other, they have lived through, and in large measure are thought to be the products of, the hyper-commercialization of youth culture in the age of "cool hunting," Tommy Hilfiger and designer consumerism. As I will argue throughout this book, these poles—youth as deviant versus youth as savvy consumers—continue to frame public perceptions of young Canadians and even to inform public policy debate in this country. The real lives of Canadian youth—what cultural studies scholars call their "lived experience"—are, in fact, as complicated and as varied as the lives of *any* Canadians, the more so perhaps because young people today are even more likely than the population at large to be new immigrants or aboriginal people. As I will demonstrate, if there is a single defining characteristic of Canadian youth and young adults today—persons who were 35 or younger in the year 2000—it is their *downward mobility*, that is, their seemingly intractable economic marginalization, dependency (for the middle class), poverty (for the working class), isolation and alienation. Young people may, indeed, "live in their own worlds," as their older critics like to say, but these are worlds not of their own making or choosing. "Youth" today live in worlds into which adults have consigned them, sometimes well into their thirties.

Methodologically, this book reflects my disciplinary training as an historian and relies heavily upon documentary sources, including published books, articles, surveys, statistical analyses, polls, etc. Although there have been relatively few recent attempts to synthesize the existing literature into broadly accessible analyses—Paul Audley's *Canada's Cultural Industries: Broadcasting, Publishing, Records and Film* (1983) and Rowland Lorimer's more cursory "Book Publishing in Canada" (1995) are important exceptions—there is no shortage of primary published documents from which to work. The Canadian publishing industry has its own trade journals, associations and lobbyists; and the American publishing industry, of which Canada is in some important respects an adjunct, regularly directs its gaze northward. I have made extensive use of documents commissioned and published by Statistics Canada and by the National Library of Canada, two truly great national institutions whose contributions to Canadian social scientific research are incalculable (and whose historic commitment to *public* accessibility now appears to be threatened). As Canadians probably do not need to be reminded in this age of seemingly relentless "globalization," Canada's "cultural industries" are now more than ever subject to forces originating beyond their border; the same thing may also be said of "youth culture," at least insofar as trends in the lives of young people in the industrialized West (and arguably elsewhere) are themselves the products of global mass media. For this reason, I have attempted to inform my analysis, wherever possible, with reference to what is happening outside of Canada, since this seems crucial to any understanding of what is going on within.

Broadly speaking, public interest in the kinds of questions posed by my study—whether and how much young people are reading—has tended to be cyclical, and seemingly prompted as much by "political" as by socio-cultural criteria. This fact alone is of great interest to the study of youth culture, since it suggests that there is always more to these issues than meets the eye and, indeed, that agendas often having very little to do with young people themselves are sometimes being advanced at their expense.In the late 1980s, for example, there was a cluster of research exploring the role of "adolescent literature" in the amelioration of what appeared to be increasingly grave psychological and social problems then facing young people, including suicidality, adjustment to urban life, alienation among gay and lesbian youth, and the ostracization of immigrant and "ethnic" youth.[3] Simultaneously, though for more obviously mercenary reasons, the publishing trade seemed to be preoccupied with developing the "teen market," which was thought to be especially promising via-à-vis the saturation of the adult book market.[4] Today, by contrast, North Americans are obsessed—the word is not too strong—with *literacy*. The common perception that youth are illiterate has produced a singlemindedness in the research literature and especially the popular press that has eclipsed virtually all other discourses, casting a long shadow over the ways in which young people's relationship to literature and publishing is understood.

As thorough as I have attempted to be in my reading of the literature on youth and reading, there are two gaps in the documentary record of which some mention should be made at the outset. The first is that there has been no major statistical analysis of young Canadians' reading and book purchasing habits since the publication of Frank L. Graves' and Timothy Dugas' *Reading in Canada 1991* and Nancy Duxbury's *The Reading and Purchasing Public* (1995). This means that, for now at least, researchers are left to consider less rigorous data on, for example, the impact of new technologies and pastimes, most notably the Internet. I take the view that this is not an especially worrisome gap in the literature since, despite the hype, there is little evidence to suggest that people actually *read* much online (and a good deal of data showing just how little concentrated effort is expended in "surfing"); indeed, to date the Internet has actually increased book sales.[5] Moreover, the promise of the Internet as an essentially text-based medium is now giving way inexorably to a radically less democratic incarnation of the Web as a mostly corporate-dominated entertainment medium—a tendency that will be cemented before long in the "convergence" of "broad band" applications designed to carry televisual and audio entertainment, thereby effectively reproducing the biases of existing media, most notably television.[6] For the near term at least, nobody in the publishing industry seems overly worried about the possibility that the Internet might somehow "replace" books (the way it seems to be replacing compact discs, for example) and, indeed, many have discovered in the Net an exciting new means of promoting and distributing their print publications. Even Coach House Books, a Canadian firm that is quite literally pioneering the use of the Internet in the publishing and promotion of literature, has positioned itself in such a manner as to affirm that the "threat" of the Net eclipsing book publishing has been exaggerated.[7] "Net fatigue" also seems to be having a salutary effect upon book retailing—most obviously in the new emphasis on "social" space in the superstore chains—and, indeed, in the resurrection of an almost fetish-like appreciation of the "book as object." I tend to agree with Jim Allen of the Canadian publishing firm Thomas Allen and Son, who said recently: "Technology, wonderful as it is, has a monochromatic aesthetic. Let's face it, it's boring. There will always be human beings who require a sense of peace and contemplation, which they will never get from computers." [8]

The second limitation inherent in this kind of research is unique to the book publishing enterprise, and sooner or later all researchers must make their peace with it. Bluntly stated, there is no accurate means of calculating book readership, in Canada or elsewhere. On the one hand, as Rowland Lorimer has noted, book publishing is simultaneously "a cultural industry, an entertainment industry, and/or an information industry," making it "a challenge to differentiate between the cultural elements of the book publishing industry and the entertainment and informational elements."[9] Secondly, unlike newspaper and magazine publishers, who are in the business of selling audiences to advertisers, book publishers do not sell advertising and cannot say, with any degree of accuracy, whether the books they sell are ever actually read. I am reminded of a joke that circulated widely in the wake of the publication of Stephen Hawking's bestseller *A Brief History of Time*, namely that everybody bought it, few people read it and nobody understood it! (I was one of the brave souls who made it about half-way). As Walter Kirn and William Dowell have suggested sardonically, "Reading is a lot like sex. People who rarely read can feel abnormal. People who read all the time can feel abnormal. And because so much reading is done in private behind closed doors (often bedroom doors), no one really knows what normal is. A book a day? A month? A year? Do self-help books count, or only novels? What if they're on tape?" Kirn and Dowell correctly note that there seems to be a "reading renaissance" these days based upon the increasing visibility of reading in North American popular culture, from "espresso-serving superstores to the emergence on American TV and in countless living rooms of book clubs and reading groups." It is entirely possible, they conclude, that "reading books (or listening to them in the Jeep) is to the 1990s what gym-going was to the 80s: something we Americans plan to do, something we want to do and, by all appearances, something everyone else is doing, even Oprah viewers."[10]

The problem is not merely that books do not trade in advertising and, hence, that publishers have little incentive to track their readerships. Like the murky relationship between book reading and book purchasing, it is also impossible to know precisely the impact of book *borrowing* (from friends, institutions and, most obviously, libraries) and, hence, of determining which books have been more widely read than their raw sales figures might indicate. This is an especially crucial issue when it comes to the reading habits of youth since, according to the most reliable survey data, they are among the heaviest library users and also among the least likely to purchase new books at retail or through book clubs. Young people tend, moreover, to "hear about" good books through informal channels (word of mouth) rather than through official promotional channels (book reviews, ads, in-store displays). According to a 1991 survey, roughly half of the books read by Canadians are obtained from non-commercial sources, and only about 35% are purchased from bookstores or book clubs. Significantly, the number of books borrowed was estimated to more or less *equal* the number of new books purchased.[11] Used and antiquarian bookstores, exchanges and book fairs do not figure in these data, further complicating the question since, in my experience at least, the most voracious readers and collectors are often the most idiosyncratic and obsessive in their patronage of used bookstores. (My favourite shops are *all* used bookstores, and together they constitute a regular "route" through the city of Toronto over which I regularly travel for good deals and unexpected treats.) To all of this ambiguity the researcher must also add what is perhaps the most significant variable of all, namely the tendency of Canadians to exaggerate their love of books (and to understate their television viewing habits) because they know that reading is commonly perceived as *virtuous*!

These limitations notwithstanding, it seems to me a propitious time to be discussing the cultural condition of young people in Canada, hence my inclination to expand what began as a narrow policy study into a more broadly based study of youth culture. We seem to be living through an era of extraordinary paradox. We are rushing headlong into the celebrated "post-industrial" age and embracing the "information economy," yet we often hear that "print is dead." We live in an age of obsession about "declining literacy standards" yet we have never, at least in North America, been better educated. In many respects, it has been the young who have acted as the lightning rods for far more generalized worries—sometimes amounting to hysteria—about the socio-economic "revolutions" through which we are now said to be passing. Above all, in this era of globalization and what some observers see as the consolidation of a global commercial monoculture, we seem also to be living in the last days of nationalism and, in particular, at the end of the era in which literature, perhaps more than the other arts, has the power to represent "national identity." As *The Toronto Star* book critic Philip Marchand has observed, somewhat pessimistically, "We live in a period unfavourable to the production of great literature. Why this should be is an interesting question, with many possible answers, from the pervasive influence of new electronic media, to the poisonous effect of French literary theorists."[12] Academic critic Graham Knight agrees, suggesting that the very project of literary criticism is today haunted by "the lingering possibility that, in an age of global electronic media, literature no longer plays such a vital role in the formation and reproduction of the national, except perhaps in the movie version."[13] Robert Lecker, whose 1995 book *Making It Real* constitutes nothing less than a lament for the once robust nationalist strain in Canadian criticism, has argued specifically that literature and citizenship, once closely linked in Canada, have become unstuck and "downgraded" in Canadians' lived experience—a trend he believes is having its most pronounced impact among the young: "Although it would be nice to believe that teachers of Canadian literature could use their skills to enable students to become more critical of their country, pedagogy and criticism in recent years have encouraged students to focus on texts at the expense of questions of nation and on theoretical speculation to the exclusion of real political involvement in the events of national political life. . . . Today we seldom see examples of Canadian literary criticism that actually suggest a relation between the literature and the country. In fact, the very suggestion is often treated as a sign of bad taste."[14]

The severing of links between youth, reading and citizenship—evident practically everywhere throughout the industrialized West—has been particularly traumatic in Canada owing to the formative circumstances of the "Canadian Lit" project as it was conceived in the late 1960s and especially the early 1970s.

Indeed, the core historical thesis of this book is that, uniquely, youth were essential to the formation of the Canadian literary project because the era of heightened nationalism in which it arose coincided precisely with the formative years of the baby boom cohort, imprinting the latter indelibly with a profoundly *literary* view of the nation and, moreover, with what has turned out to be a lifelong predilection for "reading Canadian." The evidence suggests rather starkly that what has changed in the last thirty years is not so much that Canadian youth read less, or less voraciously, but that they are far less nationalist (at least in English Canada) and, hence, that they utterly lack the conviction that the act of reading literature—especially the officially sanctioned literature of the classroom—is somehow integral to national identity formation or, above all, to citizenship. In short, to overgeneralize only slightly, where the imaginative Canadian landscape of the baby boomers could literally be read off the page—in celebrated canonical works from L.M. Montgomery's *Anne of Green Gables* to Margaret Atwood's *Survival*—this is not true for the post-NAFTA youth of today. If any such imaginative landscape(s) inform the daily lives of young Canadians—and this premise is itself questionable in an era of globalized mass media, fashion and youth culture—they are far less likely to manifest themselves in literary form than, say, in the music of the Tragically Hip or in the latest Roots styles or, most symptomatically of all perhaps, in the semi-ironic emptiness of a Molson slogan: "I am Canadian." Where serious literature *is* being read—and especially written—by young Canadians, one finds little reference to what was once broadly understood as *the national*, a generalized hostility to the proposition that such a referent is meaningful or relevant, an explicit critique of its tendency towards romantic escapism and bourgeois complacency, and above all an abiding distrust of the literary/publishing establishment that has sustained it. In its stead, we seem to be witnessing the emergence of an entirely new imaginative landscape, one that Hal Niedzviecki has called the "concrete forest"—a highly "fragmented and anonymous" but nonetheless communal space "overgrown with the joys and terrors of the urban." This is the world of youth today, a world in which "[j]obs are harder to get, choices are fewer and less inviting, and everywhere people are encroaching on other people's time and space." Although he does not say so explicitly, Niedzviecki's "concrete forest" is itself an element in the internationalization of youth culture, in which the experience of being young and literary—whether in Toronto, London or New York—trades in an urban pop cultural vernacular and carries many of the same "cosmopolitan" meanings, many of which carry little currency among older readers and writers. These days, in literature and publishing as in music and fashion, the greatest divide is not so much geographic as it is demographic and especially socio-economic.[15]

Thus, although I am loathe to generalize about cohorts (or "generations") as if they are monolithic,[16] this book is informed throughout by my fundamental conviction that baby boomers are symbiotically linked to Canada's dominant literary/publishing culture as it has taken shape since the 1970s and younger cohorts simply are not. As everybody knows, the boomers are Canada's largest and most affluent demographic, and will remain so for the entirety of their life cycle; moreover, they are attaining levels of wealth (and especially of disposable income) which *both* their parents and their children can only dream of, a trend which promises to project their historic status as the publishing industry's golden goose well into the foreseeable future. Above all, though, the boomers' nationalist imprinting—their deeply rooted identification of literature, culture, citizenship and nation—has cast a long shadow over the entire Canadian literary/publishing culture, cementing a predictable, profitable and even enviable literary scene in this country, even as it has occasionally worked to marginalize alternative visions and voices.

Canadian publishers—beleaguered by a decade-long recession, deep cuts in government funding and the myriad challenges of globalization—can hardly be faulted for positioning
themselves in such a way as to continue to benefit from the massive (and massively profitable) baby boom readership base; nor,
even more obviously, can this readership itself be faulted for continuing to indulge literary tastes that are culturally specific to its
own time and place. Moreover, as I have taken pains to document in this book, the claim that the large Canadian publishers
and even the small established presses have ceased to innovate, to
take risks, or to reach out to youth has been grossly exaggerated.
It is true that a sort of "division of labour" akin to the relationship of "independent" and "major" record labels has grown up in
Canadian publishing, in which smaller firms do much of the
reconnaissance for the larger ones; it is also true that the small
and micro-publishers in Canada are better situated to react
quickly to changing trends at "street level," a comparative advantage which contributes to the perception that larger presses are
lagging. This is not, however, to valorize "underground" publishers as if they alone represent the literary tastes and aspirations of
youth. Young writers and especially readers represent the future
for even the largest and reputedly most risk-averse presses, and
they know it. (That it was McClelland and Stewart that published *Concrete Forest* speaks directly to this point.) As academic
critic Allan Hepburn suggested recently in *Quill & Quire*, echoing Niedzviecki, the urban fiction being pioneered by young
Canadian writers has already begun to challenge some of the core
elements in the Canadian Lit tradition, and in some of the most
"conservative" corners of the publishing industry:

> Canadian fiction has grown up, got a degree, moved to the
> big city and snagged a bad-ass job. It has taken some vacations
> abroad. It has become, in a word, cosmopolitan. Instead of

Group-of-Seven devotion to landscape, contemporary writers deal with urban realities: blind dates, chance encounters, clubbing, homelessness, nepotism, the pursuit of fame, dot-com jobs. Canadian protagonists used to go to the local rink for a hockey game; now they go to Paris or Beijing. They used to drink rye-and-coke; now they drink Chardonnay in summer and Merlot in winter. They can identify Armani, but they can't quite place Massey-Ferguson. Historical expansiveness, international sophistication, and stylistic elegance have become signatures of the best new Canadian writing.[17]

If the main historical aspect of this book is to emphasize the perhaps predictable dominance of the baby boom over Canada's literary/publishing culture, its core sociological claim may come as something of a revelation: though far less enamoured of *the national* in Canadian literature than their forebears, *Canadian youth and young adults are today better educated, more worldly, more media savvy, and more comfortable with the world of print culture than any prior cohort.* With the extremely important exception of those youth who, for whatever reason, have found themselves forced to the margins of Canadian society— most notably those who have dropped out of school—young people in Canada have been extremely well served by Canada's "culture of literacy" as it has taken shape since the 1970s. Young Canadians have, in fact, been the primary beneficiaries of what the *National Library News* has called "the public awareness of the importance of literacy practices, opportunities for using literacy skills in the workplace to keep pace with technological advances, access to libraries, support for family literacy awareness and initiatives to foster good literacy practices as part of daily life."[18] In short, as I shall demonstrate, Canadian youth have never been better equipped to enjoy a lifelong relationship with the printed word.

Because so much of the jargon of the publishing world is used rather casually, some clarification of the terminology I use throughout this book is warranted at the outset. Firstly, for reasons that will be elaborated below, I tend to use the terms "youth" and "young people" interchangeably to signify persons who are between fourteen and 22 years of age, and the term "young adult" for those between 23 and 35. (In the world of publishing and bookselling, the age range for readers of "children's" and "young adult" literature terminates at between twelve and fourteen, hence even the youngest adolescents are, from the vantage point of book *marketing*, considered consumers of "adult" literature.) I delimit the categories "youth" and "young adult" at age 22 simply because this is the approximate age at which most full-time university students graduate with their first degree—a transition into the "adult" world that often carries important consequences for their reading habits, most notably the end of "mandatory" curricular reading and increased "voluntary" reading for pleasure.

Secondly, some codification of the various kinds of publishing enterprises in this country is also in order, though here I tend to keep to established practise. I use the term "multinational" to refer to firms that have operations in Canada but which are headed elsewhere, i.e. in the United States or Europe, and I use the terms "subsidiary" and "branch plant" interchangeably to refer to the largely subordinate Canadian operations of such firms. (The recently merged Doubleday/Bantam Canada, now part of the global Bertelsmann empire, is an obvious example of this multinational/subsidiary arrangement.) "Large" Canadian firms are those which enjoy a national (rather than merely regional) presence, as well as access to resources (capital, personnel, distribution, promotion, etc.) on a scale roughly comparable to those of the foreign-owned firms with which they compete in the domestic market. (McClelland and Stewart and Canada Publishing Corporation are examples.) "Micro-publishers" are at the other end of the size/resources spectrum. They have no national presence and are often localized in a single city, they lack access either to private capital or to state subsidy, they are likely to be run as a non-profit venture (or as a money-losing labour of love), they are typically in the business of publishing low-cost zines or chapbooks rather than conventional perfect-bound books, and they are often so marginal (or impermanent) as to be excluded from official industry statistics. "Small" publishers —the great majority of the roughly 320 Canadian-owned presses tracked by Statistics Canada—occupy the rather vast space between the large and micro-publishers, having stable but relatively limited access to capital, state subsidies and other resources, and usually serving a regional or, more likely, a "niche" market (e.g. children's books or academic textbooks).

Thirdly, I must emphasize that the general tendency of this study, especially insofar as it examines literary nationalism in the context of an increasingly globalized, market-driven competitive environment, is to focus on English-Canadian literature and publishing. I have tried, wherever possible (and especially where the data permit) to note important variations as they manifest themselves within Québec publishing—most notably the evidence that young Québecois are now only about half as likely as their English-Canadian counterparts to "identify strongly with Canada." I hasten to add, however, that my analysis of "national" data on the socio-economic condition of Nineties youth in Canada—as published, for example, by Statistics Canada—takes Québec youth explicitly into account. As noted above, this study is also informed by my view that young people in Canada, including Québec, increasingly occupy the same mass-mediated cultural spaces as youth elsewhere in the industrialized world, and hence that local, regional and even national differences in young people's experience of mass culture—television, magazines, rock music, movies, fashion, etc.—matter less today than ever.

Lastly, on a more personal note, I should add that this study has been informed implicitly by my fifteen-year career teaching undergraduates and explicitly by my conversations with my students (and other young people) as the research was in progress. I am also indebted to the roughly 400 young people who responded to a questionnaire I posted on the Internet while my research was in progress; though I am by no means an expert in polling or survey-styled methodology, I have made occasional reference to their responses in such cases where they buttress other, more rigorous data.

1

BACKGROUND

The Canadian
Lit Boom

"CANADIAN LITERATURE" has been written and published
since the colonial period but "Canadian Lit" (or "Can-
Lit")—a term signifying the achievement of a critical
mass of institutional strength, commercial viability and critical
respectability—dates only from the Centennial (1967) era and,
indeed, is now widely considered to have been one of the
essential elements in the nationalist resurgence of that time. Like
the emergence and consolidation of interdisciplinary Canadian
Studies in the 1960s and early 1970s, the Canadian Lit phenomenon owed its rather meteoric success to the coincidence of several
demographic and cultural factors: the maturation into adulthood of the baby boom and the massive institutional growth this
demographic trend occasioned (most notably in higher education), the significant improvement in the national literacy rate,
the emergence of a highly visible (and literate) youth counterculture, the igniting of latent anti-Americanism (centred on a

broadly based "left-nationalist" critique of US foreign policy and the "imperialistic" practices of multinational corporations) and the dramatic expansion of state regulation and subsidy in the realm of cultural production. The Canadian Lit phenomenon is, in short, little more than thirty years old and is inextricably bound up both with the formative socio-cultural experience of the massive (and massively profitable) baby boom cohort and also to an historically specific project of national "identity" formation. These have been, generally speaking, the decisive factors in the evolution of hegemonic Canadian literary conventions and publishing strategies up to the present.

As Rowland Lorimer suggests in *Book Publishing in Canada*, apart from the 1921 Copyright Act, book publishing was not a matter for public policy in Canada until the Centennial era; nor, apparently, was the domination of the Canadian market by books from British and American publishers of much concern to Canadians.[1] Only after the sale in 1970 of W. J. Gage and the United Church-owned Ryerson Press to US firms Scott, Foresman and McGraw-Hill, respectively, did Canadians apprehend the threat of a foreign "takeover" of "their" publishing industry. Reviews of the Canadian publishing industry were undertaken by the private consulting firm Ernst & Ernst on behalf of the federal Department of Industry, Trade and Commerce in 1970 and by a Government of Ontario royal commission the following year. The latter recommended a "bailout" for McClelland and Stewart, which was also known to be ripe for foreign takeover, as well as loan guarantees for other Canadian-owned publishers—policies that were implemented over the next two years. In 1979 the Canadian Book Publishing Development Program (CBPDP) was created to "address the financial and economic base of the Canadian-controlled sector" through operating subsidies; and in 1993 its successor, the Book Publishing Industry Development Program (BPIDP), was recast with what Lorimer calls its "leadership into profitability" measures strengthened.[2]

The available data suggest that the Canadian Lit boom produced not only more and "better" literature in the 1970s but significantly increased revenues for Canadian publishers (See Figure 1.1, which shows the value of sales in the Canadian domestic book market for the period 1969-80). According to estimates in the Ernst and Ernst study, the total value of the Canadian book publishing industry in 1969 was C$222 million, indicating that sales had grown steadily at an average annual rate of 13 per cent in the previous five years—a rate of growth only slightly greater than that of the Canadian GNP. According to industry analyst Paul Audley, who is doubtful of the accuracy of the Ernst & Ernst figures, data from the annual "printing, publishing and allied industries survey" show that revenue from book sales in Canada increased by 95.4 percent between 1975 and 1980, while the GNP grew by only 75.3 per cent. In this period, Canadian-published books accounted for 27.6 per cent of total revenue from book sales in the Canadian market. In 1978 sales of Canadian-manufactured books were valued at C$224.3 million (compared with C$77.2 million in 1969), a ten-year increase of 190.5 per cent. Concludes Audley, "if the Ernst & Ernst estimates for 1969 were accurate, total book sales in the Canadian market over that same period increased by 208.6 per cent, from $222 million to $685 million."[3]

ESTIMATES OF THE CANADIAN DOMESTIC BOOK MARKET, 1969–80

($ millions % increase)

	1969	1975		1978		1979		1980	
Book sales	222	476.7	114.7%	685	43.7%	816.5	19.2%	931.7	14.1%
GNP	79,815	165,343	107.2%	230,353	39.3%	261,961	13.2%	289,859	10.6%

Figure 1.1
Source: Paul Audley, *Canada's Cultural Industries: Broadcasting, Publishing, Records and Film* (Toronto: Lorimer, 1983), p. 87.

Audley's 1983 analysis of data from the 1970s and early 1980s also revealed what Canadian-owned publishers had long known about their place in the national marketplace, namely that while they were producing the lion's share of Canadian content, foreign-controlled firms were taking the lion's share of revenues (see Figure 1.2). Concluded Audley: "While Canadian-controlled book publishing companies account for less than one-third of the industry's total sales, they produce most of the new titles that are published in Canada each year. In 1975, Canadian-controlled firms published 2,193 titles, which represented 70 per cent of the 3,127 titles the industry published that year. Canadian-controlled companies produced 3,556 titles in 1979, which represented 78 per cent of the new titles published that year. While foreign-controlled companies accounted for roughly 70 per cent of total industry revenue in 1979, and were operating very profitably, they produced only 21.6 per cent of all new Canadian titles."[4] This dilemma, one that is common to all cultural producers in

BOOKS PUBLISHED, REPRINTED AND IN PRINT FOR FOREIGN AND CANADIAN-CONTROLLED PUBLISHERS, 1975 AND 1979

Country of Control	1975			1979		
	Titles Published	Titles Reprinted	Titles in Print	Titles Published	Titles Reprinted	Titles In Print
Canada	2,193	1,892	16,563	3,556	2,525	27,264
U. S.	786	868	4,903	751	758	5,036
U. K.	148	250	1,037	227	347	2,259
TOTAL	3,127	2,010	22,503	4,534	3,630	34,559

Figure 1.2
Source: Paul Audley, *Canada's Cultural Industries: Broadcasting, Publishing, Records and Film* (Toronto: Lorimer, 1983), p. 102.

Canada, has obtained in Canadian publishing up to the present and constitutes the essential *raison d'etre* for "protectionist" government policies up to and including the BPIDP.

Literary critic Robert Lecker is one of many academic observers to lament that, in retrospect, the rise of Canadian Lit was simply *too* meteoric. Writing in 1995, he noted: "Too much had been accomplished. Too fast. In three decades we had witnessed the creation of a full-blown industry—a powerful government-supported network comprised of academics and publishers involved in the teaching, study and promotion of Canadian literature and literary criticism. This industry contributed to the formation of the institution of English Canadian literature, a university-based culture devoted to the study of the nation's literature, a culture defined by rules, customs, and ways of speaking that made the members of the institution (and the literature it studied) seem separate, special, and powerfully self-sustaining." Such an intensity was not, in fact, sustainable. As early as the 1980s Canadian literature seemed to be suffering from a creeping complacency: "Orthodoxy was up. Passion was down. The operative metaphor was closure."[5]

The apparent rise and fall of Canadian Lit, at least insofar as it was an "institution" that engaged the public, is of more than academic interest to Lecker and other critics. They worry that Canadians have lost interest in a fundamental question, namely "What [is] the relationship between Canadian literature and citizenship?" Lecker has, in fact, extended his disillusionment with the current state of literary criticism into a full-blown analysis of this once-potent relationship, concluding that the historic Canadian concern for identity (or, as he prefers to put it in the pluralistic vernacular of today, *identities*) must be rejuvenated: "[T]he formation of the English Canadian literary institution was driven by the desire to see literature as a force that verified one's sense of community and place. In this view, literature becomes a medium that refers us to the connection between writing, culture, and nation. . . . This assumption inspires most Canadian criticism written up to the 1980s; in fact ever since the nineteenth century, canonical activity in Canada has been driven by different applications of the national-referential ideal, and by the assumption that *a country without a national literature is not a country at all*" (emphasis added). These days, Lecker notes pessimistically, under the considerable pressure of postmodernism and especially post-structural cultural theory, critics simply "assume that the relation between literature and nation is tainted—a subject to be avoided—even though it is precisely this relation that inspired the formation of the [literary] institution and allowed it to (briefly) thrive."[6]

Though written primarily for his fellow academics, Lecker's concerns about the dislocation of literature and citizenship are crucially important for Canadians' relationship to "their" literature, and especially for young people's encounters with Canadian writing. Lecker makes an important distinction between the "private" and "public" worlds of reading, noting that the once "popular" practise of discussing Canadian literature among academic *and* non-academic readers has been usurped by a formal "criticism" that is today irrelevant outside of the classroom: "[I]n most contemporary discussions of Canadian literature (including my own) the public is left outside, while professionals develop the orthodoxy of specialization in the confines of an increasingly privatized club. . . . [T]he idea that there might be a public audience for Canadian criticism now seems absurd to most specialists in the field. . . . [T]here is no discussion about the relationship between literature and community. We don't seem to believe that the public audience has any literary competence, or that it belongs at our academic affairs. We talk privately. We hoard what we own."[7]

The goal for the literati, Lecker implies—and this observation may be extended to all who work in what he calls the literature "industry," including publishers—is not merely to engage once again with the public readership for Canadian literature but also to acknowledge openly that, whatever it *might* have been in the heyday of Canadian Lit, the Canada of the twenty-first century is pluralistic, multicultural and postmodern: "The argument that there is no monolithic Canada is self-evident. Once this is accepted, there is no choice but to imagine the 'actual society' in an entirely new way." This is, for Lecker at least, a populist and even a democratizing project: "We have to explain that whatever idea we have of the country is constructed, and that everyone can participate in this construction. Everyone can make it real, which means that the country can become a collective fiction that is constantly renewed. After all, Canada is nothing less than a dramatic narrative about community. The strongest expressions of this new community will be those that recreate the country by imagining it anew." The situation is critical, Lecker warns, because already "the noncurricular audience for Canadian literature is extremely small." The implications for Canadian youth (though he does not single out young people explicitly) would seem to be ominous: "[T]he reality is that the actual reading community inhabits a tiny island in a sea of illiteracy. There is no way that, under current circumstances, the study of Canadian literature will have any effect on the public at large."[8]

Read Canadian

The claim that Canadian readers today inhabit "a tiny island in a sea of illiteracy" is overstated, but concerns about the dislocation of Canadian literature and its popular readership—especially young readers—do indeed stand in marked contrast to the late 1960s and early 1970s, when young people were commonly thought to have "discovered" Canadian literature! (More than one observer has noted, for example, the characteristic cross-pollenization of the poetry, fiction and popular music of the Sixties counterculture in Canada, most obviously in the work of Leonard Cohen, whose second novel, *Beautiful Losers*, became a blockbuster only *after* he was signed to Columbia Records.)[9] The sense of nationalist *urgency* in the Centennial era—characterized by an unprecedented desire to assert Canadian cultural, political and especially economic autonomy vis-à-vis the United States—set the tone for the Canadian Lit renaissance and, in myth if not in reality, young people were at the centre of the movement. Fusing left-nationalist ideology (much of it borrowed, ironically, from the New Left in the US), the energy and ideas of the counterculture (many of which were borrowed, equally ironically, from older Canadian nationalists like George Grant), and the crusading entrepreneurial spirit made possible by a relatively healthy economy, the largesse of the state and the emergence of the massive "youth market," the goal of building Canadian literature/publishing into what would today be called a "world class" enterprise was literally awash with the exuberance of Sixties youth.

Many texts from the Centennial era capture this spirit of youthful confidence and enthusiasm for the new nationalist literary project—Margaret Atwood's *Survival* in particular stands out as one of the most exemplary (and now arguably the most maligned) standardbearer of the period.[10] The book that seems to best capture the literary *zeitgeist* of its times, however, especially where Canadian publishing is concerned, is *Read Canadian: A Book About Canadian Books*, a now largely forgotten (and for many, no doubt, anachronistic) compendium edited jointly by Robert Fulford, David Godfrey and Abraham Rotstein.[11] Published the same year as *Survival* (1972) but lacking both its coherent thematic focus and the seductive elegance of Atwood's prose, *Read Canadian* offers a glimpse not only at the undiluted and unabashed nationalist exuberance of the early 1970s but, more importantly, at the subtle and not-so-subtle ways in which this enthusiasm translated into what might be called the militant, youth-oriented CanLit project.

Fulford, then editor of *Saturday Night* magazine and a well known author in his own right, introduced *Read Canadian* as "a handbook, a guide to a couple of dozen separate fields of expertise that can be approached in a Canadian context." Ever the public intellectual, he added that it would "serve equally well for the citizen exploring a subject that has begun to interest him, a student working on his own or a teacher exploring a field new to him" [*sic*]. For Fulford, the pressing need for a book on Canadian books had become most obvious in his encounters with English teachers who were well trained in literature but who had practically no exposure to Canadian writing and certainly no sense of how to teach it. Thus, with a casualness typical of the era, nationalism and pedagogy were fused: "Canadian books should be part of the curriculum in our high schools, our community colleges and our universities. . . . [I]t is self-evident that in Canadian education, Canadian books should play a major role: without them we cannot begin to understand Canada's situation, values and problems."[12]

Read Canadian was divided into five broad fields—history, economics and politics, society, literature and the arts, books and publishers—and further into subsections, most of which were written by academic specialists. Virtually all of the authors selected for inclusion were explicitly nationalist and progressive, hence the book's concern with subjects that in some cases now seem quite dated, including Lynn McDonald's extraordinarily liberal treatment of "Drugs" and Abe Rotstein's characteristically partisan survey of "Foreign Control of the Economy." Nowhere is the book's strident, activist agenda more striking than in the final section, written jointly by David Godfrey and James Lorimer

and entitled "Publishing in Canada." Godfrey was then a professor of English at the University of Toronto, a recent Governor
General's Award-winner for fiction and a celebrated independent
publisher, while Lorimer, also a U of T professor, had just com-
menced his lifelong career in Canadian publishing as a founding partner of James, Lewis & Samuel (publisher of *Read
Canadian*). They began with the commonsensical observation
that, contrary to popular opinion, there already existed plenty of
writing on Canada and by Canadians; only because of the colonized condition of Canadian culture was it unknown to its citizens. Lest readers jump to the conclusion that they advocated a
"narrow nationalism" of the kind that cuts Canada off from the
"great international free flow of ideas," Godfrey and Lorimer put
forward an argument which has since become commonplace for
cultural nationalists in Canada: "Of course no one is saying that
people should stop reading American books or British books, or
Dutch or Swedish or Belgian books for that matter. What we
both would say, however, is that Canadians should learn about
themselves and their own country, and that they have an obligation to do that before they become better informed than most
Americans about the US, or more English than the English. Only
in a country as colonized and as deprived of its own sense of itself
as this one would such a position be regarded as anything other
than obvious." They regarded literature, moreover, as a cultural
pursuit uniquely worthy of nurture and protection: "Writing and
publishing is at the heart of every country's cultural and intellectual life, and book publishing is a key activity whose importance
to national life is far greater than the small contribution it makes
as an industry to a country's gross national product."[13]

Godfrey's and Lorimer's analysis of the book publishing
industry in Canada borrowed heavily from the critique of foreign
investment and especially branch plant-style corporate management popularized by their *Read Canadian* co-authors, Mel

Watkins and Abe Rotstein: "[T]he best estimates available suggest that no more than 5 per cent of the books bought every year in Canada are books written by Canadians and published by Canadian-owned firms. The book-publishing industry is at present dominated by foreign branch plants, some of them British but most of them American. Publishing is not quite in the same category as the oil industry, the auto industry, or the computer industry, which are almost totally American owned. But it has come perilously close." In most industrialized nations, they noted, book publishing accounted for between 0.21 and 0.24 per cent of annual GNP, whereas in Canada it accounted for only for 0.06 per cent. They surmised, therefore, that with a GNP of $100 billion in Canada in 1972, "the national book-publishing industry—including the output of those foreign subsidiaries operating in the country—is producing something like $60 million worth of books instead of $210 million." In short, they concluded: "The present gross underdevelopment of our branch-plant-dominated publishing industry connects directly to the gross underdevelopment of our national cultural life at every level, from books on gardening and travel to poetry and philosophy."[14]

Godfrey and Lorimer were pleased to report that, in the aftermath of the Ryerson sale, the remaining "Canadian-owned English-language publishers" had formed a new trade organization, the Independent Publishers' Association, the explicit goal of which was to agitate for "government measures to halt the US takeover and to make available the capital that these firms needed in order to continue to operate and to expand their activities." Virtually all Canadian-owned book publishers affiliated themselves with the IPA, which came to embrace both the "small, relatively new young houses" (Peter Martin Associates, Hurtig Publishers, Tundra Books, House of Anansi) as well as several larger firms including Clarke-Irwin and University of Toronto Press; only McClelland and Stewart declined membership, they noted, "apparently considering itself big and important enough not to need the strength of a trade association for protection."[15] This would not be the last time that dissention between small and large presses would assume a nationalist tone.

For Godfrey and Lorimer, as for the editors of *Read Canadian* and other cultural nationalists of the day, the debate over Canadian ownership of Canadian publishing houses (and the broader debate over American control of the Canadian economy) was timely for precisely the reason that Canadians' interest in "their" literature had achieved critical mass. They bluntly accused Canadian subsidiaries of American firms of ignoring Canadian writing for decades while Canadian firms had been painstakingly (and thanklessly) building up an audience for it, then creaming off the best Canadian writers once they had become profitable. The time was right, they insisted, for a concerted effort by Canadians in support of their own publishers: "We are all aware of the growing interest of Canadians in their country, and accompanying this has been a growing interest in Canadian books of all kinds. Good work is being done in a wide range of fields; new writers are appearing all the time; and publishers—almost without exception the Canadian-owned houses, particularly the small and relatively new ones—are bringing out more and more books and managing not to lose money in the process."[16]

In the final pages of "Publishing in Canada," Godfrey and Lorimer set out an extremely aggressive activist agenda by which Canadians—and in particular young Canadians—were urged to support Canadian-owned publishing and resist the encroachments of US-owned branch plants. Students were urged to "refuse to buy books published by branch plants even if they're required reading. Rely on library copies or Xeroxes instead." Librarians were to be lobbied to purchase and stock "every book mentioned in *Read Canadian*." Canadian book lovers were urged to join the only "All Canadian book club" (the Readers' Club of

Canada) and to cancel their memberships in the (American) Book of the Month Club; they were also urged to join the mailing lists of Canadian-owned publishers, and to write letters to the editors of newspapers complaining that they do not carry regular reviews of "important new Canadian books." Students were encouraged to "check to see if there aren't Canadian books" on subjects for which American books were being used in their classrooms and, if so, to "unilaterally substitute the Canadian for the American." Canadian university students were especially encouraged to "give an inscribed presentation copy of *Read Canadian* to every one of your US professors."[17]

Taken as a whole, *Read Canadian* emerges as a pivotal text in what might be called the politicization of Canadian literature/ publishing in a climate of resurgent nationalism and virtually unprecedented anti-Americanism. Like *Survival*, it represented what was by the early 1970s commonly understood to be a seamless fusion of the left-nationalist critique of cultural imperialism and the anti-establishment politics of the youth counterculture. In the years since its publication, the essential fragility of this fusion—and, more obviously, the waning of economic nationalism and of countercultural idealism generally—has eroded the relevance of *Read Canadian*'s activist strategies. Yet the vestiges of this powerful alliance are everywhere to be seen today—in the content, style and even the institutional *structures* of contemporary Canadian writing/publishing. Forged in the crucible of left-nationalism and the youth counterculture, it may be argued, the publishing industry in Canada remains, even now, wedded both to the aesthetic sensibility of this formative period—as evinced by the seemingly indefatigable dominance of the likes of Margaret Atwood—and, more particularly, to the baby boom cohort itself, whose numbers, affluence and love of books have anchored it ever since.

Canada's Literary Culture

In October 1997 Philip Marchand wrote a bluntly worded, highly controversial article for *Saturday Night* entitled "What I really think about Margaret Laurence, Michael Ondaatje, Margaret Atwood, Timothy Findley, and the rest of the CanLit crowd." After eight years as book review editor for the *Toronto Star,* Marchand was fed up with the Canadian literary *status quo*, and he did not mince words explaining why. Taking aim at the group of ageing, established writers Margaret Laurence had once affectionately called the "tribe," Marchand attacked the Canadian Lit canon mercilessly: "No-one who has read them at all widely can read, say, Laurence or Atwood or Davies, and not recognize that they are, when all is said, minor writers." Echoing Robert Lecker's observation that "too much had been accomplished" since the 1970s, Marchand mocked the largely government-funded infrastructure that sustains Canadian writers: "During the years of Laurence's matriarchate, more and more people discovered that they could devote most, if not all, of their working hours to writing and not starve to death. Not only was there in place a social safety net—pogey, welfare, and so on—but there was a range of benefits targeted to writers. Federal and provincial grants. Jobs as teachers of creative-writing courses and writers-in-residence at universities, colleges, libraries." The problem, said Marchand, had became endemic: "For a couple of decades . . . economic survival became ever more assured for Canadian writers, and, in Darwinian fashion, the species multiplied accordingly. The majority had modest claims to literary glory, but firm identities as writers. The notion of belonging to a 'tribe' strongly appealed to them because it shored up that identity."[18]

Marchand's critique was framed by what might be called a "generational" perspective; however much one might agree or disagree with his claims about established Canadian writers, his observations about the failure of Canadian writing/publishing to renew itself are not easily dismissed. As far as Marchand was concerned, the Canadian literary establishment that had coalesced in the 1970s and entrenched itself in the 1980s had, by the 1990s, simply ossified. Protecting their own claims to public affection (and, perhaps more importantly, to public subsidy), the tribe had circled the wagons and established a literary/publishing culture that had become risk-averse in the extreme, abetting mediocrity among established writers, and locking out new talent and fresh ideas. Speculating that Margaret Atwood's acclaim as a writer of fiction will probably not endure beyond her own time, for example, Marchand specifically suggested that her "prodigious reputation in English Canada . . . stems in large part from her ability to express, in almost all facets of her career, a mental outlook widely shared by her contemporaries." Like Tennyson, he predicted, Atwood "will have her literary reputation undergo the scrutiny of readers who no longer find her thoughts on social issues bracing and revelatory."[19] However indelicate, few arguments for succession in the world of Canadian literature/publishing are so provocative: to be "bracing and revelatory," literature must be renewed.

For Marchand, ever the iconoclast, the important question for the literary critic ought to be a simple one: "What do you actually like to read, as opposed to what you think people should read?" Unfortunately, he mused, "Too many novels I've read in the past eight years have been the kind where you mentally keep subtracting the pages you've read from the total number, like an unruly child in the backseat of a car asking his parents, 'When are we going to get there.'" Comparing a couple of sentences from Russell Smith's *How Insensitive* to Michael Ondaatje's *The English Patient*, Marchand praised the spare prose of the former and asserted bluntly that the latter is comprised of "the kind of verbal embroidery that is called 'beautiful prose' by people who like

gobs of marmalade on their toast."[20] Further, in a sardonic allu-
sion to the fact that people often purchase books they do not (or
cannot) read, he quipped that *The English Patient* is the book
"most frequently begun by readers and not finished since Stephen
Hawking's *A Brief History of Time.*" Verbose, self-important,
pedantic—for Marchand, Canadian literature itself had become
as staid as the academic criticism described by Lecker; established
Canadian writers had lost their edge, while younger, lesser known
writers were having all the "fun." Noting that the "new journalism" (among other stylistic innovations) has had a salutary effect
upon younger Canadian authors, Marchand suggested provocatively that non-fiction had assumed an unprecedented importance vis-à-vis fiction in Canada: "How much more fun . . . to
read about the new, elaborate subcultures of high school students
than, say, the reverie of some character remembering how rotten
his father was, or how a sunny day on the prairie once revealed to
him the numinous mystery of the universe."[21]

Andrew Pyper is an acclaimed "new" Canadian novelist (born
1968) who has been published by both small and large publishing
houses; he has also taught creative writing at the university level
and reading seminars for students of both high school and university levels. For Pyper, echoing Marchand, the problem of renewal in the world of Canadian fiction has become critical. He
believes that "younger readers are feeling increasingly alienated
from mainstream CanLit" and that this "pronounced generational divide in Canadian writing" is based not merely on age,
but also on aesthetics:

> While we as Canadian readers are right in celebrating the
> enormous success of the generation of writers currently dom-
> inating the mainstream (i.e., everyone from Bonnie Burnard
> on up) there is a conspicuous lack of widespread acknowl-
> edgement of the writers immediately behind this generation

(roughly in the age group from 25 to 40). For example, of the 10 titles shortlisted for the Giller and Governor General's prizes [in 1999], only two were offered by a writer under the age of 47. This in a year notable for the very work of many younger writers (Zsuszi Gartner, Michael Winter, Lynn Crosbie, Michael Turner, to name only a few. . . .)."22

Pyper speaks specifically of an "institutional bias" which maintains that the only "real" Canadian literature of value is that which represents the "dominant (i.e., 45-plus) generation and their attendant concerns." He notes that younger writers are sometimes viewed as "provocative novelties" but also that there is "a distancing between the powers-that-be in literary recognition (i.e., the CBC, universities, school boards, prize juries) and the up-and-comers. The 45-plussers are doing the noble, good work, and the rest of us are attention-hungry shit disturbers who write about nothing but the superficiality of sex, drugs and rock and roll. This, as with all stereotypes, is untrue."23

Like Marchand, Andrew Pyper is highly critical of the failure of what he calls "taught literature" to renew itself. He notes that books chosen for undergraduate and high school reading lists, for example, "tend to be quiet, earnest, uneventful, 'reaffirming,' morally obvious (if also technically accomplished) texts." He also believes that, while this tradition may be "expedient for inherently cautious and conservative school boards," it does "little to inflame the contemporary imaginations of today's youth." Pyper argues for "a more equitable mix between 'established' texts and those of younger voices" in the hope that a better balance would "show young people that reading CanLit need not be an exercise in fawning repetition, but an exploration of our country's true diversity." He admits that it is easier to criticize the status quo than it is to offer practical solutions for renewal but there are, he notes, some hopeful signs: the "healthy existence of small literary

presses are essential in this regard," as is "the continued vibrancy
of literary festivals and public readings that introduce younger
writers to audiences." Pyper's appeal, not only for renewal generally but for a renewed emphasis on diversity in Canadian litera-
ture/publishing, is eloquent and impassioned: "Diversity is often
cited as a value that Canadian culture holds in high regard. But
real cultural diversity is not achieved through the reassuring
rhetoric of equal regional/ethnic/gender representation. It is a
matter of opening the doors wide to a broad range of perspectives, attitudes and aesthetics. It requires our society to look at
things in its literature it may not be used to seeing there, un-
savoury or weird or troubling aspects of our contemporary reality
that have not previously been considered as properly occupying
the rarefied space of 'literary.'"[24]

If, as Marchand and Pyper suggest, there are mounting worries within Canada about the failure of the national literary/
publishing culture to foster renewal and innovation—especially
where youth are concerned—it must be conceded, somewhat paradoxically, that from the vantage point of many authors and industry observers the consolidation of this culture over several decades
has produced one of the world's most enviable literary scenes.
Guy Vanderhaeghe, for example, winner of the 1998 Governor-
General's Literary Award for *The Englishman's Boy*, has observed
that "[n]ames like Margaret Atwood and Alice Munro and Carol
Shields have created a huge amount of pride. And there's now
a generation of people who have studied Canadian literature in
school and university. We don't have a highly developed pop
culture, and writers have a much higher profile, comparatively
speaking, than in other countries. I can't think of a comparable
figure in the United States who has the kind of presence of an
Atwood or a Richler."[25] Similarly, John Pearce, editor-in-chief of
Doubleday Canada, credits the Canadian system of grants and
subsidies with having nurtured a first-class literary/publishing

environment: "The way Canada has funded literature has meant that in this country literary figures are sitting up there on the bestseller list along with the big American blockbuster writers. There's help not only for writers and literary publishing programs but also for author tours, support for writing schools, and amazingly, the public has followed all this, and so has the bookselling community. People here still have visions of writing the Great Canadian Novel." (He adds, parenthetically, that "sometimes American fiction can be a hard sell [in Canada], because there's this sense of obligation to support Canadian writers.")[26] Ever the optimist, Jack Stoddart, head of General Publishing in Canada, has boasted more than once recently that Canada has a "more serious reading public" than the United States.[27]

In publishing as elsewhere, nothing succeeds like success. There is evidence, most notably in the American trade press, that such high opinions of the Canadian literary scene as Pearce's and Stoddart's are not only widely shared outside Canada but integral to the international reputation of Canadian writers (and, at least theoretically, to the value of Canadian literary exports). Writing in the US-based trade magazine *Publishers Weekly* in May 1998, John F. Baker praised the "growing international repute of Canadian writers," among whom he named the late Robertson Davies, Margaret Atwood, Alice Munro, Mavis Gallant and the "apparently reborn Mordecai Richler," as well as a "new generation of widely respected writers with an international following—Anne Michaels, Barbara Gowdy, Carol Shields, Michael Ondaatje, Guy Vanderhaeghe, Rohinton Mistry, and Jane Urquhart."[28] The benefits to the book publishing industry of Canada's maturing literary culture, he enthused, were everywhere to be seen: "The publishing capital of Toronto, once seen as a provincial backwater, is now one of the compelling North American cities, with a vibrant book community, lively scouts and agents, an internationally acclaimed author event in the annual Harbourfront Festival, and a reputation as a city second only to New York as a port of call for overseas scouts and publishing folk."[29] Echoing Pearce and Stoddart, Baker added that "Canada has a reading public that seems to care deeply for the literary works its best writers produce, and a government policy that has helped encourage the growth and publication of such writers."[30]

Whether Canada's growing international reputation as a literary powerhouse is mere boosterism is not easy to tell. Noting somewhat sardonically that Canada has become "the country of the literary gabfest" in recent years, *Maclean's* journalist Diana Turbide has suggested, perceptively, that the apparent success of authors' festivals and other promotional strategies must be gauged within a broad cultural context: "All these literary love-ins are occurring at a time when conventional wisdom holds that the word is dead while the image is paramount, that North America is becoming increasingly illiterate. All this at a time when government support for the arts has declined precipitously."[31] Carleton University professor and author Tom Henighan is equally critical, arguing that "publishers' marketing strategies and the media have glamorized the image of the author," and not always to the benefit of literature. "The writer has become a minor cult figure," he notes. "It is the name, the image, that's being marketed: 'come see the famous Ondaatje or Atwood.' It has got very little to do with the intimate experience of reading an author's books. The name precedes the experience—that's how our culture works."[32] Turbide would seem to agree, noting that, in spite of their growing audiences—the Toronto International Festival of Authors alone attracts upwards of 14 000 fans these days—Canadian publishers are not unambiguously prepared to say that the festivals "translate into sales."[33] The anecdotal evidence suggests, however, that the festivals do indeed "rely on a hard-core of passionate readers" and that this experience of participating in literature, however superficially, can only be good for the cause of reading.

As Greg Gatenby, artistic director of the Toronto festival, points out: "Literature is the only art form that you take naked into bed with you. Good writers have a unique ability to get inside your head. They can articulate things that you may not have even realized you felt. People still come up to me at readings and tell me, 'You know, that book changed my life. And I'm thrilled to finally see the person who wrote it.'"[34]

2

PUBLISHING
IN CANADA

The Publishing
Recession of
the 1990s

E VEN THE MOST CURSORY GLANCE at the sales figures for
Canadian book publishers in the 1990s seems to illuminate
the paradox suggested by Diana Turbide and others: Canada
is commonly thought to have developed into one of the world's
most vital and enviable literary cultures in the 1990s, yet for virtually the entirety of this decade the Canadian publishing industry
has been hobbled by sluggish growth, diminishing margins,
declining subsidies and—according to some observers—poor
morale. Canadian publishing appears never to have fully recov-
ered from the economic recession of the early 1990s, nor from
severe cuts to government grants at mid-decade. At the time of

writing, the Canadian publishing industry had only just begun to partake of the economic recovery in Canada.

In 1996–97, the most recent year for which Statistics Canada has published comprehensive longitudinal data on the Canadian publishing industry, there were 321 Canadian publishers.[1] In that year they published a total of 10 497 titles, of which 2 319 were textbooks, 950 children's books, 4 487 trade books and 2 741 titles classified as "other." The total number of reprinted titles for the year was 7 210, while the total number of books in print was 81 216. Total sales in the Canadian market in 1996–97 amounted to C$1.47 billion—up from C$1.24 billion in 1991–2 and C$1.25 billion in 1992–3, the hardest years of the recession. Total revenue —in all markets, including exports—for 1996–97 were C$1.94 billion, up from C$1.52 from the early 1990s. Before-tax profits on all sales for 1996–97 amounted to C$77 million, or 4.0 percent of revenues. In 1996–97, only half (53.9 percent) of the publishing firms surveyed by Statistics Canada showed any profit; given the reputedly dire financial situation of Canadian micropublishers, many of which are not represented in official statistics, the general state of Canadian-owned firms' profitability is probably even worse. According to an industry rule of thumb, a typical Canadian work of fiction currently sells 2 500, and nonfiction, 3 500. Because of the economies of scale in the publishing industry, however, profits usually only begin after sales of 5 000 units, and even then provide publishers with only modest margins.[2] Writing for *Maclean's* in late 1997, journalist Anita Elash summarized the situation facing Canadian book publishers: "The publishing industry has persevered through hard times when no one believed there was much of a future. Only a handful of companies consistently make a profit or even expect to. In fact, most independent Canadian houses pride themselves on their willingness to ignore economics in favour of worthy projects that might otherwise never see the light of day. Most are buffered by the ever-diminishing government grants, and a few make up for their losses by distributing imported titles." Given that only 30 percent were ever likely to see profit, however, Elash insisted that the health of a company at any given time remained as precarious as ever. One or two poor-selling titles can bankrupt a Canadian publisher, while a well-selling title can buoy it up well beyond expectation. (She cited the example of David K. Foote's and Daniel Stoffman's *Boom Bust and Echo*, which by mid-August 1996 had sold 212 000 copies and had, therefore, effectively subsidized the publication of lesser books by its publisher Macfarlane, Walter & Ross. By 1999 sales of this title had reached roughly 600 000, making this best selling Canadian non-fiction book ever.)[3]

As Paul Audley and other industry analysts have known for decades, Canadian publishers—like virtually all cultural producers—face numerous challenges which might be called "systemic," some of which are common to all small-market countries and others, unique to Canada.[4] Chief among these is the obvious limitation of having a linguistically divided population (with only 19 million English-speakers) spread across a vast territory. Further, as nationalists within the Canadian publishing industry have been claiming since the *Read Canadian* era, Canada is singularly exposed to the competition of English-language titles from U.K. and U.S. publishing houses, leaving the Canadian market perennially saturated with more books than it can "absorb." A further problem, according to some American observers, is that Canada has traditionally been "underbook-shopped," meaning that there have been not only too few bookstores but a rather lethargic bookstore culture—something that had begun to change in the late 1990s with the introduction of "superstores" (Chapters and Indigo) and innovative online programs.[5]

At least as dramatic as the recession in their impact upon Canadian-owned book publishers have been cuts to government funding. (According to *Government Expenditures on Culture*, a

Statistics Canada document published in October 1999, "1997–98 represents the eighth straight year that total government spending on culture has declined." Further: "Over the last five years [1994–9], federal spending per person fell $13 to $89 in 1997–98, while provincial-territorial spending was down $12 to $57.")[6] In 1997 Anita Elash described the impact that federal belt-tightening was having upon the book publishing industry specifically, noting that the 55 percent (C$25 million) cut in federal publishing grants announced that year were pushing many publishers, especially the small houses, "perilously close to the edge." Already, she reported, declining grants had forced smaller presses to undertake much more aggressive marketing strategies and, indeed, much more mercenary ones. ECW Press in Toronto, for example, acclaimed for its scholarly works on Canadian literature, had responded to cuts in grants and library budgets by reducing the number of titles it produces annually by a third, and also by adopting a strategy of publishing "moneymakers"— including hockey books and celebrity biographies—designed to subsidize the serious half of its list.[7]

The most sensational "failure"—said to have sent "shockwaves through Canada's small press industry"—was that of Coach House Press in Toronto, one of Canada's most "prestigious" small houses (and one-time home to Margaret Atwood and Michael Ondaatje). According to reports in the trade press, the 31-year-old firm had adjusted reasonably well to the nearly C$190 000 in federal funding cuts with which they were faced between 1994 and 1996, largely because they had known about the reductions in advance and had had time to downsize (they reduced their staff to two employees and adjusted their publication schedule for maximum profitability in the fall season). Having accommodated to the federal cuts, however, Coach House was "completely unprepared" for the 74 percent reduction (equalling C$54 202) in its provincial grants announced in 1996, and could see no alternative but to close. (Committed to a dramatic reduction in the size of government in Ontario, the Conservatives under Premier Mike Harris also dissolved the Ontario Development Corporation, which had guaranteed loans for book publishers, reduced the budget of the Ontario Arts Council by 29 percent, and cut funding for schools and libraries. Asked about the demise of Coach House in July of 1996, Premier Harris was reported as saying that budget cuts were not to blame; the publisher was simply "the victim of poor management.")[8] Fortunately, Coach House *Press* has since been re-born as Coach House *Books*, with vigorous print and online lists in the late 1990s.

The question of government subsidy for the publishing industry remains (or perhaps is *again*) contentious, even after the budget-slashing exercises of the mid-1990s. Foreign-controlled publishers seem generally to take the position, as David Kent of Random House puts it, that there is "too much government support going to publishers that don't really need it."[9] On the other hand, as Beverley Slopen has argued recently in *Publishers Weekly*, there is a general perception even among outside observers that "relatively small" grants from government have "contributed to the development of one of the liveliest literary cultures in English today." Slopen quite correctly (and eloquently) notes that the dictates of the free market are no guarantee of a quality literary/publishing culture: "It is not true that all good books get published eventually; good books don't even get written without a vigorous publishing and bookselling community and receptive readers. The results are visible in Canadian bookshops and on Canadian bestseller lists. And many of the fruits are available in American and international bookstores."[10] Critic Robert Lecker is even more emphatic, asserting that it is really only through the support of the federal and provincial funding agencies that "literary life in Canada" survives at all—a claim substantiated by the longitudinal data on Canadian publishers' marginal profitability.

"Without such support, the remaining signs of literary life in Canada would probably vanish. There would be no more readings, no more authors on tour, hardly any advertising, few new books. Most publishing companies would fold. Academics would find it impossible to publish their studies. . . . [W]hile this scenario may seem extreme, anyone who is involved in writing about or publishing Canadian literature knows (or needs to know) that the end of government support is the end of the game."[11]

Given that the funding crisis has passed, and that the economic tide appears to be turning in Canada generally, it would seem to be a propitious time to be discussing the renewal of Canadian publishing. Early in 1998, after almost a decade of lacklustre performance from Canadian publishers, *Publishers Weekly* reported optimistically that there finally seemed to be a break in the "long, long book trade recession" in Canada, in large measure because the "revolution" in publishing and bookselling occasioned by globalization and new electronic media had finally begun to pay dividends.[12] As recently as May 1999, the same trade journal reported of the future of Canadian book publishing: "[B]y and large what was once a struggling industry trying to reach a small but vastly extended readership by fairly antiquated retail and distribution channels has continued to improve its profits and prospects in the [last] year. . . ."[13] Jack Stoddart, for one, is wildly optimistic about the future: "In Canada we'll have a market growth of at least 20 percent in the next two years. When we hit our recession, it was more severe than in the US. We've had almost no growth in the sales of books since 1990, whereas the US market has had an annual increase of 7 percent to 9 percent."[14] Paul Davidson, former executive director of the Association of Canadian Publishers (ACP) and now a VP at Stoddart, put the case more realistically: "There has never been a good time to be a publisher in Canada, but if there is one, Canada is seeing it now."[15]

Globalization

With what may well turn out to be only a *slight* exaggeration, Bridget Kinsella introduced the "millennial" edition of *Fiction Writer* magazine with the observation that the last few years have seen the most "dramatic metamorphosis for the printed word since Gutenberg invented moveable type in 1450." One the one hand, she suggested, the introduction of book superstores, online sellers like Amazon.com and more recently the introduction of the electronic book (e-book) and other digital media seemed poised to transform the publishing industry in one fell swoop. On the other hand, book publishing was passing through an era of dramatic corporate consolidation, with fifteen acquisition deals in 1998 alone, worth more than US$11 billion.[16] (The evidence that we are, indeed, in a new period of global consolidation In the entertainment/mass media sector mounts practically daily. To cite only the most sensational example, in mid-January 2000 Internet giant America Online [AOL] purchased media giant Time-Warner, and a week later the new combined company purchased the British music industry giant EMI. The world has entered, it would seem, an era of unprecedented *vertical* integration in this sector, in which the goal is to achieve not only a global presence but to fully integrate information/entertainment *content* with multimedia *service provision*.) The most noteworthy of the "mergers and acquisitions" in the publishing industry was the Bertelsmann purchase of Random House for US$1.4 billion, a deal that coupled what was already the largest US publishing company with the giant Bantam Doubleday Dell, which Bertelsmann already owned. Bertelsmann is now said to control anywhere from 11 to 35 percent of the American adult trade market in books, according to Kinsella, "depending on whom you ask."[17]

In Canada, the "merger mania" of 1998 produced controversy along an historic fault line, pitting the Canadian-owned publishers—represented by the "vocal" 145-member ACP—against not only the multinationals but the federal government (which, they insisted, ought to disallow the merger in Canada on the grounds that the combined company would wield too much power in the domestic marketplace).[18] In the end, the merging of Random House/Knopf Canada and Doubleday/Bantam Canada (under the Bertelsmann Entertainment conglomerate as Random House Limited) was approved by Ottawa. The new merged company makes for "a complete horizontal publisher," according to industry observers, since Random/Knopf has Vintage for trade paperbacks, and Doubleday/Bantam has Seal for the mass market. It can now offer "a complete publication package," which includes the packaging of new hardcover titles and "paperbacking" by one of the mass marketing lines.[19] Even now, the decision of the federal government to approve the merger remains divisive. Some insiders have suggested that the publishing industry in Canada in general is now so prosperous that there is plenty of profit to go around. As John Neale, formerly of Doubleday Canada and now chairman of the merged company, put it: "There's a huge amount of young talent here [in Canada], and we all benefit when we bring the best of Canadian writers to the world."[20] From the vantage point of the ACP, in contrast, this kind of concentration can only further weaken Canadian-owned publishing. Laments Paul Davidson: "The five top Canadian firms combined don't play as large a role in the trade market as Doubleday-Random will do as a combination."[21] (There is, notwithstanding the nationalist sentiments of the ACP, evidence to suggest that the dubious tradition of having personnel "graduate" from a Canadian-owned firm to a multinational is alive and well, and perhaps even contributing to Canada's literary/publishing culture. The most celebrated case in recent years is that of Louise Dennys, who in 1991 folded her own

Canadian-owned company, Lester & Orpen Dennys, only to be recruited by Knopf Canada. Part of her "mission" at Knopf today, says Dennys, is to "seek out new Canadian writing." Among other strategies, she has inaugurated a program called the *New Face of Fiction*, which introduces and promotes up to five first novelists per year.)[22] To the surprise of many within the Canadian publishing industry, in late June 2000 McClelland & Stewart owner Avie Bennett announced that he would be donating 75 percent of M&S to the University of Toronto, and selling the remaining 25 percent to Random House Canada.[23]

Although it is probably too early to tell, it appears that the global trend towards mergers and acquisitions in the publishing industry—as in the entertainment and mass media industries generally—will fundamentally alter the relationship of independent publishers to the multinationals, even as it transforms the relationship between authors and publishers. On the one hand, the consolidation of ever-larger global publishing firms seems to have increased the level of "commercialization" on the world's bestseller lists. U.S. industry observers, for example, have begun to notice the increased dominance of big name authors from the major publishing houses, a trend which makes it far more difficult, as Bridget Kinsella puts it, "for unknowns to score big on the lists."[24] Like the global music conglomerates, which are less interested than ever in artist development, the worry is that the major publishing houses have charted a course in which it will be nearly impossible to nurture new talent, since it can take many years and, indeed, many books to establish a new "world class" author. Says Morgan Entrekin, president of Grove/Atlantic Press in the U.S., "Ten years ago the system allowed a writer to find an audience by the fourth or fifth book. Nowadays if writers don't sell enough of their first and second books, they can be labelled 'damaged goods.'"[25] The "plus side to the merger madness," according to Kinsella—and this has important implications for

Canadian publishers—is that "independent presses have never had a better crop of writers to publish."[26] Independents, she notes, often serve as "feeders and filters" for emerging authors, many of whom achieve their initial acclaim with a small press and later get picked up by a big one. The contrary is also true. Writers who have been dropped from the major publishing houses often find their way to the small presses as well.[27] Avie Bennett and others worry, however, that the trend towards globalization ultimately disadvantages Canadian-owned publishers because the multinationals are so attractive to authors and their agents: "Agents are trying more and more to find a one-world market for their authors. At present the multinationals are trying to be good Canadians, and buying big for Canadian authors—but how long will it last once they control the market?"[28]

A second and no less dramatic change affecting the Canadian literary/publishing culture in the late 1990s has been the introduction of the Barnes & Noble-styled retail superstores, Chapters and Indigo. As noted above, book retailing was one area in which Canadians had been accused of lagging (though why Canadian booksellers were reticent about adopting the U.S. superstore model is not clear). Judging from the trade press, some Canadian book publishers are pleased with the introduction of Chapters and Indigo, suggesting that they have not only glamorized bookselling but broadened the market for books. Jackie Hushion, described as the "face and voice of the Canadian Publishers' Council," believes Chapters has done a good job of bringing "non-readers" into the stores and, in particular, of promoting Canadian book prize winners and shortlisted authors: "They've really enhanced their market, and I think the superstore growth has energized Canadian publishing."[29] Adds Cynthia Good of Penguin Canada, "They're bringing in a wide range of new customers, and they've been very supportive of Canadian books, which is what my program here is all about. They believe that highlighting Canadiana is only good for business, and that, of course, is good for us."[30] The massive influence of Chapters in the Canadian marketplace today—estimated by the company to be in the range of a 23 percent market share but by some of its adversaries to be over 50 percent—has not, however, been an unmitigated blessing, either for small Canadian-owned publishers, some of whom claim that getting shelf space in the chains is more difficult than ever, nor especially for independent bookstores, many of which have recently closed up shop after decades in business. The closing of The Children's Bookstore in Toronto in January 2000, for example, after literally pioneering children's bookselling in Canada in the mid-1970s, is a case in point. Media coverage of the closing suggested that owners Judy and Hy Sarick were simply ready for retirement. But, as Charlotte Teeple, executive director of the Children's Book Centre in Toronto, points out, the Saricks' decision can only be understood in the context of increasing competition from the superstores—a suggestion buttressed by the fact that they were unable to find a buyer for their retail operation, even though they had sold their distribution business to Pegasus, Chapters' wholesaler. Laments Teeple: "It's another important independent gone, and for us in the children's book community, it's a huge loss."[31] In November 1999, owing largely to pressure from the CBA, Chapters' domination of Canadian book retailing became the focus of an inquiry by the federal Competition Bureau, which concluded that the chain had not "broken any rules."[32] In early 2000, following in the wake of some high profile store closings in Toronto and Vancouver, the dispute shifted to a series of highly publicized hearings before the Standing Committee on Canadian Heritage.[33]

Jean Baird, publisher of a Canadian magazine for and by young people, *In 2 Print*, has been frank in her concern about what she sees as the industry's (and more specifically Chapters') failure to meet the needs of young people. "Years of trying to develop a relationship" between her magazine and the chain, says Baird, has produced a consistent refrain from its upper management: "The teen market does not work for us." Further, "When I have suggested that the situation might be changed by aggressively supporting the reading interests of teens the response has been indifference. If the major bookseller in Canada does not care about the teen marketplace, I think we have a problem." Referring to recent claims made by Sheryl McKean, executive director of the Canadian Booksellers' Association (CBA), Baird notes as well that publishers now seem to be making decisions about what books they publish based on the criterion of what Chapters will carry and promote. Baird asks rhetorically: "Since Chapters has no expressed interest in the teen marketplace, as a publisher what decision would you make?" Worse yet, publishers have been cowed into not publicly criticizing the superstores since, as she puts it, "Everyone in the book industry knows that if you want to stay in business you don't deliberately offend Chapters." As for *In 2 Print* and similarly styled Canadian magazines, Baird notes that the situation has gone from bad to worse: "Through deals with wholesale distributors, Chapters directly affects the access of consumers to magazines as well as access to books. Management at Chapters say that Coles and Smithbooks will only carry 'mass marketing American titles.' So much for Canadian content on newsstands."[34]

Perhaps the most dramatic impact of globalization on Canadian publishing has been the meteoric rise of Internet-based bookselling, though the full-blown impact of this phenomenon remains to be seen. At the centre of this highly sensational (and, for shareholders, profitable) trend has been Amazon.com, the online book superstore launched in 1995 by former Wall Street hedge fund executive Jeff Bezos, as well as Barnes & Noble, the biggest U.S. bookseller and, as of 1997, another major player in online bookselling. In Canada, both Chapters and Indigo are online with sophisticated, widely promoted e-commerce sites, as are many smaller booksellers. Like the claims in praise of the superstore retailers noted above, industry observers seem to believe that Internet selling has increased consumers' interest in books, adding a new intimacy to the experience of literature.[35] Amazon.com's proposal to locate customer service and distribution centres in Canada has, however, been controversial, not least because the corporation has hired former New Brunswick premier Frank McKenna to "help pave a path into the Canadian book retailing market."[36]

Publishers themselves are now well established in the "creative" use of the Net to promote and sell their goods, though, significantly, many large publishers are not selling their books online because they don't want to compete with giants like Amazon.com.[37] HarperCollins/Salon has featured a contest for a trip to London on a page promoting the book *The Professor and the Madman*, for example, while Avon Books has created an e-mail update system for fans of their authors. Chat rooms and community sites are popular with publishers because they have turned out to be "a boon for niche titles," most notably among readers of science-fiction and romance.[38] A relatively new strategy is to post the first chapter of a forthcoming book online before its actual release. This has the advantage of reaching a fan base, capturing the e-mail addresses of those fans and in the process compiling "a robust mailing list for use on future projects."[39] (The first major book release to post a chapter ahead of publication came in February 1997 when Bantam Doubleday Bell released the first two chapters of John Grisham's *The Partner*, in collaboration with AOL). Excerpts for virtually all books are now posted on the Web as "standard practice" in the publishing industry. Says Danya Ruttenberg of *E Business Magazine*, "Whether through Amazon.com, the corporate site, or other promotions, it makes good business sense: a consumer is more apt to buy if s/he knows what s/he's getting. And with the infinite Candyland of titles and data available, it won't take long for a browser at any online book venue to find something worth purchasing." Ruttenberg speculates, interestingly, that "this new genre of store will prove an economic boon to smaller presses. Online venues, with unlimited shelving space, can carry a wider selection of titles irrespective of salability. And, since it benefits the retailer to have the most possible information available on every title, publishers are oft granted the luxury of posting their marketing copy on a retail site free of charge. For a small house with a shoestring budget, this opportunity can be quite a blessing."[40]

Already, however, there is evidence that book buyers are growing bored with what has been called the "mallification of the web."[41] Some observers are predicting a return to the more intimate environment of smaller, independent bookstores, and to the tactile, even fetishistic fascination of the book-as-object. As Pat Holt of the San Francisco *Chronicle* puts it: "When it comes down to it, the tangible bits of book loving—from browsing in a store and flipping through the chapters to folding down the corners of beautifully-written pages—are still, for many, the most magical. Whether the title is discovered in an online review or purchased with a click of a button matters less than the moment when the new binding first cracks. And e-commerce can't change that."[42]

Publishing Succession

Applied to the Canadian publishing industry, the term "succession" has two important meanings, both of which relate directly to the ageing of the industry's demographic centre of gravity, namely the baby boomer cohort. The first and, for the purpose of this study, most pressing question is, who will succeed the boomers as readers and purchasers of published work; the second is, who will assume the leadership of the industry itself once the "early" boomers who have built up the Canadian-owned industry since the 1970s begin retiring *en masse*? As the ACP's Roy Mac-Skimming has observed: "A lot of the Canadian companies now are managed by people who are growing older, and I'd like to see some beneficial tax changes that could draw new investment as people die or move on. The Canadian-owned sector is very under-capitalized compared to the foreign-owned competition." Mac-Skimming no doubt speaks for many in the Canadian-owned sector when he asserts that "a new generation of publishers is needed, and needs to be encouraged."[43]

As noted in the Introduction, book publishers have no particular reason for (nor any proven method of) precisely calculating the demographic basis of their readership. This is because, unlike newspapers and magazines, books do not carry advertising and, hence, book publishers are not in the business of selling their readerships to advertisers. Even the most cursory review of the publishing trade literature confirms that book publishers have expended very little energy (or money) on the matter of reader-ship succession; the magazine and especially the newspaper indus-tries, by contrast, have addressed the matter with a sometimes obsessive fervour. Throughout the 1990s, newspaper publishers and editors worldwide have been commissioning research, hold-ing conferences and even lobbying governments—especially on the need for increased "literacy training"—in the hope of thwart-ing what they have come to see as an imminent crisis in their readership. This crisis is, to judge from the voluminous research they have produced—essentially "generational." *The young, it is feared, do not read newspapers, if they read at all.* For this reason, it is appropriate to review briefly recent trends pertinent to newspa-per succession since, in theory at least, they are somewhat analo-gous to succession in book publishing. More significantly, the newspaper industry's worry about succession has contributed greatly to the popular stereotype of young people as illiterate or too lazy to read.

The newspapers' interest in youth began in earnest in the early 1990s when it was discovered that young people were neither engaged by the content of traditional newspapers, nor inclined to subscribe to them. A 1991 study of U.S. college students' attitudes towards newspapers, for example, concluded that "[a]lthough they acknowledge the received definition of newspapers as factual sources for citizens, young adults experience the newspaper as a ritual, a symbol, and a tool. They consider the facts in newspapers boring because they deal with contexts unrelated to their lives."[44] For the academic demographers who conducted this study, these results confirmed mounting fears within the industry: "American newspaper executives and conservative critics complain that young adults who don't read newspapers and lack a knowledge of basic facts may be unprepared to become informed citizens. Studies also correlate newspaper reading with political interest. Young readers, who begin with comics and turn to newspapers for entertainment, do not find political news meaningful."[45]

Significantly, by the mid-1990s the earnest tone of such reports—centring on the civic virtue of political engagement—had been displaced by a far more mercenary agenda: if young people could not be persuaded to come to the newspapers, then the newspapers would have to go to the "kids." As Diane McFarlin put it in the *Bulletin of the American Society of Newspaper Editors*: "The inclination of people to read newspapers is determined by their appeal to the readers, and the sustainability and success of a newspaper depends on its circulation. Newspapers should personalize themselves, be distributed better, be interesting and comprehensible and attract youngsters who perceive newspapers as adult-oriented for them to be successful."[46] Predictably, polls commissioned by the Newspaper Features Council in the United

States affirmed "syndicate executives' belief that more young people's features could help newspapers attract new readers."[47] Lee Salem, vice president/editorial director of the Universal Press Syndicate, captured what was thought to be the essence of the problem when he equated declining newspaper readership with the cultural condition of North American youth: "There are so many activities other than newspaper reading to attract young people. Many not only do not care to read newspapers, they do not care to read much of anything. They have been raised on a diet of TV, so why should they switch to newspapers now?"[48] Thereafter, the newspapers' preoccupation with youth assumed an increasingly urgent, even desperate tone, as they shifted away from the question of what youth might *need* to the matter of what they *want*. Various conferences, panel discussions and polls gauging young people's tastes and opinions revealed that "adults did not have a proper perspective on the lives of teenagers. Reports on teenagers tended to reflect the opinions of the writer and adults rather than that of the teenagers."[49] Research in the United States concluded that "[t]he young feel that newspapers are irresponsible in reporting matters related to sex and race. Youngsters also dislike newspapers publishing stories that portray a negative picture of youth. Youngsters read newspapers for three reasons, 'connections, community, and continuity.' Measures such as publishing investigative stories on topics related to youth and starting a classified section for youth will attract more young readers."[50]

As if to signal the *global* magnitude of the problem, in 1994 the first World Editors Forum was held in Vienna and attended by 100 editors from 27 nations. According to William B. Ketter, reporting on the conference for *Editor & Publisher*, "[t]he focus of the meeting was on how to recapture readers. Problems and suggested solutions were found to be similar worldwide. Common problems included small budgets and a lack of reading by youth. The solutions offered were to provide more imaginative content, improved format and be innovative." Participants discovered that "[t]he everyday problems, it turned out, are remarkably similar—from illiteracy in South Africa and Slovenia to smaller editorial budgets in the United States and the United Kingdom to young people with no time to read in Indonesia and Ireland to newsroom discomfort with marketing departments in Belgium and Brazil."[51] A consensus emerged: newspapers must shift their emphasis to what young people "want" and place "less accent on what editors think they need, like it or not."[52]

By late 1996, evidence that the Internet was already enormously popular among North American young people had heightened newspaper editors' fears about loss of readership, redoubling their efforts to target youth (and, significantly, *children*). When the Interactive Newspapers '97 conference convened in Houston, for example, little remained of the lofty argument from "citizenship." The Internet generation was at risk of "never developing the newspaper habit," the participants agreed, and desperate times called for desperate measures. Youth-oriented innovations praised at the conference included online features like the *Chicago Tribune's* "Bit Storm" section, which reviews video games, and the "Tall Tales Forum," a New Jersey-based online area for discussions about "roaches, bugs and other gross-out topics."[53] Not to be outdone by these American trend-setters, many Canadian newspapers accepted the same logic and began to expand their offerings for children and youth. In October 1999, even the venerable *Globe and Mail,* perceived to be in a life or death struggle with the upstart *National Post,* adopted this mercenary strategy, retooling its Saturday edition for a younger audience, complete with stories on "penis length, the frequency of sex, and a photo feature on how to deliver the two-cheek kiss."[54]

That North American newspaper editors seem to believe, firstly, that contemporary youth are *dramatically* unlike their elders (at least in their reading habits) and secondly, that they must be pandered to if they are ever to be won over to "serious" print media may have significant implications for book publishers. At the very least, the sensational coverage of young people's cultural and especially political "illiteracy" occasioned by the newspapers' preoccupation with succession has helped to foster an unflattering stereotype—youth as mindless captives of mostly televisual mass media. (David Kent of Random House Canada undoubtedly speaks for many in the book publishing industry when he alludes to the seemingly intractable problem of attracting young readers: "How do you compete with motion picture companies, which are huge? Then you have the whole cable TV industry, and the Internet, which makes the world available to your home. That did not exist 10 years ago.")[55] At their worst, such claims run the risk of polarizing serious discussion about young people—and especially their encounters with literature—into one of two condescending generalizations: youth as irredeemably illiterate, or youth as utterly alien to the established traditions of print. For book publishers, as for newspaper editors, such stereotypes can result in only two, equally superficial strategies: either young people are to be ignored, as publishers chase the baby boomer market into oblivion, or they are to be hived off as a "niche market," unable or unwilling to be engaged by "serious" ("adult") print culture.

3

YOUTH
CULTURE
IN CANADA

Demographics:
A Widening
Generation Gap

ANY DISCUSSION of contemporary Canadian youth must begin with one seemingly incontrovertible demographic reality: Canadians born in the wake of the baby boom are numerically fewer and, hence, far less economically and culturally significant to the shaping of the broader social fabric than the cohort of boomers advancing "ahead" of them. The hegemony of the baby boom generation in the setting of North American social and cultural trends has, in fact, been the hallmark of the cohort since it entered childhood; indeed, the assumed dominance of this cohort at every phase in its life cycle has itself become a commonplace, thanks to enormously popular books by Canadians David K. Foote, Don Tapscott and others.[1] As noted in Chapter One, Canada's literary/publishing culture has been dominated by the baby boom generation since the 1970s, not only by virtue of its numbers and affluence, but also because of the nationalist resurgence that coincided with its formative years. This publishing culture may be said, then, to be potentially resistant to contemporary youth on two mutually reinforcing grounds, firstly, that young people tend not to share the nationalist cast of mind with which the baby boom generation seems so indelibly imprinted, and secondly, that they currently have neither the numerical strength nor the cultural clout (i.e., purchasing power) to inspire or perhaps even to warrant any significant departure from the publishing *status quo* in Canada.

Recent Statistics Canada data on the demographic composition of contemporary Canadian society serve to illustrate the magnitude of this "generational" impediment to renewal in the Canadian publishing industry. (Note: Statistics Canada defines children as "all persons 0 to 14 years" and youth as "all individuals 15 to 24 years"). According to *Children and Youth: An Overview*, published in 1994, the national birth rate began to drop "steeply" in the mid-1960s, producing significantly fewer children and youth as a proportion of the overall population. The 1991 census showed a "modest upturn" in the relative percentage of children in the population (the bulge now commonly known as the baby boom "echo"). But while the number of children in Canada may be on the "rebound," this is not true for teenagers and young adults: "The number of youth in Canada grew over the period 1961–1981, then declined thereafter. Accordingly, the absolute number of youth steadily increased from about 2.6 million in 1961 to 4.7 million by 1981, then declined to 3.8 million by 1991." Further, "the relative proportion of Canada's population under the age of 25 has fallen consistently since 1966. Almost half of

Canada's population (49.4 percent) was under 25 in 1966, but this fell steadily to only 34.4 percent by 1991.[2] The authors of *Children and Youth* extend their analysis of the demographic data to the question of cultural hegemony, confirming the general dominance of the baby boom noted above:

> Throughout the 1960s and 1970s, Canada experienced a boom in the construction of elementary and high schools to accommodate the sizable numbers of persons passing through childhood and youth. Recently a shifting age distribution has led to alternate accommodations. . . . With fewer younger Canadians, the demand for various consumer goods has been affected (e.g., for specific types of clothing, sports equipment, etc.) as has the availability of jobs on graduation, the potential pool of college and university students, and so on. The size of the baby boom contributed to a distinctive youth culture during the 1960s and 1970s which no longer appears to be pervasive. The smaller numbers that follow the baby boomers have yet to gain the same influence, demographically or culturally.[3]

Another demographic trend having a direct bearing on Canadian publishing concerns the educational attainment of various cohorts. Between 1971 and 1991 young people in Canada became progressively better educated: not only were more Canadians than ever attending postsecondary institutions but "the proportion of youth with less than Grade 9 dropped steadily from 12.4 percent in 1971 to 4.8 percent in 1991," while "the percentage of those with grades 9-13 also dropped from 64.4 percent in 1971 to 60.3 percent in 1991."[4] This trend towards higher levels of educational attainment has continued in the 1990s, and it is likely to continue for the foreseeable future. Taken together, the data suggest that in the next decade or two there will be relatively larger numbers of youth in the overall Canadian population (the "echo"), and that they will be better educated than any prior cohort—a pattern corroborated by recent Canadian literacy data (see the section entitled "The International Adult Literacy Survey" in Chapter Four). This bodes well for the future of all Canadian cultural industries, at least potentially, and may provide an opportunity for the publishing industry in particular to address itself to young people to an extent that may not have been practical (or profitable) previously.

In the meanwhile, however, and for the foreseeable future, two serious demographic obstacles will continue to face the project of large-scale renewal in Canadian publishing. The first remains the overwhelming dominance of the baby boom, now heading into its retirement years. Ever the book publishers' golden goose, this cohort is generally expected to have more leisure time, a more "active" approach to retirement and, above all, more disposable income than any prior cohort of Canadian "seniors." For the near future at least, the baby boom will continue to predominate demographically, both by inflating Canada's median age as it ages and by maintaining its disproportionate size relative to the general population. There is no reason to suspect that the massive shift of the North American consumer economy towards the so-called "silver" generation, which has now begun in earnest, will be displaced any time soon, and it is highly likely that Canadian publishers will continue to see this cohort as their primary market. Secondly, there remains the matter of subsequent youth cohorts, which, for the purposes of this study may be said to include anyone born between the late 1960s and the mid 1980s. Downwardly mobile, demographically insignificant, politically apathetic and culturally benighted—they have been called "Generation X," "the MTVgeneration," "the slacker generation"—young people (including many young adults who are no longer technically "youths") are reputed to have spent the last decade alienated from the mainstream of Canadian life at virtually every level. Little wonder, given the power and pervasiveness of this stereotype, that some boomer-fixated publishers (and others) are thought to have given them up as a "lost generation."

The Economic Condition of Canadian Youth

Contemporary Canadian youth and young adults—that is, anyone under the age of 35 in the year 2000[5]—have been mired in an economic crisis unprecedented since the Great Depression, and one which future historians may well describe in similarly bleak terms. Judging by the relative lack of public interest in this crisis until only recently, however, its magnitude has been largely hidden from public view and, thus, for the young Canadians who have experienced it, all the more frustrating. Public perceptions that 1990s youth are "slackers" and "whiners"—or that "alienation" from "McJobs" is a pose that they have assumed as a kind of lifestyle accessory—has helped to silence the victims of this crisis, while the indifference (and in some cases, the antipathy) of public policy towards young people—for example, the recent Provincial crackdown on so-called "squeegee kids" in Ontario and the sensational "toughening up" of the federal Young Offenders Act—has helped to divert attention away from its root causes. That young Canadians' economic plight has received almost no attention from either organized labour or the social democratic left in Canada has no doubt exaggerated not only their reputed "political apathy" but their already considerable sense of isolation.[6]

The economic crisis among Canadian youth has been fuelled by what has become a familiar litany of "revolutionary changes" in the late twentieth century Canadian economy: global competitiveness, corporate downsizing, government restructuring, new technologies demanding higher skills, more "competitive" labour markets, etc. The transition to the post-industrial "information age" through which the Canadian economy is now passing is commonly thought to be having its worst impact upon older workers with antiquated skills (and, no doubt, such persons have suffered greatly); yet paradoxically, it is entry-level workers, most of them young and better educated than their elders, who have borne the brunt of this revolution in the workplace. The unemployment data for the 1990s tell part of the story. Throughout the decade young people had the highest unemployment rate of any group in Canada—sometimes at a rate of nearly twice the national average. In 1992, the worst year of the recession, 184 000 15 to 19-year-olds (19.7 percent of all labour force participants in this age range) were unemployed, compared with 16.6 percent of those aged 20–24 and 9.9 percent among those aged 25 and over.[7] For most of the decade, youth unemployment hovered in the 16 percent range. Only recently, according to labour market survey data from Statistics Canada, has there been any sign of relief, with the unemployment rate among Canadians aged 15 to 24 dropping from 15.8 percent at the beginning of 1998 to 13.2 percent in November 1999 (the lowest it has been since August 1990).[8]

As bad as they are, what the recent unemployment statistics do not show is the long-term, systemic degradation of the value of the labour of young Canadians since the late 1970s—a trend that has been laid bare in an important Statistics Canada document entitled *What is Happening to Earnings Inequalities and Youth Wages in the 1990s?* Written by statistician Garnett Picot and published in 1998, this report is based upon data from the Survey of Consumer Finances (scf) for "selected years" between 1975 and 1995, and concerns itself not with the customary "cyclical" changes in the Canadian economy but with "structural change." Picot's findings, while confirming that the recession "cycle" of the 1990s was especially hard on Canadian youth, point to even more dramatic and worrisome trends in the Canadian economy over what amounts to an entire generation. Picot demonstrates what many middle and working class Canadians have sensed in their day-to-day lives in recent years, namely that there has been a "clear trend towards a 'declining middle' in the earnings distribution." This trend has been exacerbated by what he calls a long-term "polarizing trend" among male workers in Canada, in which "the rich are getting richer, the poor poorer," and also by "continuing inequality in men's and women's earnings."[9] One of the more dramatic trends in the "inequality story," he writes, "has been the increasing gap in annual earnings between younger and older workers, particularly among men. This has been largely due to declines in real earnings among young workers. . . ." For Canadian men aged 18–24 real earnings dropped 36 percent between 1979 and the 1990s; among 25 to 34-year-olds (young adults), earnings have fallen 14 percent in the same period—an extremely significant finding insofar as it implies that young men today have downward mobility and declining socio-economic status in common with contemporary Canadian youth. For men "the ratio of annual earnings of workers under 35 to those over 35 fell from .64 in 1981 to .57 in 1989, and .55 in 1993." Among the variables that account for this dramatic decline, the most crucial, says Picot, would seem to be declining hourly wages, since the number of weeks worked (as well as the number of hours per week worked) have changed relatively little since the late 1970s. The real annual earnings of young women in Canada fell 29 percent between the late 1970s and the 1990s; in their case, this decline is attributable to a combination of declining real wages and a decline in the number of hours per week worked.[10]

Cautious about extending his analysis beyond what is statistically demonstrable, Picot speculates that employers have found it expedient to "adjust the wages of entry (or near entry) level jobs downward in the face of decreased labour demands"—a phenomenon borne out by young Canadians' experience of low-wage service sector jobs and exacerbated by the disinclination of the labour movement in Canada to organize them. Another critical factor is the relative increase in the educational level of older workers vis-à-vis younger workers. The baby boom was far better educated than earlier cohorts, affirms Picot, thus "the educational advantage that younger workers once had over their older counterparts has largely disappeared in the 1990s." The data suggest—with worrying implications for the future—that these younger cohorts simply "do not 'catch up' to earlier cohorts as they age and acquire more experience." Most worrisome of all, arguably, in this era of dramatically increasing tuition fees and student loan debt, is Picot's blunt observation that "[h]aving a university degree did not protect younger male workers from this downward shift in the age-earnings profile."[11] Picot's study shows, in general terms, that while the overall numbers in earnings inequality/polarization in Canada have remained relatively stable, this generalized tendency hides the "offsetting" nature of some groups' gains set against the enormous losses of others. This may help to explain why youth unemployment and especially the abysmal drop in young people's real wages has failed to register in public policy debates, in the media and even among organized labour groups in Canada. As Picot himself concludes, "Understanding these [offsetting] trends is important if we are not to be deceived by the stability in the aggregate, and possibly become complacent regarding labour market earnings trends."[12]

INDEXED REAL ANNUAL EARNINGS OF PAID MALE WORKERS,
BY AGE GROUP, 1965–95 (1969 = 100)

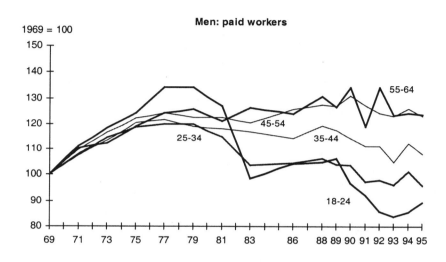

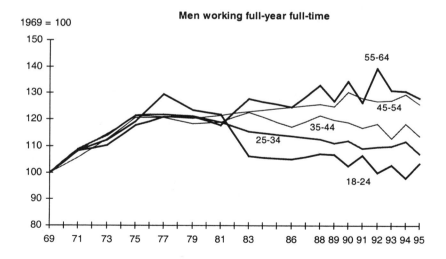

Figure 3.1

Source: Garnett Picot, *What is Happening to youth Wages in the 1990s?* (Ottawa : Statistics Canada, 1988), p. 22.

Compared to their elders, the numbers, especially for young Canadian men, remain disheartening. As Statistics Canada analyst Myles Corack reported in 1999, young men entering the Canadian job market between 1983 and 1993 earned 11 percent less than their counterparts a decade earlier, *regardless of their occupation, the industry they worked in or the prevailing unemployment rate.* "Young men aged 18 to 24 who were working *full-time* in 1994 earned on average the same as their counterparts in 1969, after adjusting for inflation." By contrast, "workers in their 40s and 50s earned a third more than their counterparts 25 years earlier."[13] Not only are youth wages down, but "labour force participation"—i.e., the number of young people with jobs—has also declined dramatically. In early 1999, a report released by the Canadian Council on Social Development noted that "[m]ore than half of today's 16-year-olds have never found paid work, compared to only about a quarter in 1989," while fewer than half of 15 to 19-year-olds were able to find summer jobs in 1997, down from two-thirds in 1989. "Despite the economic recovery between 1993 and 1997," the report asserted, "the youth labour force participation rate continued to fall and now stands at its lowest point in 25 years."[14] Judging from a 1999 report issued by the Corporate Council on Youth in the Economy—a free market think tank sponsored by the Royal Bank, YTV, Environics, The Body Shop and others—youth unemployment appears finally to have registered on the national agenda. As Anne Cira, senior vice-president of the "youth strategy team" at the CIBC put it: "This is a wake-up call for corporate Canada. Tackling the youth unemployment problem is not just a matter of social responsibility nor philanthropic contribution. The cost of ignoring this crisis will have enormous long-term impact on our country's future prosperity and productivity."[15]

**AVERAGE INCOME FOR YOUTH IN CONSTANT (1990) DOLLARS
BY AGE, CANADA, 1980, 1985 AND 1990**

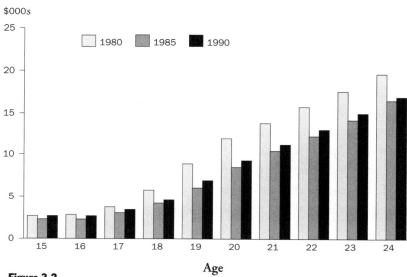

Figure 3.2

Source: Don Kerr, et al., *Children and Youth: An Overview* (Ottawa: Statistics Canada and Prentice Hall Canada Inc., 1994), p. 58.

Though somewhat dated, Figure 3.2 confirms the impact that the long-term economic crisis described by Picot has had on young Canadians' purchasing power (even *before* the recession of the 1990s). It shows average income for youth in constant 1990 dollars, illustrating that between 1980 and 1990, the real income of Canadians aged 15 to 24 declined dramatically—the more so the older they were. For those between 15 and 17 and making less than C$5 000 the relative decline was marginal; but for those between 20 and 24 making between C$12 000 and C$20 000, the decline was significant, suggesting a profound loss of surplus purchasing power in a cohort which was relatively small (and relatively poor) to begin with.[16] These data illustrate quite clearly that the baby boomer cohort, which already enjoys the advantage of numbers, has also enjoyed steadily increasing real incomes in recent decades; the children who followed them, by contrast, namely the youth of the late 1980s and the 1990s, are not only numerically less significant but they enjoy significantly less consumer clout in the economy. (This is to say nothing of the *billions* of dollars Canadian baby boomers are expected to inherit from their parents; in the U.S. estimates of this "windfall" range into the *trillions*.) For the book publishing industry, which may be characterized as a non-essential sector of the economy whose fortunes depend greatly on the availability of "disposable" income, these data speak volumes; for no matter how much Eighties and especially Nineties youth might have been *inclined* to read, the evidence suggests rather starkly that they could ill-afford to spend much of their own earned income on the purchase of books.

The Cultural Condition of Canadian Youth

Canadian youth are today widely perceived to be both *in social crisis* (as evinced by high suicide rates, high unemployment, homelessness, a declining standard of living, declining academic standards, and declining expectations of the Canadian state, etc.) and to be *the agents of social crisis* (increasing criminality and violence, gangs, sexual promiscuity, drug and alcohol abuse, declining morality and deference to authority, the creation of "deviant" cultural and subcultural forms, etc.). Heightening this apparent crisis is the sense that *this* generation of youth is somehow qualitatively different than its predecessors—the products of disintegrating families, schools and communities, and more particularly of a selfish, superficial popular culture centred on television and shopping malls. As *Maclean's* put the case in 1991: "To many

Canadian adults, the present generation of teenagers often seems rootless and pessimistic. Unlike their parents, many of whom grew up protesting against war and advocating the liberalization of drug laws, today's young people are often depicted by social observers as self-centred and directionless."[17] Even Canada's university students, lamented historian J. L. Granatstein in 1998, are "totally ignorant of anything not beamed into their brains via TV, movies, comic books, and the Internet."[18]

As I have argued elsewhere, the notion of "youth" itself has undergone a radical transformation in Canada in the era of corporate culture, globalization and the retreat of the welfare state, and this revolution has in turn dramatically transformed Canadians' understanding of the perennial "generation gap."[19] Whereas "youth" and its claims to independence, rebellion and even deviance were once understood within social and political discourses —as evinced most strikingly in the "countercultural" rebelliousness of the Sixties generation—it has been transformed in the 1990s by the discourses of the free market and especially by its ideological vanguard, advertising. Once viewed as social and political actors with legitimate claims on Canadian public life, young people have in the 1990s been reconstituted as essentially commercial actors—"viewers" to be targeted, "consumers" to be courted, a supposedly rich cohort promising vast profits to the pollsters and demographers who can crack its enigmatic cultural codes. To judge from the likes of *Maclean's*, which has regularly featured stories on "the vast and often bewildering world of teenagers" in the 1990s, the most authoritative public voices on young people today are not social workers or teachers or even parents, but pollsters and "youth-marketing research companies."[20] As they themselves well know, young people today are "sold" virtually everything, from baggy pants and piercings to fashionable opinions and even university degrees; and in the marketplace, if almost nowhere else, they command respect. They may not be the *Pepsi Generation* but in a world in which surveys of their most deeply held beliefs and desires are "jointly commissioned" by Health and Welfare Canada and Pepsi-Cola Canada Ltd.,[21] popular distinctions between young people's personal lives and their consumer tastes, and especially between their collective identities (or sub-cultures) and the market share they represent, have all but lost their meaning.

The degraded socio-economic and cultural condition of youth in the industrialized West—which may be said to include Canada at least insofar as the mass-mediated bases of youth culture are now *global*—has alarmed European and American scholars throughout the 1990s. Lawrence Grossberg, for example, locates the reputed "aimlessness" of young people today in neo-conservative political and cultural discourses and, in particular, contends that the baby boom cohort has co-opted the very idea of "youth." He writes: "Youth itself has become a battlefield on which the current generation of adolescents, baby boomers, parents and corporate media interests are fighting for control of its meanings, investments and powers. . . . Youth today is caught in the contradictions between those who experience the powerlessness of their age (adolescents and college students) and the generations of baby boomers who have attached the category of youth to their life trajectory, in part by redefining it as an attitude ("You're only as old as you feel"). . . . To put it quite simply, kids today know too much and they are, at some deep level, too cynical to mark any difference from older generations. . . . Not only do many young people not believe in the inevitability of progress, they do not place any particular faith in traditional institutions, images or authorities. . . ."[22] Henry A. Giroux has carried Grossberg's critique even further, suggesting that young people are today subjected to systematic processes of social reconstruction and depoliticization: "At stake here is not merely how [North] American culture is redefining the meaning of youth, but how it constructs children in relation to a future devoid of the moral and political obligations of citizenship, social responsibility, and democracy. Caught up in an age of increasing despair, youth no longer appear to inspire adults to reaffirm their commitment to a public discourse that envisions a future in which human suffering is diminished while the general welfare of society is increased. Constructed primarily within the language of the market and the increasingly conservative politics of media culture, contemporary youth appear unable to constitute themselves through a defining generational referent that gives them a sense of distinctiveness and vision, as did the generation of youth in the 1960s."[23] In what is arguably the finest book on the subject of Nineties youth to date, *The Scapegoat Generation,* Mike A. Males has placed the blame for the grievous condition of young people squarely at the feet of self-interested older cohorts who have manipulated public policy (welfare, education, taxes) to their own advantage: "Much, if not virtually all, of the phenomenal economic success of today's senior and Baby Boom generations owes itself to the support of prior generations, including government employment, educa-tion, housing, and welfare subsidy programs. Like so much else, today's adults say to the young: 'Welfare was okay for us, not for you.' Much of the economic throes of today's young are founded in the steady withdrawal of public and private support by elder from younger over the past two decades. It isn't the quality of American youth that has deteriorated over the last half century; it is the attitudes and policies of adults towards the young."[24]

In Canada, as in the US, young people have been blamed for any number of moral panics in the 1990s. Despite incontrovert-ible evidence that youth crime has been *declining* in Canada in the late 1990s, for example, polls show that Canadian adults— subjected practically daily to sensationalised news reports of such tragedies as the Reena Virk and Dmitri Baranovsky murders— believe it is actually increasing (and are garrisoning themselves

accordingly).[25] Heavy metal, hip-hop and more recently industrial and goth music have been blamed for inciting violent, suicidal and even murderous behaviour in young people.[26] Rave
culture has been impugned for its connection to what public officials are now calling "ecstasy-related" deaths.[27] That teens appear
to be smoking in increasing numbers has produced a highly theatrical feud between the federal health minister and the "tobacco
industry"—enhancing a public perception of Canadian youth as
naive or reckless in the process. Adding fuel to the fire, the suggestion is now routinely made in the media that various social
pathologies once limited to youth are manifesting themselves
increasingly among children. A recent story in the *Globe and
Mail* published under the headline "Alarm Raised Over Students
Behaving Badly" typifies the tone of much of this reportage: "An
alarming number of Canadian students are smoking, getting
'really drunk' and cutting class, says a comprehensive new Health
Canada study to be released soon. Drug use is up, bullying is
common and there is a lot of unsupervised 'hanging out,' Health
Canada said, documenting disturbing behaviour that affects
school performance for students from Grade 6 to Grade 10."[28]
Demonizing youth also makes for good politics in Canada these
days, judging from the crackdown on so-called "squeegee kids,"
youth "gangs" and especially young offenders. The only youth-
related crisis that seems to have registered on the national agenda
at all (and then only recently) is "child poverty," but even here
there has been more political posturing than public policy reform.
A poll taken in 1995 revealed that close to one in ten Canadians
"would feel uneasy around a person, if the only thing they knew
about them was that they were a teenager."[29]

The distance between *public* discourses about Canadian youth
—as deviant, apathetic, uncaring, alien—and the *private* world
of young people's aspirations and values simply cannot be overstated. Young people who came of age in the late 1980s and the

1990s are, according to the most reliable sociological data available, far more like older Canadians than perhaps any other recent youth cohort, *including the baby boomers*. If anything, the dire economic circumstances of their lives has fashioned Canadians under 35 into a more *conservative* group, taken as a whole, than their elders—and for good reason. Education, especially higher education, tends to be a conservatizing force in the lives of young people, emphasizing discipline, delayed gratification and, to a greater or lesser degree, identification with the promise of upward mobility. With more young Canadians than ever in school, youth are more likely to identify with the socio-economic *status quo* in Canada than to challenge it. Debt alone—which many young graduates must now bear as a kind of mortgage, sometimes running into the tens of thousands of dollars—is a sobering, conservatizing force, notwithstanding the sensational claims frequently made in the news media that defaulting is a common strategy for young Canadians.[30] The evidence suggests, moreover, that young people are today more tolerant, more sensitive to issues of gender and ethnicity, more environmentally conscious and perhaps even more conscientious in general than their elders—trends to which I can attest myself after fifteen years of teaching Canadian undergraduates. In short, *despite* the horrendous conditions of their economic lives and the myriad challenges with which they must cope in the near and longer terms, *the kids are alright*.

Reginald W. Bibby and Donald C. Posterski's *Teen Trends: A Nation in Motion*, published in 1992, remains the definitive study of the "generation" of Canadian youth ("Generation X," those now in their twenties and early thirties) that has caused so much public derision and official hand-wringing in recent years. Mindful of the negative stereotyping that was already underway in the early 1990s, the authors introduced their book as "an effort to provide Canadians with a clear picture of where young people are headed, along with some thoughts on how we might respond to what is taking place." Drawing on their earlier study of Canadian youth, *The Emerging Generation*, published in 1984 and focused on the lives of young Canadians in the late 1970s and early 1980s, *Teen Trends* has the advantage of Bibby's and Posterski's longitudinal, comparative analysis. It is also unique for its singular *indifference* to young people's consumption habits, a refreshing (and methodologically rigorous) departure from the market-oriented "research" to which this cohort has been relentlessly subjected (and about which they are rightly cynical). Finally, Bibby's and Posterski's study is important because it explicitly compared young people's attitudes and aspirations not only to earlier cohorts of youth but to adults. As the authors themselves put it, this is historically significant because the young people they were studying comprised "the first generation to live in the space age, to welcome cable television, to live among computers, to be part of a society with an economy increasingly based on service and information," while their parents were "the first generation to have to adjust to the extensive fragmenting of the family, the marginalizing of religious institutions, and the personalizing of morality."[31]

In broad outline, *Teen Trends* was organized around two major themes. The first was that, like their elders, Canadian youth in the early 1990s valued interpersonal relationships, communal well-being and non-material values above all else, but that these commitments were eroding under the pressure of heightened materialism, individualism and competitiveness—values Bibby and Posterski identified with the "Americanization" of Canadian culture under the inexorable influence of mass media. The second theme was that Canadian youth in the 1990s were overwhelmed by a sense of *crisis* in their own lives and in the world at large.

Significantly, Bibby and Posterski opened *Teen Trends* with a blunt refutation of what they called "The Callousness Myth." Acknowledging that there was a widely held "stereotype that

young people are callous and detached, not willing or even wanting to experience warmth and affection," they asserted that the
data simply did not support this stereotype and speculated that
"[s]uch propaganda may be a salve for parents who are not connecting well with their teenagers." The evidence suggested rather
that "Canada's young people place tremendous value on good
relationships." Under the subheading "What Teens Want," Bibby
and Posterski affirmed that youth ranked *freedom, friendship* and
respect as their first, second and third priorities, respectively, followed by "the material goals of success and a comfortable life."
The authors were clearly pleased to report that teens placed such
a high value on the quality of their personal lives (including
"being loved") but they added that elsewhere "the news is less
encouraging and, in places, a bit troubling." In particular, the
"ideal of social compassion gets mixed reviews," with only 6 out
of 10 teenagers saying that "concern for others" is "very important" to them. (The authors noted that these data were especially
significant because it is "inappropriate, officially, for individuals,
groups, or organizations to be indifferent to people.")[32]

Throughout *Teen Trends*, Bibby and Posterski emphasized
that young Canadians' sense of themselves, their communities
and schools, Canada and the world was filtered through their
apprehension of pervasive *crisis*. Since "at least 1976," they noted,
young people have been "overwhelmed by the negative portray-
als of both the country and the planet" and by issues that include
"racial discrimination, gender inequality, aboriginal issues, the
environment, sexual assault, child abuse, abortion, and the rights
of the physically disabled."[33] The authors were eloquent in
expressing their sympathy for the young and their pessimism
about the world they were to inherit:

> When you think about it, today's teens have not seen many
> solutions in their lifetime. The one major exception is the

dissipation of the Cold War between the U.S. and what was formerly the U.S.S.R., along with an equivalent dissolving of the former fear of a nuclear holocaust. Certainly, young people have seen technological advances, but the difficulties first registered in their early memories still remain unresolved. Whether the problem is famine and hunger, overpopulation, the national debt, drug-trafficking, violent crime, political instability, unending wars, or a dread of cancer, what was still is. And to further complicate matters, more recent concerns such as the depletion of the ozone layer, global warming, the discovery of buried toxic wastes, racial discrimination, and AIDS only compound their impression that solving problems is not just improbable, but close to impossible. No wonder modern young people are feeling powerless.[34]

In the end, Bibby and Posterski concluded, not particularly optimistically, Nineties youth exhibited virtually none of the idealism that characterized young people in the 1960s, nor did they have much reason to do so: "Canadian young people in the 1990s do not see themselves as agents of change. They are like mirrors on the wall of society. Their attitudes and behaviour mainly reflect the *status quo*. They have not been able to carve out much of a world that is uniquely their own." In a word, the authors asserted, Canadian youth are *under control*. "Only a few cause society much trouble. The great majority are quiet and rather conventional. They are more inclined to conform than to innovate; more comfortable being quietly passive than radically active."[35]

Subsequent studies have corroborated Bibby's and Posterski's suggestion that, in general, Canadian youth are conservative, quiet and under control. *Healthy Connections: Listening To B.C. Youth*, published in the fall of 1999 and billed as "the largest-ever survey" of British Columbia teenagers, found that, "contrary to the media portrayal, more than 90 percent of teenagers are in excellent health and feel good about themselves." The majority of BC adolescents do not smoke, drink, have sex or fight, and more than 80 percent do volunteer work in their communities. Said Roger Tonkin, executive director of the McCreary Centre Society, the Burnaby-based research organization that conducted the study: "We hope the results will calm current fears about the physical and emotional health of youth. Today's young people are not more violent, more alienated from their parents or less interested in their education. Though they are bombarded by sexual images in film and advertising, more teens are deciding to delay sexual activity. Most are coping well with the challenges of a complicated world."[36] The *National Longitudinal Survey of Children and Youth*, a massive, ongoing study of Canadians' transition from childhood to adulthood, also reported in 1999 that "most youth have a happy and positive outlook on life." Significantly, 93 percent of Canadians who were 12 and 13 years old in 1996–7 (the study's core sample) reported that they were "happy with the way things were in their lives" and 95 percent indicated that "their futures looked good."[37]

As even this brief survey of young Canadians' socio-economic and cultural circumstances suggests, a paradox of enormous significance lies at the heart of the lived experience of youth today: young people in Canada have not been as *economically* disadvantaged since the Great Depression, and yet they have been heralded throughout the 1990s as a "market" with seemingly limitless disposable income, consumer clout and marketing savvy. It is now a commonplace that the "cool hunters," advertisers, market analysts, music and movie promoters, and sloganeers who today dominate public life situate young people as members of a highly lucrative "niche" market designated according to specifically demographic criteria. To judge from the mountains of youth-oriented marketing "research"—published not only in the specialized periodical literature (*American Demographics, Futurist,*

Marketing, Adweek, MediaWeek, Marketing News) but in the business press generally (*Forbes, Money, Report on Business*) and even in general interest periodicals *(Maclean's, Time, Newsweek)* —corporations from Gap to Nike have fallen over themselves in the 1990s to "brand" youth, that is, to cement their enormously lucrative allegiance to this brand of jeans or that style of music.

The truth is that this pattern is not paradoxical at all but, rather, the product of a profound cultural shift in the lives of young people throughout the industrialized West. Contemporary youth, in Canada and elsewhere, have been consigned to unprecedented levels of economic *dependency*—primarily on their parents or other family members—and this dependent state has been so thoroughly "naturalized" over the last two decades that few researchers or commentators have even acknowledged its existence. That "children" in their thirties and even their forties continue to live with their parents, or to have their lifestyles subsidized by them, speaks volumes, both about the extent to which the very idea of *dependence* has been privatized (dependence on the *state* is today more stigmatizing than ever) and also about the extent to which earlier notions of adult independence have been undermined. There is, for example, a growing quasi-academic self-help literature in Canada aimed at the members of the so-called "sandwich" generation who are now "responsible" both for their ageing parents and their adult children, none of which addresses the question of how public policy has contributed to this shift.[38] Yet the evidence mounts daily. In early 1999, for example, Statistics Canada reported that roughly *half* of Canadians between the ages of 20 and 34 still lived "at home." Even more remarkably, *one-third* of single Canadian men earning C$40 000 annually or more still live with their parents.[39] Though largely unacknowledged and under-studied, this phenomenon—the extension of childlike dependence well into adulthood—may turn out to be one of the most dramatic "psycho-demographic" revolutions of our time, with grave consequences for the future. As Bob Glossop, director of programs at the Vanier Institute of the Family has observed: "It changes fundamentally the life course for adults and suggests young people really are prolonging the period of adolescence."[40] For the present, suffice it to say that the "youth market" so celebrated in commercial discourses today is, in fact, largely comprised of middle class youths and young adults who, via their families' subsidies, can purchase all of the superficial trappings of the good life—designer clothing, compact discs, even mutual funds—but who cannot, in the end, afford to pay their own rent. For young Canadians without such private subsidy, the situation is grave: one in five Canadian young people lives in poverty (a total of 1.4 million people), and fully *half* of the patrons of Canada's food banks are now children and youth. As a *Toronto Star* editorial put the case recently, "No one knows how many children are homeless. The emergency shelters are too overwhelmed to count."[41]

The misrepresentation of youth and young adults as rich consumers is but one symptom of an even more pronounced tendency in Canadian life today, namely the habit of generalizing about young people as if, by virtue of their age alone, *they are all alike.* Indeed, "youth" remain the one social group about which the most casual and stereotypical generalizations may still be made—generalizations which, if applied to other ethnic, gender or age groups, would be regarded as the prejudicial nonsense they are. Media coverage of a shooting incident outside Emery Collegiate in Toronto in mid-February 2000, for example, once again raised public anxiety about "youth violence" in the city to fever pitch, implying that age alone signifies a propensity towards this or that social pathology. (One does not hear similar generalizations about "middle aged" or "geriatric" violence when a murder has been committed by a Canadian adult.) Such tendencies are, of course, potentially prejudicial to *all* young people; even where prejudice of this kind is not explicitly stated this pattern of over-generalization perpetuates an inclination to see young people as fundamentally alien.

This tendency to generalize about youth contributes to two further prejudices against them. One is to imagine that all young people are somehow represented by the "worst" exemplars of their cohort, hence common platitudes such as "Young people have no respect for authority" or "Youth today have no attention span." The second and perhaps far more serious tendency—which relates as well to the *hiddenness* of young people's dire socio-economic situation—is to blame youth for circumstances neither of their own making or choosing, that is, to forget that they live almost entirely in worlds created and delimited by adults. That this latter bias colours even the work of ostensibly "serious" researchers can be seen, for example, in Michael Adams' recent book, *Sex in the Snow: Canadian Social Values at the End of the Millennium*. A veteran Canadian pollster, Adams divides con-temporary Canadian society into twelve labelled cohorts or "val-ues tribes," of which three are comprised of Canadians 50 years of age or older, four of baby boomers, and five of "post-boomers." Of the latter, the most socially and culturally significant is a group the author labels "Aimless Dependents," the largest of the five youth tribes, comprising 1.9 million Canadians in 1995 (fully eight percent of the total population). The content and especially the tone of Adams' treatment of this group—which is often flip-pant, occasionally grave and always condescending—hinges on his observation that its members tend to "approach life in a some-what unemotional way, scoring low on values measuring an adventurous, open attitude towards life." The most significant attribute of this tribe is its *anxiety* and *rage*—symptoms, says Adams, of "a very weak sense of being in control of their lives." Although he does nothing whatsoever to contextualize the socio-economic plight of these young Canadians, he observes that

"their anxiety is expressed through an obsession with job security" and concludes that "they have found nothing satisfactory to
replace tradition and as a result are 'slackers without a cause.'"
They are, says Adams, "people who have allowed their fears—and
sometimes their laziness or inertia—to shut them off from much
of what the world has to offer in terms of social, spiritual and
material pleasures. . . . Aimless Dependents are poor navigators in
the consumer marketplace and in life in general."[42] Thus does he
dispose of the almost 2 million Canadian young people whose life
circumstances—family life, social class, ethnicity, education, language skills, cultural capital, etc.—have relegated them to the
margins of society.

Though one would not know it from such condescending and
generalizing discourses about Canadian youth, it is crucial to reiterate that *young people in Canada are as varied as any other social
group*. This seemingly obvious truth ought to guide serious public debate on any number of youth-related questions, including
violence, crime, poverty, sexual abuse, homelessness, drug abuse,
illiteracy, etc., but as yet it does not (to the perennial frustration
of young people and their professional advocates).[43] That
Toronto police officials and even Ontario premier Mike Harris
responded to the Emery Collegiate shooting with the suggestion
that video games be subjected to a special tax speaks volumes
about the continuing ease with which superficial stigmatization
(and political opportunism) passes for serious policy debate when
it comes to contemporary Canadian youth. Again, to reiterate, it
is incumbent on serious researchers of youth culture, if not Canadian society more generally, to extend to young people the same
general latitude accorded other social groups and to concede,
despite all of the misrepresentation to the contrary, that youth are
far more like "us" than not.

MEDIA/
LITERACY

Alarms about
Mass Media

READING is one realm in which the worst stereotypes about young people persist; the perception that contemporary Canadian youth are either illiterate or too lazy to pick up a book is now such a commonplace as to go largely unchallenged. From subway posters to university senior common rooms, hand-wringing about the "dumbing down" of contemporary youth seems to be the order of the day throughout North America.[1] There is evidence to suggest that within the publishing industry, the stereotype of the TV-addicted youth influences not only what is published—especially under "YA" (young adult) auspices—but how it is promoted. A recent publishing trade ad for Simon and Schuster/Pocket Books announced "This Just In: Teens *Do* Read!", ostensibly challenging the dominant stereotype but arguably merely reinforcing it.[2] When it comes to the mainstream publishing world generally, young people are thus not only disadvantaged demographically and socio-economically but subject to an almost wholesale discursive impediment to inclusion: the perception that even if they had the numbers and the money, they would remain stubbornly unresponsive to the printed word.

Before turning to the important matter of illiteracy among the young, it is worth reviewing the ostensibly degraded cultural condition of youth within which the literacy obsession operates, particularly the worry that young people have been so thoroughly inundated by televisual media that they have simply lost the habit of, or the capacity for, reading. Though it has been roundly criticized in some quarters in the thirteen years since it was first published, Allan Bloom's *The Closing of the American Mind* remains in some respects the definitive critique of young people's presumed cultural retardation, and it is worth revisiting if only because Bloom was so profoundly ambivalent about whether or not young people were themselves to blame for their disengagement from what he called "the great books." Starting with his own experience of undergraduates' indifference to literature—which, he claimed, had increased palpably between the 1960s and the 1980s—Bloom went on to generalize broadly: "[O]ur students have lost the practise of and the taste for reading. They have not learned how to read, nor do they have the expectation of delight or improvement from reading." Further, "the notion of books as companions is foreign to them. . . . There is no printed word to which they look for counsel, inspiration or joy." While Bloom could be poignant and eloquent in his historical analysis of American family life, and even sympathetic to the myriad ways in which he believed his students had been intellectually betrayed by their parents, educators and especially commercial interests, he seemed incapable of resisting the temptation to attack the very earnestness in his undergraduates he had once hoped to cultivate:

After such sessions [class discussions about important books] I am pursued by a student or two who wants to make it clear that he or she is really influenced by books, not just by one or two but by many. Then he [sic] recites a list of classics he may have grazed in high school. . . . The psychological obtuseness of our students is appalling. . . . As the awareness that we owed almost exclusively to literary genius falters, people become more alike, for want of knowing they can be otherwise. What poor substitutes for real diversity are the wild rainbows of dyed hair and other external differences that tell the observer nothing about what is inside.3

Whereas in the 1980s and the early 1990s self-styled "elitist" critics like Bloom and E.D. Hirsch showed an implicit tendency to indict young people for their cultural ignorance, lack of erudition, short attention spans and preference for popular culture over more cerebral pursuits, today even some of the most progressive observers of youth culture seem to accept the premise that the cultural condition of young people is more or less the sum total of a lifetime spent playing video games or watching television. This tendency is evident, for example, in a recent critique of *Beavis and Butt-Head,* the MTV cartoon series that seems to epitomize marginal North American youth today. According to authors Steven Best and Douglas Kellner, "*Beavis and Butt-Head* underlines the catastrophic effects on the current generation of youth raised primarily on media culture, showing how they have become 'dumbed down' by image machines. This generation was likely conceived in the sights and sounds of media culture, weaned on it, and socialized by the glass teat of television used as pacifier, babysitter, and educator by a generation of parents for whom media culture, especially television, was a natural background and constitutive part of everyday life. The digital skills of this generation most likely have been formed more through video games than sports or musical training. . . ." Echoing Bloom, Best and Kellner assert that "*Beavis and Butt-Head* depicts the disillusion of the rational subject, the Recline of Western Civilization, and perhaps the End of the Enlightenment in today's media culture." Beavis and Butt-Head are archetypal characters, and all the more tragic therefore, because they seem to live in a netherworld of unbridgeable distance from print culture, yet they lack the critical tools applicable to what might be called the new, televisual literacy: "[L]ike so many youth and even adults in our own world, they are illiterate, a problem that frequently lands them in trouble when they misread various signs. The rational, linear modes of thought imparted to the citizens of the Enlightenment and Gutenberg Galaxy is abandoned by the post modern vidiots who seek scopophilic escape from everyday life, finding visceral satisfaction through subliminal immersion in the images and sounds of corporate media." Citing Neil Postman's *Amusing Ourselves to Death* at length, Best and Kellner conclude that mass media, and television in particular, have produced a "dramatic decline in literacy, a loss of the skills associated with rational argumentation, linear and analytical thought, and critical and public discourse."[4]

Robert Fulford, a veteran of Canada's literary/publishing culture and a sympathetic observer of Canadian youth since the 1960s, seems to agree. Speaking in 1997 at an American conference on "The Closing of the American Mind Revisited," Fulford reminded his presumably "adult" audience of Bloom's claim that "what we are required to do—in matters of the mind and spirit . . . [is] to pass the Torah or its equivalent to the generations that follow." The assumption of an attitude of "humility" is the only appropriate way to read the great works of the past whatever one's age, argued Fulford, since one "must approach material that at first appears incomprehensible or boring, and trust that it will turn out to be so enriching that the effort made to assimilate it will be justified, even if no professional advantage can be anticipated." And yet, "humility is precisely what the contemporary world opposes. The very tone of our lives (partly the tone of the media, but not only that) actively discourages it." The acquisition of an attitude of humility is a virtually impossible task for young readers in particular, concludes Fulford, because youth today have been deprived of the existential cast of mind required for the very act of reading:

> The advantages of humility are not something we find easy to explain to the young. For one thing, we are often too busy flattering them. Advertising and the media flatter the young in order to profit from them. Educators flatter the young in order to win their attention. We tell the young that self-esteem is a human right, whether earned or not, and that one person's opinion is as good as another's. Our culture encourages everyone to be assertive, to speak out, but those who enthusiastically accept this advice may find themselves unable to respond attentively to culture. When confronted by some aspect of the world that is hard to understand, their impulse is not to search for the way to understand it but either to reject it outright or to demand that the world make itself simpler.[5]

It is crucial to reiterate that this common lamentation—the worry that youth no longer possess the cultural capital that would provide them even basic *access* to the world of reading—conceals a deeply rooted ambivalence about young people's own complicity in this state of affairs, something which is palpably evident in academics' public and especially private conversations about the lack of erudition among their students. For all of their emphasis upon the *structural* impediments to young people's acquisition of critical reading skills in a world so obviously dominated by televisual mass media, there remains more than a little residue in these quarters of the kind of reproach that was so striking in *The Closing of the American Mind*. Though nebulous, this attitude seems to consist in the commonsensical belief that, *all of these cultural impediments notwithstanding*, a young person need only undertake the most modest exploration of her local library and the "counsel, inspiration [and] joy" that comes from books shall, willy nilly, prompt an indomitable awakening of her mind and spirit. Within the universities in Canada, this belief has become especially noteworthy. Some of the nation's most progressive humanities professors now complain openly that they cannot get their undergraduates to do required course readings, resorting to inducement strategies that include critical reading workshops, bonus grades for students who complete library tours, and even the acceptance of video projects in lieu of written essays. The syndrome does indeed sometimes seem daunting; in the fall of 1999, I had a first-year history major boast in a tutorial that he had "never read a book"—a comment which I shall not soon forget, regardless of how many of that student's peers may have been dedicated readers. For many teachers, librarians and other "knowledge workers," it is not easy to know how to frame such experiences, nor to reconcile such admittedly anecdotal evidence with documentary evidence to the contrary. It is clear, however, that the power (beauty, joy, virtue, etc.) of reading is often taken as self-evident by those with a passion for it and, hence, that anything short of the fullest appreciation of books is among the most egregious cultural deprivations imaginable. Virginia Davis, past president of the Canadian Association of Children's Librarians, put the case this way: "We do look to literature, both fiction and non-fiction, as a means of finding out we're not alone, helping us working out problems by seeing how someone else handled them, and dispelling some of the mystery about the future."[6] Similarly, Roch Carrier, former head of the Canada Council for the Arts, author of "The Hockey Sweater," one of the best known

Canadian short stories, and now National Librarian, has recalled: "Without books I would sell gas at the pumps or be a lumberjack or construction worker. I had the privilege of having parents who gave me the taste for books. *It opened up my life.*"[7]

Peter C. Emberley's recent book, *Zero Tolerance: Hot Button Politics in Canada's Universities,* represents one of the finest attempts in recent years to work through this profound ambiguity, that is, the inclination to project young people's perceived indifference to print culture onto youth themselves or, worse yet, to simply valorize a canonical standard of "classic books" against which all "un-cultured" people may be impugned. Though Emberley is broadly interested in defending the claims of "liberal" education in Canada, his observations about reading, learning and citizenship carry profound implications both for contemporary youth and for older Canadians working to inspire in them a taste for books. He begins with the observation that "[a]s in other literate cultures, books in the Western world serve as the main medium for self-interpretation and exploration of meaning. They offer us the opportunity to enter a great dialogue spanning millennia and continents. It is a distinctive characteristic of our culture that it is defined by a pedigree of books, a continuous lineage that runs parallel to, and that has shaped, the history of our institutions and our social practices." What Emberley says about the formal institutional exposure of students to books may equally be said of the informal exposure of *all* young people to the world of reading: "In being given a selection of great literary and philosophic books, narratives of history, and works of art, music and drama, students are invited to encounter heroes and demons, saints and martyrs, fanatics and wise persons—the human condition in all its superlative virtue and all its depraved evil. The purpose of these adventures is to invite students to acquire the discipline of intelligence, to pursue intimations of wholeness, to cultivate a discerning appreciation of meaning, to fine-tune their moral vision and to learn how to respond to the contingencies of their existence with courage and hope." Emberley reminds us that there is something extraordinary in seeing the blossoming of a young person's encounter with books: "Few teachers fail to be moved when they see their students transported out of the here and now, driven by an unalloyed intellectual curiosity and wonder, oblivious to daily matters."[8] He takes pains to distinguish between this understanding of reading as an empowering, contextualizing exercise and contrasts it not only with the "increasingly sterile" canon wars but with the elitist claims of works like E. D. Hirsch's *The Dictionary of Cultural Literacy*, which presume to list all of the books that every "cultured" person ought to know. Emberley argues that it is an imprecise business to attempt to judge "what exactly should be read" and, moreover, that the project of compiling lists of "great books" merely renders "adventure into a pilgrimage, where one holy shrine after another is checked off." He is explicitly critical of the ideological bias in *The Closing of the American Mind* and similar works, observing that "[l]ists of books are political instruments, and while affirming the possibility of an education that transcends politics, we would be foolish to deny that political power and knowledge has been interconnected especially at those historical moments when fluid experience has been transformed into doctrine and dogma." Emberley insists that reading must be celebrated as a means of self-discovery rather than as some kind of ideological affirmation: "Above all else, we read to be given a narrative in which the contingencies and predicaments of our lives are given meaning. A book is a small cosmos that takes up the intimations, adventures and longings of our lives and sings them into a rhythm."[9]

Such an impassioned and even optimistic reminder about the pleasures and potentialities of reading may help to assuage the sometimes overwhelming sense that contemporary youth are hopelessly or irretrievably "post-literate." So, too, is empirical data on the *actual* impact of televisual media, particularly television, on book reading and publishing—a relationship that simply cannot be gleaned from the sort of content analysis put forward by Best and Kellner (in which *fictional* television characters like Beavis and Butt-Head are presumed to represent *actual* young people). Paul Rutherford's massive history of the first two decades of television in Canada, for example, shows that "the idiot box"—a term Canadians adopted from the outset—did not displace book reading and, moreover, that it occasioned only minor adjustments within the publishing industry. Rutherford —who explicitly rejects the "demon theory of television," as well as the "typical views of highbrows or cultural nationalists . . . about the baneful effects of TV"—notes that the impact of television on book publishing was far from catastrophic:

> Fiction borrowing at libraries was hurt: one analyst, Rodolphe Laplante, found that there was a modest decline in the lending of novels (though not biography or history) at a Montreal library between 1953 and 1955. . . . The American publishing industry, the source of so much of the reading matter consumed by Canadians, adjusted to the new times: between 1950 and 1970 the number of new titles in the realms of fantasy fell from 22 percent to 13 percent of trade books. But titles promising aid to the individual (the pocket-book, the body, the diet, and the mind), true stories of the past or present, exposés and reminiscences, and so on were in increasing demand. Brian Stewart, writing in the CBC *Times* in 1959 about children and television, detected a definite tendency towards "non-fiction in reading." A government leisure report in 1972 claimed that 70 percent of the Canadian population did read in their leisure time, although the reading group included "relatively fewer people" with a below grade 9 education and in the blue-collar work-force of the people

under twenty-five. Overall, then, television worked to limit the popularity of reading fiction, especially among people with a limited education, but not of reading fact. It should be added, as well, that television apparently didn't harm quality fiction: that brand flourished in English Canada during the 1960s and beyond.10

Empirical research on the reading and television viewing habits of nineties youth affirm that Rutherford's essential thesis continues to obtain: the relationship between televisual media and books is not merely a zero-sum game. Reginald Bibby's and Donald Posterski's research on Canadian youth, for example, centred heavily upon the increasing role of mass media in young people's lives but, like Rutherford, they concluded that this trend was not altogether bad; indeed, these researchers were at pains to refute the accusation that young people are not as knowledgeable as their parents and grandparents were when *they* were teenagers, calling this claim "nonsense." On the contrary, "[t]oday's young people are the best informed teenagers in Canadian history. When it comes to a basic awareness of what is happening in the world, they leave their counterparts of the past three generations in the dust." Bibby and Posterski correctly emphasize that far more young people today have university degrees than their parents (and especially their grandparents); they also invert the highbrow critique of mass culture and insist that young people are "better informed" today not because of the traditional "three Rs" but because of the "three Ts"—television, technology and travel. Taking direct aim at the likes of Bloom, Postman, Best and Kellner, they assert: "Television has revolutionized perception. The endless array of channels available through cable has put young Canadians in contact with the entire world." The only concession Bibby and Posterski are prepared to make to critics of mass media is this: "[W]e are not saying that the information teenagers

AVERAGE DAILY TIME SPENT ON SELECTED ACTIVITIES, 1992

	People aged 15-18			Total population		
	Men	Women	Total	Men	Women	Total
			Hours per day			
Productive activities:						
Paid work and related activities	1.6	1.4	1.5	4.5	2.7	3.6
Unpaid work	1.0	1.9	1.4	2.6	4.5	3.6
Education and related activities	3.1	4.1	3.6	0.6	0.6	0.6
Total productive activities	5.7	7.4	6.5	7.7	7.8	7.8
Sleep	8.9	8.6	8.7	7.9	8.2	8.1
Other personal care activities	2.0	2.2	2.1	2.4	2.6	2.4
Free time activities:						
Socializing	2.3	2.3	2.3	1.8	1.9	1.8
Television viewing	2.5	1.8	2.2	2.4	2.0	2.2
Reading and other passive leisure	0.4	0.5	0.5	0.6	0.6	0.6
Attending movies, sport events and other entertainment events	0.3	0.4	0.3	0.1	0.1	0.1
Active sports	1.2	0.5	0.9	0.6	0.3	0.4
Other active leisure	0.7	0.3	0.5	0.4	0.6	0.5
Total free time	7.4	5.8	6.7	6.0	5.4	5.7
Total time	24.0	24.0	24.0	24.0	24.0	24.0

Figure 4.1

Source: Colin Lindsay et al., *Youth in Canada: Second Edition* (Ottawa:Statistics Canada, 1994), p. 36.

have about events and issues nationally and globally is necessarily deep. But when it comes to broad general knowledge, today's teen dwarfs previous generations."[11]

It is true, however, as one might expect given the historic trend described by Rutherford, that televisual media have made their greatest inroads among young—*and* older—Canadians in the realm of leisure (or what Bloom and other elitist critics would call the realm of *distraction*). Bibby and Posterski put the case this way: "Before television, books were a popular form of entertainment. Sometimes the reading allowed vicarious adventures, or engaged our minds with puzzles, or taught history in the context of fiction, but whatever the text, books used to be more important than they are today. TV has replaced them, and there has been a cost. Today, only 18 percent of [Canadian] teenagers say they enjoy reading 'a great deal.'" Television has not only challenged reading as a leisure pursuit, they argue; more fundamentally, it has "diminished our patience with reading." Again, it is critical to note that Bibby and Posterski, both of whom are serious scholars, do not regard this media revolution as an unmitigated disaster, at least not regarding young people's ability to *learn*, or to function intelligently in the world. They reject the commonsensical claims of book enthusiasts noted above, namely that print media are somehow uniquely empowering; contemporary youth may be inclined to read less now than in the past but for Bibby and Posterski (and even for highbrow critics like Kellner and Best) this merely means that they constitute a generation of "visual learners." Bibby and Posterski assert explicitly that "young people, who are products of the television society, think differently than those who lived before the advent of television. In the past, society leaned more toward the literary. When people read more and watched less they naturally developed their abilities for reflective and analytical thought." Thus, in contrast with many of their elders, "today's youth have video screens in their heads to interpret the world around them. Daily doses of television reinforce the already entrenched pattern of visual perception and understanding. Is it superior or inferior to other ways of thinking? The answer to that question remains a matter of debate, but the modern way of perceiving has changed how young people learn and how we can effectively communicate with them."[12]

In the end, all of this intellectual agonizing over the displacement of reading by television may be, from an historical perspective at least, somewhat moot. On the one hand, highbrow fears of commercial (American) mass media have been germinating in Canada since at least the arrival of radio in the 1920s, inspiring the founding of the CBC and later, in the era of the Massey Commission (1949-51), helping to institutionalize the prevailing elitist view of mass culture as "monolithic, manipulative, and mind-numbing."[13] On the other hand, as Paul Rutherford has demonstrated, Canadians have always enjoyed television as primarily an entertainment medium, adapting it to their "existing patterns of family life and social activities."[14] Contemporary youth are hardly the first to "grow up" on commercial mass media; indeed, it may be said of the baby boom that many of *its* formative cultural influences were those most feared by highbrow critics like Bloom, especially television and rock music. Complicating the critique of mass culture even further is evidence that the heaviest television viewers in Canada have tended to be the elderly, who also happen to be the heaviest book readers as well as the least "functionally literate" Canadians.[15] Lastly, after five decades of obsessive research on the effects of television viewing on children and youth, the jury is *still* out. In a paper presented at the 1998 conference of the International Federation of Library Associations and Institutions, for example, Danish researcher Kirsten Drotner found "a positive correlation between television and leisure reading in the adolescent group." In contrast with the common (*Beavis and Butt-Head*) stereotype, Drotner reported that "the most avid TV-consumers amongst those aged 15–18 are also the most avid readers: 30 percent of those who spend more than four hours per day watching TV read for pleasure for an hour or more."[16]

Perhaps the best way of understanding the relationships between various media is not through an implicitly Darwinian paradigm of competition (and *extinction*) but through the prism of what culture critic Paul Levinson calls "anthropotropism." A lifelong technophile who rejects the highbrow critique of mass culture out of hand, Levinson coined this term to describe "the powerful tendency to bring media ever more fully into human consonance." In his most recent book, *The Soft Edge*, he elaborates a three-part model in which human beings "(a) initially enjoyed a balanced though unextended communication environment (eyesight, earshot, and memory were its limits), (b) developed media to break beyond such limits, but paid a price for these breakthroughs in the balance and other human factors they sacrificed (the total lack of resemblance of the alphabet to the real world is a prime example), so (c) increasingly seek media which preserve and continue the extensional breakthroughs of the past, while retrieving the elements of the naturally human communicative world that were lost." As Levinson himself notes, one critical advantage of his anthropotropic model is that it "refutes the cynical, unexamined but widely accepted assumption of much of the twentieth century that new media and technology serve to dehumanize us."[17] And, although his optimistic claims about the seemingly timeless durability of *text* now seem in doubt—he wrote *The Soft Edge* in 1996 when it was widely assumed that the "fundamental currency [of the Internet] remains the written word"[18]—there remains an essential pragmatism in his thinking that transcends the dogmatism of the zero-sum paradigm and allows for a far more nuanced treatment of the complex relationship between televisual and print media.

Alarms about Illiteracy

If the highbrow critique of mass culture represents an historic anxiety about the survival of print culture, dating in Canada from at least the 1920s, hysteria about Canadians' supposedly abominable literacy standards has emerged as a relatively recent phenomenon. Indeed, one of the leading social reform crusades in North America in the 1990s—a decade in which the downsizing of the welfare state and the privatization of dependency produced comparatively little attention to "traditional" social problems like poverty—has been the so-called war on illiteracy. US President Bill Clinton put the issue at the top of his reform agenda, for example, taking every opportunity to associate literacy with American educational and especially workplace competitiveness, and also to reward literacy workers like Nancye Gaj, founder of "Motheread," with prestigious civic honours.[19] Contemporary studies of literacy in Canada and the United States now number in the hundreds, even spawning specialized indices to guide researchers through their voluminous data. The literacy "crisis" has been informed by a generalized insecurity about rapid economic change in the 1990s and, in particular, about the transition to an "information economy" in which literacy and "numeracy" skills in the workforce are thought to be displacing the manufacturing-based "skill sets" of the industrial era. That Canadian "educational" software companies like the Ottawa-based Auto-Skills International are now frantically trying to cash in on the "fledgling field of reading skills software" speaks volumes about what might be called the trendiness of the North American literacy obsession. As AutoSkills president John Wandell suggested matter-of-factly in late 1999, "the focus on this issue will eventually be overtaken by another social or education issue within two to five years."[20]

In Canada, the literacy crisis was heralded in 1987 with the publication of *Broken Words*, an alarmist report commissioned by newspaper giant Southam Inc. and edited by journalist Peter Calamai. "Five million Canadians cannot read, write or handle numbers well enough to meet the literacy demands of today's society," the report declared, "and one-third are high school graduates." Canadians were said to be "marching against their will in an army of illiterates. . . . [D]arkness and hopelessness are usually their banners." The authors of *Broken Words* were meticulous in clarifying their research methodology and especially in justifying their own definition of literacy. (Having spent almost C$300 000 on the survey Southam was presumably at pains to refute the charge that it was manufacturing a crisis in order to pressure governments for literacy programs that would, in turn, produce more newspaper readers). The UNESCO standard for literacy was inadequate, they suggested, because it maintained simply that anyone with eight years of education is literate—a dubious claim, at least when applied to grade nine students in Canada. Thus, a more rigorous and nuanced standard, based upon the day-to-day need for various reading and comprehension skills, was proposed by a "jury" ostensibly composed of Canadians from all walks of life (including Margaret Atwood, Thomas D'Aquino, Ken Dryden, Farley Mowat, Bob White, and a number of "ordinary" people variously described as "steel worker," "smelter worker," "grain farmer," "cattleman"). The survey data were drawn from "tests" of 2 398 adults conducted in May and June 1987 and comprised of "a battery of more than 40 literacy-related questions."[21]

Broken Words boasted that it had "identified 4.5 million Canadian residents who failed to reach a minimum level of functional literacy. . . ."[22] Further, to the surprise of few who had been working on the front lines of literacy training, it found that:

- Illiteracy increases from west to east, rising from a low of 17 percent among adults in British Columbia to an astonishing high of 44 percent in Newfoundland;
- Illiteracy is higher among francophones than anglophones—29 percent to 23 percent—but the gap is biggest among the oldest and vanishes among the young;
- Nearly half of the 4.5 million functional illiterates identified in the survey are 55 or older, even though this group only accounts for 29 percent of the total population;
- Half of the illiterates say they went to high school and one-third say they graduated. One in 12 who claimed to be university graduates still tested as functionally illiterate;
- Poverty and education play major roles in deciding whether illiteracy is transmitted from one generation to the next. The children of the jobless, the working class and the poorly educated are much more liable to be illiterate.[23]

The report concluded that the "dangers" of illiteracy in Canada were "stark": ten percent of Canadian adults "can't understand the dosage directions on a medicine bottle; 20 percent can't correctly select a fact from a simple newspaper article; 40 percent can't figure out the tip on a lunch bill; more than 50 percent have serious troubles using bus schedules; and nearly 60 percent misinterpret the key section of the Charter of Rights and Freedoms."[24]

Significantly, the *Broken Words* survey included a "special over-sample of 21- to 25-year-olds," implying an extraordinary concern with young adults' literacy skills and, as suggested in Chapter Two, with the question of newspaper readership succession. The standard for functional literacy in "youth" (defined as age 21 to 25) was set out in a section entitled "Canadian Youth Score Lower in Literacy Survey than American Counterparts." It centred on "general reading proficiency" and the use of "everyday documents such as bus schedules and the Yellow Pages." Seventy-eight percent of

American youth were found to meet this standard, compared with 74 percent for Canadian youth. Notwithstanding the hyperbolic tone of this headline, the report concluded that "[y]outh on both sides of the border perform *reasonably well on school-type reading* but have trouble with real-life written material that requires more complicated 'information processing,' like finding headings in the Yellow Pages or summarizing general themes" (emphasis added).[25] A section entitled "Universities Graduate Functional Illiterates" claimed boldly that eight percent of Canadian university graduates fell below the basic standard for literacy. In the discussion that followed, however, it was admitted that: a) some respondents had exaggerated their level of educational attainment, suggesting for example that they had graduated from university rather than merely taken some courses or flunked out; b) illiteracy rises steadily with age, meaning that people who had graduated from university years or decades earlier often find their reading skills eroding; and c) recent immigrants and foreign-born Canadians may have trouble functioning in English or French even if they came to Canada with relatively high levels of educational attainment from their home countries. Of all of *Broken Words'* findings, the most significant with respect to Canadian youth was simply that "*illiterates are older*—30 percent over 65 years old compared to 16 percent of the general population" (emphasis added).[26] (Most ironic of all perhaps, especially given Southam's concern for readership succession, was the study's curious discovery that "illiterates are only slightly less likely than literates to read a newspaper at least once a week—87 percent versus 95 percent. . . .")[27]

By the mid-1990s, the literacy crisis heralded by *Broken Words* had escalated; bolstered not only by a deluge of national literacy polls but by high-profile celebrity endorsements and even corporate sponsorships, literacy training was placed squarely on the public policy agenda, where it remains. Predictably, scapegoats have been sought, and found. Television viewing has been singled out as a leading cause of illiteracy; so, too, has the poor parental supervision of children and youth. In particular, the literacy crisis has produced a pitched battle throughout North America over reading pedagogy in primary schools, in which progressive teachers favouring "whole language" reading instruction have been pitted against traditionalists who claim that the "phonics" approach was demonstrably superior.[28] Self-styled neo-conservative critics, many of whom perceive contemporary youth generally to be "wild" and out of control, have interpreted the literacy crisis as a symptom of a more broadly based "liberal" tendency in public policy. Borrowing from the Republican Right in the U.S., for example, the right-wing *Alberta Report* has in the late 1990s regularly featured stories like "A Hidebound Education Monopoly is Blamed for the Rising Tide of Illiteracy."[29] Suspicious of the hyperbole that has accompanied the literacy debate in Canada, conservative *Financial Post* columnist Michael Coren has even accused Statistics Canada and the OECD of "manipulating [their] studies to produce artificially high levels of illiteracy in order to push for more government programs." Said Coren in 1995, "Of course many [Canadians] might be uncomfortable with Dostoevsky or Kant but not with a *TV Guide* or phone directory."[30]

Echoing historian J.L. Granatstein, whose derision of Canadian university students' cognitive skills was noted above, academic observers have also waded into the literacy debate. In 1995, for example, critic Robert Lecker linked the decline of Canada's literary/publishing culture directly to the literacy crisis, citing evidence from *Broken Words*. We should remember, he cautioned,

> just how few literate readers Canada actually has. Despite the frequently made assertions that "Canadians are voracious book readers" and that we have a "robust literary culture" . . . a recent Decima survey indicates that "only 10 percent of

Canadians buy books from bookstores". Perhaps this is because we are not a nation of readers. In the first survey to provide real statistics about the state of literacy in Canada, the Southam Literacy Report *Broken Words* (1987) revealed that "five million Canadians cannot read, write or use numbers well enough to meet the literacy demands of today's society," and that 50 percent of Canadian adults have serious trouble using bus schedules and can't find a store listing in the yellow pages. . . . [E]ight percent of Canadian university graduates are functionally illiterate.

On the matter of public policy, Lecker did not pull his punches: "All the government funding directed toward the identification and promotion of Canadian culture through the reading and study of Canadian literature might have been better invested in creating a nation that, first, could read."[31] With even respectable academic researchers echoing the claims of private sector documents like *Broken Words*, little wonder that Canadians have come to believe that they are indeed "marching in an army of illiterates."

The International Adult Literacy Survey

In 1994-95 seven OECD nations—Canada, Germany, the Netherlands, Poland, Sweden, Switzerland and the U.S.—collaborated in a massive statistical analysis of their citizens' literacy skills known as the International Adult Literacy Survey (IALS). The Canadian component of the IALS, which was sponsored by the applied research branch of Human Resources Development Canada and facilitated by Statistics Canada, was published in

1996 and has subsequently has provided the raw data for any number of cohort-specific national analyses. Generally speaking, what these data reveal about literacy among youth in Canada stands in rather stark contrast with both the hysterical claims of Southam's *Broken Words* report and worries within the universities that, as Robert Lecker put it, the Canadian "reading community inhabits a tiny island in a sea of illiteracy." The truth, according to the IALS, is that young Canadians have never been more literate, that their literacy skills tend to correlate with socio-economic and regional disparities in Canada (which are matters of public policy) and, above all, that young people are today *the most literate Canadians*.

The IALS distinguished between "three literacy domains," namely prose, document, and quantitative: "Prose literacy required participants to read, understand, and use information from texts such as stories and editorials. Document literacy required readers to locate and use information from texts such as job applications, transportation schedules, and maps. Quantitative literacy required the ability to find, understand, and use mathematical operations imbedded in texts—to read weather charts found in the newspaper, for instance, or to calculate interest using a loan chart." For all nations involved in the survey, the evidence suggested, predictably, that "practices such as using libraries and reading daily reinforce strong individual literacy skills." Newspaper reading was found to be common throughout the OECD, with over 80 percent of respondents in every country reporting that they read a newspaper at least weekly; significantly, "reading books was found to be much less common than reading newspapers." (Fewer than 40 percent of respondents in all participating nations reported reading books daily, although "about 66 percent read books at least once a month." Not surprisingly, it was found that "[t]hose who read books every day tend to be at the highest literacy level.") There was a rather predictable economic emphasis in the international IALS results, a common characteristic of most literacy research since, as noted above, literacy and economic productivity in the new "information economy" are thought to be closely correlated: "the survey shows that literacy skills such as reading, writing and numeracy are also essential to a nation's economic success and social well-being."

As for the Canadian data, the IALS found that "Canada's overall literacy ratings were comparable to the United States" but that "a high proportion of [the Canadian] population achieved the lowest level of literacy in all three domains." Further, "[t]he Canadian and American results are markedly worse than those of the European countries in the study, and stand in sharp contrast to Sweden which had only about 8 percent of its adult population score at level one [the lowest level]."[32] Three broad implications for Canada of the IALS data were summarized in the *National Library News* in 1996, and correlated explicitly with the country's economic performance:

- Those who have achieved a high level of education can lose their literacy skills. Conversely, those with little formal schooling can develop, through practice and effort, sophisticated literacy competence.
- Members of Canada's "reserve labour force" (the unemployed and those currently not seeking employment) are less literate than those in similar situations in several other countries surveyed. Further, most Canadians identified as "reading but not reading well" are presently employed but have limited training opportunities.
- Public policy infrastructure is needed to create a culture of literacy in Canada (e.g., public awareness of the importance of literacy practices, opportunities for using literacy skills in the workplace to keep pace with technological advances, access to libraries, support for family literacy

awareness and initiatives to foster good literacy practices
as part of daily life).[33]

One of the most provocative of the many Canadian analyses
based upon the IALS data was J. Douglas Willms' *Literacy Skills of
Canadian Youth*, published by Statistics Canada in 1997. Willms
was interested in probing the linkages between reading skills and
upward mobility, especially as they affected the young. He began
by asserting the conventional wisdom on literacy and economic
success: "Inequalities in literacy . . . contribute directly to
inequalities in income and occupational status, in that those
[Canadians] with low literacy skills have restricted access to certain labour markets. Those with high literacy skills are more
likely to attain high-paying jobs and be rewarded for their skills."
Citing the work of French cultural theorist Pierre Bourdieu,
Willms eloquently described the socio-cultural context of literacy
in Canada, emphasizing the crucial role of reading in the demar-
cation of *class*: "Literacy is, itself, a defining characteristic of social
class. People become part of a culture by learning to interpret and
use its particular signs and symbols. They use language in social
relations that increase their knowledge and develop their potential. As such, literacy is an instrument of social power." He
reminded his readers that variations in literacy skills tend to contribute not only economic polarization in Canada but also—and
relatedly—to the degradation of the Canadian social fabric:
"Because literacy is so central to social and economic status, policy measures that decrease inequalities in literacy are fundamental to achieving tolerance [and] social cohesion. . . ."[34]

The primary task of *Literacy Skills of Canadian Youth* was to
correlate the three forms of literacy identified by the IALS (prose,
document, and quantitative) with the performance of various
Canadian age cohorts. Willms found, firstly, that each of the IALS
literacy measures "essentially follow the average literacy scores at

each age," meaning that, for Canadians in general, there were only negligible variations *between* the three literacy types in Canada (see Figure 4.2). This finding directly challenges the contention of *Broken Words* that young Canadians "perform reasonably well on school-type reading but have trouble with real-life written material that requires more complicated 'information processing'. . . ."[35] Relatedly, Willms found that "[t]he relationship between literacy and age is dramatic," not because youth are becoming increasingly illiterate, as the common stereotype would suggest, but precisely because young people's unprecedented literacy competence has so dramatically heightened the inadequacies of *older* Canadians: "The highest literacy scores on these tests were attained by adults aged (approximately) 20 to 40. After age 40, the scores declined sharply, and continued to decline through to age 90." As Figure 4.2 shows rather starkly, there is an almost inverse relationship between age and functional literacy in Canada, suggesting that, in general, literacy has steadily improved over the lifetimes of living Canadians (and, indeed, over the better part of the twentieth century). One important caveat Willms notes under the heading of "Age Effects" is that "[f]or the prose and quantitative scores, the figure indicates a modest decline in literacy scores between age 16 and 25, and thereafter, virtually no relationship with age until age 65, when it declines further." What may account for this "modest decline" he does not venture to say; it seems likely, however, that the above-average number of 16- to 25-year-olds whose first language is neither French nor English would have a significant statistical effect on the performance of this cohort. (He did, in fact, confirm that for the Canadian population at large "[a] large difference exists . . . between the literacy scores of people whose first language was English or French compared with those who had a different first language.")

LITERACY SCORES BY AGE, ADJUSTED FOR RESPONDENTS' BACK-GROUND, 1994 INTERNATIONAL ADULT LITERACY SURVEY, CANADA

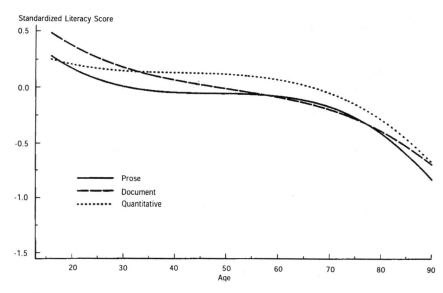

Figure 4.2
Source: J. Douglas Willms, *Literacy Skills of Canadian Youth* (Ottawa: Statistics Canada, 1997), p. 14.

As well as correlating the IALS data for Canadians with age, Willms correlated them with "years of education" and, interestingly, with the "education levels of respondents' parents." Here he confirmed the claims that literacy workers have been making for decades, namely that whether or not a young person stays in school is of paramount importance to his or her acquisition of literacy skills: "[T]he effects associated with dropping out of school remained large and statistically significant. Dropouts had prose and document literacy scores about 30 percent of a standard deviation lower than those who had completed high school; the gap for quantitative literacy was less at six percent of the standard deviation." Interestingly, with respect to parents' influence on youth literacy, the statistically significant variations were found to correlate with the mother's level of educational attainment and with the father's occupation, but not vice versa. Finally, Willms' analysis of regional variations in Canadians' IALS scores revealed that the provinces were "clustered into two distinct groups," those which have "relatively shallow gradients," meaning that the *range* of literacy skills in a given province was modest, and those which have "relatively steep gradients," or more pronounced variations (see Figure 4.3). (Manitoba and Saskatchewan scored more than one year of schooling above the national average; British Columbia, Alberta, Nova Scotia, and Quebec scored near the national average; and Ontario, New Brunswick, Newfoundland and Prince Edward Island scored the equivalent of one year of schooling below the national average.) Although, as Willms noted, "the IALS data are inadequate for addressing the causes of the steep gradients," he observed that "provinces which do well overall do so by raising the levels of performance of their youth from lower socioeconomic backgrounds." Generally, he argued, "part, but not all, of the explanation for the large variations in gradients may be explained by young adults from lower socioeconomic backgrounds remaining in school longer in provinces with shallow gradients."[36] Willms concluded *Literacy Skills of Canadian Youth* by reiterating his thesis that the greatest variation in the IALS literacy data for Canadians was indeed "associated with age" and that the significant lack of literacy skills in Canadians *older than 24* ought to be cause for immediate national attention. In contrast with *Broken Words*, he offered a cautiously optimistic prognostication for Canada's future prospects based upon the impressive literacy levels attained by the baby boom and subsequent youth cohorts: "A more uplifting aspect of the literacy-age relationship is that the baby-boomers—those aged 28 to 47 at the time of the survey—have strong literacy skills. . . . Consequently as our population ages over the next decade, the 'pool of ability', in terms of literacy skills, will increase dramatically. This should strengthen the Canadian economy. . . ."[37]

SES GRADIENTS FOR YOUTH BY PROVINCE,
1994 INTERNATIONAL ADULT LITERARY SURVEY

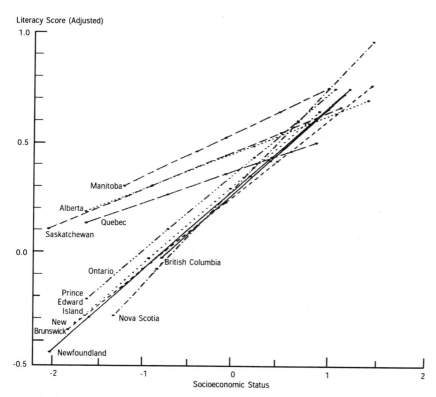

Figure 4.3
Source: J. Douglas Willms, *Literacy Skills of Canadian Youth* (Ottawa: Statistics Canada, 1997), p. 23.

As for young Canadians' performance in the IALS, though they showed demonstrably superior scores relative to older people, Willms and others Canadian researchers have continued to emphasize that they remain consistently below European literacy standards for youth. This finding was singled out in a 1999 Statistics Canada document entitled *Inequalities in Literacy Skills Among Youth in Canada and the United States,* for example: "A typical Canadian youth, whose parents had completed high school, scored about the same on the prose and document tests as their counterparts in Germany and Switzerland, but considerably lower than those in Sweden and the Netherlands. On the quantitative test, Canadians were outscored by youths in all other European countries except Poland." Vis-à-vis the United States, in contrast, Canadian youth literacy scores remain superior: "American youth whose parents had a similar level of education (secondary completion) scored about two to three years of schooling lower than Canadians."[38] Given the socio-economic stratification revealed by the IALS data, subsequent Canadian research has justifiably sought to "explore and experiment with different ways of enabling out-of-school/out-of-work ('at risk') youth to get back into learning." Significantly—at least with respect to strategies for getting "at risk" Canadian youth to read (and this may, indeed, have implications for many young Canadians *not* at risk) —researcher Burt Perrin has concluded that "Literacy approaches need to start from the unique perspectives of youth. A basic prerequisite is to adapt programming to what interests youth. This requires creative ways of constantly exploring means of getting youth interested and keeping them involved. Youth in general tend to live in the present. All projects [in the cluster] have found that a 'hook' of some form is critical."[39]

Vivian Shalla's and Grant Schellenberg's *The Value of Words: Literacy and Economic Security in Canada* (1998)—another study based on IALS data—raises important questions about not only literacy skills but the familial context in which Canadians acquire the habit of reading. In particular, these researchers posited a correlation between familial reading habits and economic inequality in Canada—a relationship with broad implications for young Canadians' relationship with print culture generally: "Literacy skills are doubtless important, but it is becoming abundantly clear that the processes by which individuals acquire, maintain and enhance literacy and other skills occur within a socio-economic context rife with inequality. Inequality of opportunity creates an environment conducive of unequal outcomes." Specifically, Shalla and Schellenberg asserted that "families' economic well-being and literacy affect how their children face the future—the outcomes of one generation lay the foundation for the conditions and opportunities of the next." They explored in detail "the relationship between parents' economic security and their literacy-enhancing practices and activities, as well as those of their children." What they discovered was that

> [t]he presence of reading material in the home may encourage both parents and children to pursue literacy activities. While parents from non-low-income households with children between the ages of 6 and 18 were more likely than those from low-income households to have reading material in the home, the differences were slight, except for the presence of daily newspapers—70 percent of non-low-income homes and 48 percent of low-income homes received daily newspapers. Although reading material was more likely to be found in non-low-income homes than in low-income homes, it was far from absent in low-income homes. Indeed, almost all low-income homes had a dictionary, a sizable majority owned more than 25 books or had weekly newspapers or magazines, a substantial number owned a multi-volume encyclopedia, and many had daily newspapers. (see Figure 4.4)[40]

Turning to the specific sources of Canadian families' reading materials, the authors observed, "Children from both types of households most often obtained their books from school libraries. Purchases by parents and borrowing from public libraries were the next most often mentioned sources for both low-income and non-low-income homes. These findings show that most children, regardless of economic circumstances, have access to reading

READING MATERIAL FOUND IN HOUSEHOLDS IN WHICH CHILDREN AGED 6 TO 18 ARE PRESENT, BY INCOME STATUS, CANADA, 1994

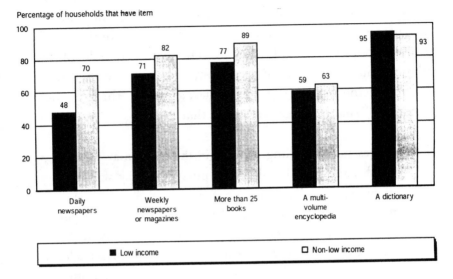

Percentage of households that have item

- Daily newspapers: 48 / 70
- Weekly newspapers or magazines: 71 / 82
- More than 25 books: 77 / 89
- A multi-volume encyclopedia: 59 / 63
- A dictionary: 95 / 93

■ Low income   □ Non-low income

Figure 4.4
Source: Vivian Shalla and Grant Schellenberg, *The Value of Words: Literacy and Economic Security in Canada* (Ottawa: Statistics Canada, 1998), p. 44.

material at home, giving them at least some of the conditions needed to engage in literacy practices."[41]

Shalla and Schellenberg concluded *The Value of Words* with several important observations. The first was that "[p]arental support for, and encouragement of, literacy-related activities is an important factor in the development of children's literacy practices. Evidence from the IALS indicates that parents from non-low-income households are only slightly more likely to encourage the development of their children's reading habits" (see Figure 4.5). Indeed, "[w]hile it appears that economic circumstances impose some constraints on literacy practices and activities in the home, parents and children from low-income homes are obviously finding ways to develop literacy skills despite financial obstacles." The authors were disposed to minimize differences between wealthy and low-income households, highlighting instead the relative similarity of these environments in the promotion of good reading habits. What is worrisome, they asserted, is a far more *generalized* pattern in Canada, namely that "a significant number of children, regardless of their economic circumstances, did not have a dedicated time to read at home, and many did not have limits set on the number of hours of television they watched each day." They concluded that these data suggest "potential problems for current and future labour market participants, given rapidly-changing employment structures and the shift to an information-based economy." For Canadians, the challenge is clear: "The strong link between literacy and economic security shown in this study should concern policy makers, especially in the context of global economic restructuring. The new economy is characterized, not only by an explosion in the production, dissemination and use of information, but also by a polarization of the labour market into good jobs and bad jobs, and by high levels of unemployment and underemployment. Because strong literacy skills are key to success in the information-based economy, those with weak literacy abilities will have more difficulty gaining a solid foothold in the labour market and achieving economic well-being." In short, for these researchers at least, "[t]he problem of poor literacy skills is not simply an issue of education, nor is it only a private, individual matter. It is also an indicator of deeper social and economic inequalities that characterize contemporary society."[42]

Taken together, the conclusions put forward by Willms, Shalla and Schellenberg, and others challenge fundamentally the stereotypical assumptions that prevail in private sector surveys about "illiterate youth," most notably those proffered by the newspaper industry. On the one hand, the IALS data as interpreted by these Canadian researchers affirm that young Canadians are

**FREQUENCY WITH WHICH CHILDREN AGED 6 TO 18 READ FOR PLEASURE
(AS REPORTED BY PARENT), BY INCOME STATUS, CANADA, 1994**

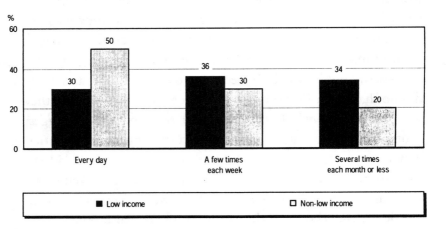

Figure 4.5
Source: Vivian Shalla and Grant Schellenberg, *The Value of Words: Literacy and Economic Security in Canada* (Ottawa: Statistics Canada, 1998), p. 46.

among the nation's most literate citizens and that, among all the other variables correlated with youth literacy, the high school drop-out rate continues to be the most significant. This finding, corroborated by the provincial variation in literacy shown so dramatically in Figure 4.3, leads to the inescapable conclusion that literacy skills continue to correlate directly with levels of *formal* educational attainment and, hence, that literacy training ought to be treated as a matter of public policy as well as a private concern. On the other hand, the evidence suggests that, *despite* their myriad socio-economic disadvantages, low-income Canadian households are not at all casual about imparting good reading habits to their children (measured against their more affluent counterparts at least). Rather, low-income parents share with their middle- and upper-income counterparts a profound awareness of the need to encourage literacy skills in their children, as evinced by their heavy use of "free" reading materials available through school and public libraries, and especially their consider-able efforts to purchase books for use at home. Though the data are not by any means conclusive, they may be interpreted as showing that families of *all* socio-economic classes are, in fact, employing these strategies to compensate for inequitable circum-stances occasioned by the Canadian class structure generally, something that should come as no surprise given the ubiquitous public preoccupation with literacy as a prerequisite for individual upward mobility and national economic prosperity.

5

READING
YOUTH

Reading to
Children

THAT CANADIANS are extraordinarily conscientious about reading to their children is evinced both by the widespread public interest in literacy issues noted above and, indeed, by the remarkable proliferation in recent years of children's literature. As journalist Wendy Cole suggested in 1998, in fact, the current North American literary obsession has produced a related preoccupation with the reading habits of children that extends even to a public fascination with baby brain development. There has been, she notes, a "media blitz about new brain research that warn of the need to provide our youngest citizens with a rich array of stimulating experiences. Everyone from Rob Reiner and Robin Williams to the Clintons embrace the cause. The White House even held a baby-brain summit."[1] Not surprisingly, many of these ostensibly scientific findings are in contention, and some researchers have expressed a worry that "their findings are being misinterpreted by the public." In an attempt to offer a more "balanced" agenda to parents, Cole advocates what has arguably become the predominant North American philosophy of child-rearing: "Books, books, and more books. Reading to a child offers wonderful bonding opportunities, and it's never too early to start. But don't race through a story or choose complicated texts. Find age-appropriate ways to engage babies in the material. If reading is merely a passive activity for toddlers, they won't learn how to be critical thinkers or to take the initiative."[2] Public interest in reading to children has coalesced around World Book Day (observed annually on 23 April) and Canada Book Day (27 April), which have become "major occasion[s] for booksellers, librarians and publishers to work together on the promotion of books and reading," especially among the young.[3] Canadians also celebrate Born To Read Day (24 April), a national project spearheaded by the late Ben Wicks, in which "nearly 2 million school children [are] given a free copy of the book *Born to Read*, which tells parents how to help their children become more literate." (In keeping with the IALS emphasis on "family literacy" noted above, Born To Read Day is said to promote a "reading-positive" atmosphere in the home.)[4] Yet another children's literature initiative is Canadian Children's Book Week, a annual festival organized and promoted by the Toronto-based Canadian Children's Book Centre. It has been estimated that this "read-in" attracts nearly 30 000 children to meet Canadian writers and illustrators in person, contributing to the children's literature star system (and, of course, to the international fame and fortune of the likes of Canadian author Robert Munsch).[5]

In 1995 *Maclean's* featured a story on the "Kidlit Boom" in Canada which chronicled the massive expansion of Canadian children's publishing since the mid-1970s, noting in particular the domestic and especially the international success of Canadian houses Annick, Groundwood, KidsCan, Owl and Tundra.

Before 1975, "only a handful" of children's books were published in Canada yearly, it noted. Yet by 1985 there were 150 titles, and by 1995 the number of children's and "young adult" titles exceeded 400 per year. Commented *Maclean's* authors Brian Bethune and Diane Turbide, "Not only are there a lot more books, but they are much better—funnier, deeper, more daring and more visually appealing—than they once were." The "kidlit boom" was, in fact, a bi-product of the 1970s Canadian Lit phenomenon explored in Chapter One and owed much of its success to the left-nationalist publishing *zeitgeist* of the times. As Bethune and Turbide imply, the "creative and entrepreneurial boom in Canadian children's books" had everything to do with demographics and good timing. The market of educated baby boomer parents with money to spend on their children was gaining momentum; so, too, was an increasing awareness of "the role of books in raising bright, imaginative children." The extension in 1975 of Canada Council funding to children's book publishing served as a powerful catalyst for myriad children's publishing ventures. As Kids Can Press publisher Valerie Hussey has recalled: "We'd been raised on British and American books, but that was a period of strong Canadian nationalism, and we decided we should have our own."[6] Similarly, Rick Wilkes, co-publisher of Toronto's Annick Press has observed: "When we started 20 years ago, we had a very strong desire to create terrific books for kids that embodied the voices and values of Canadians. And without being too self-consciously chauvinistic about it, we also knew that anything good enough for the Canadian child would be good enough for the universal child, and would travel beyond Canada."[7] *Toronto Star* columnist and one-time Morningside children's book reviewer Michele Landsberg recalled in 1995: "With a few exceptions, it used to be a patriotic chore to review Canadian children's books. Now it's a pleasure. The books being produced in this country are some of the best in the world."[8]

The children's literature "industry" is, like Canadian Lit generally, a rather unlikely success story—and one which is all the more noteworthy for having surmounted the historic obstacles to Canadian publishing, namely a small market dispersed over a huge territory. As the international publishing trade press regularly reports, Canadian children's titles are among the country's most recognizable—and profitable—literary exports. Like "adult" Canadian literature, children's books have been targeted overwhelmingly at baby boomers, the parents (and now grandparents) of 1980s and 1990s youth, institutionalizing a highly discriminating literary taste in publishing, bookselling and library acquisition. The evidence for this claim is ubiquitous—but nowhere more so than in the "boutique" bookstores whose only (or primary) business is children's books. Judy and Hy Sarick of The Children's Bookstore, for example, were "famous for refusing to carry popular series like the Babysitters' Club or the Goosebumps horror stories. . . ." Said Judy Sarick recently: "Goosebumps were terribly written and extraordinarily superficial; kids could get those someplace else. . . . Goosebumps is dead now, 80 percent off at Chapters."[9] This rather highbrow bias in Canadian children's literature is also evident in various National Library promotions, including, for example, the highly publicized launch in 1996 of *Green Eggs and Hamlet,* a two-volume anthology of poetry written by students in an Ottawa-area public school.[10]

That the dominant Canadian literary/publishing culture tends to privilege children over youth is suggested by the thirteen-year evolution of the National Library's "Read Up On It" program. Started as a pilot project in 1988 and sponsored by the CBC and the Book and Periodical Development Council (now the Book and Periodical Council), Read Up On It was, according to co-ordinator Dale Simmons, "initially designed to encourage television viewers [of all ages] to appreciate Canadian books more. The experimental project focused on the creation of 20-second television spots in which well-known actors and television personalities described books whose subject matter coincided with the program being aired." It also featured a teaching "kit," which was made available to "educators, librarians, parents and youth leaders" under National Library auspices. In the second year of the program, "libraries became essential partners," while the "spots" were still targeted at a general audience. By the third year, however, the program had drawn in a large number of corporate media sponsors, including CTV, Global, YTV and MuchMusic; and it had begun "gradually narrowing its audience to target the reading interests of children and young adults, with the materials in the kit geared to those working with children."[11] Having abandoned adults altogether, and having phased youth out of the "kit," Read Up On It was nonetheless touted as late as 1997 as a program generally aimed at "encouraging reading among the young." In the following year, however, youth were abandoned altogether in favour of a singleminded emphasis upon children. As Simons noted somewhat obliquely in his annual report for 1998, "this dynamic and evolving project has become a valuable resource tool for those interested in Canadian children's books and encouraging children to read."[12] Whether or not Read Up On It—like World Book Day and Born To Read Day—has a continuing role to play in the promotion of reading among Canadian youth, the public face of the program affirms the general rule: *children* comprise the cohort that matters most.

Given the widespread belief that Canadian youth do not or cannot read, it is not easy to know what to make of this extraordinary emphasis on "high quality" children's literature/publishing in Canada; nor, indeed, is it easy to know how to interpret the dedication with which Canadian families of all social classes make such reading materials available to their children. The salient point, at the risk of stating the obvious, is that adults are the gatekeepers of children's reading habits (and purchases) until adolescence, at which time they cease to have a commanding influence over their children's leisure pursuits. One symptom of this familial pattern, it may be argued, is the persistent "gap" in Canadian publishing and book retailing, in which children's and adults' books are well supplied but comparatively little exists in between. (Shelf space allotted to "young adult" titles in Canadian bookstores, for example, amounts by my estimate to about ten percent of the space dedicated to children's books.) As I shall suggest below, this does not necessarily mean that youth are not reading or purchasing books, but it certainly corroborates the observation of Jean Baird and others, noted in Chapter Two, that booksellers do not view young people as niche market (or at least not as one that is worth cultivating). Given the extraordinary lengths to which *competing* leisure industries have gone to carve out the "youth market" as something not only unique but on the cutting edge of North American culture generally—think of Nike, or Sega, or Interscope—this is a curious anomaly, one which cannot help but contribute to the popular stereotype that youth are not interested in books. (These days, bookstores seem to be the only outlets in Canadian shopping malls which are *not* reorienting themselves towards the youth market, which is itself curious, at least insofar as malls serve increasingly as officially sanctioned "hangouts" for young people.) Given the superior literacy skills of contemporary youth in Canada, and the rather overwhelming evidence that they were weaned on some of the world's finest children's literature, the question may not be whether young people have abandoned books but whether the book trade has abandoned young people.

This Just In: Youth *Do* Read

At the risk of overstating the case, it is worth recalling yet again—notwithstanding all of the common misperceptions about youth as illiterate or too lazy to read—that young Canadians are every bit as varied as the population at large and that, therefore, their reading and book purchasing habits are as well. What many Canadian youth and young adults *do* have in common is "downward mobility," economic dependence and entry-level wages, circumstances which inevitably affect what might be called their literary purchasing power, if not absolutely then at least insofar as they must confront hard choices about whether to buy books over clothing or computers or compact discs. A second, equally important aspect of young people's lived experience, one that sets them apart from most adults, is that they are likely to be in school—a vocation which itself limits their employment opportunities and earning potential, even if it appears to provide more leisure time than full-time paid work. To state an obvious but largely unacknowledged corollary of student life, it is also true of full- and even part-time students that they are obliged to spend much of their preparatory time for classes reading and also, especially in the case of postsecondary students, that they must devote a significant part of their incomes to the purchase of required class texts—expenses which, in turn, may contribute to their mounting educational debt load or exacerbate their state of economic dependency.

Taken together, young people's relative shortage of earned income and their already considerable *obligatory* curricular reading responsibilities mitigate against both the acquisition of vast personal libraries and the likelihood that they will spend their "free time" reading. As one of my own undergraduate students reminded me recently, "reading is my full-time job." Nor is it especially surprising that students should want to "hang" with their friends, or to "chat" with them on the phone or online, or watch television or a movie, since these are precisely the pastimes *adult* Canadians employ as antidotes to the stresses of their work-a-day lives.[13] Though obvious perhaps, these aspects of youth culture

AVERAGE DAILY TIME SPENT ON SELECTED ACTIVITIES BY PEOPLE AGED 15–19, 1992

	Employed			Students		
	Men	Women	Total	Men	Women	Total
	Hours per day					
Productive activities:						
Paid work and related activities	4.6	5.8	5.0	0.8	0.8	0.8
Unpaid work	0.9	2.0	1.3	0.9	1.4	1.2
Education and related activities	...	0.3	0.1	4.9	5.6	5.3
Total productive activities	5.4	8.1	6.4	6.5	7.9	7.2
Sleep	9.0	8.1	8.7	8.7	8.4	8.6
Other personal care activities	2.1	2.4	2.2	1.9	2.2	2.1
Free time activities:						
Socializing	2.6	2.6	2.6	1.9	2.1	2.0
Television viewing	2.4	1.2	2.0	2.4	1.6	2.0
Reading and other passive leisure	0.6	0.7	0.6	0.4	0.5	0.4
Attending movies, sport events and other entertainment events	0.2	0.1	0.1	0.3	0.4	0.3
Active sports	1.3	0.6	1.0	1.3	0.5	0.9
Other active leisure	0.4	0.3	0.4	0.6	0.4	0.5
Total free time	7.4	5.4	6.7	6.9	5.4	6.2
Total time	24.0	24.0	24.0	24.0	24.0	24.0

Figure 5.1

Source: Colin Lindsay, et al., *Youth in Canada: Second Edition* (Ottawa: Statistics Canada, 1994), p. 36.

and especially student life seem to me to go a long way towards explaining why the most literate Canadians—the young—often appear to be among the least interested in reading "for pleasure" or in purchasing books. (The same may also be said of many adult "knowledge workers;" as a 27-year-old English teacher admitted in her response to my online questionnaire, "I need to read for my job every day—that is why I don't have much time to read for pleasure." She added: "I'm trying to train myself to read a book a week.") Though admittedly anecdotal, many of the student responses to my questionnaire expressed the same sort of ambivalence, namely that "required" reading for classes diminished their interest in reading "for fun." Like so many busy Canadian adults, young people also expressed the hope that they would "get around" to reading for pleasure during their summer (and other) holidays.[14]

The definitive study of Canadians' reading practises in the 1990s remains Frank L. Graves' and Timothy Dugas' *Reading in Canada 1991,* a document commissioned by the federal Department of Communications in order to "gather up to date information on the reading behaviour and opinions of Canadians aged 14 and older." Though dated in some important respects—it does not take into account the rise of the Internet, most obviously—the data from this survey nonetheless remain extremely useful. On the one hand, they provide a singular window on one of the most heavily stigmatized youth cohorts in recent years, the so-called Gen Xers, Canadians who remain, socio-economically at least, far more like the current youth cohort than the affluent baby boomers "ahead" of them. Moreover, since Canadians who were between the ages of 14 and 24 in 1991 are today between 25 and 35, these data also provide a glimpse at the formative literary habits of the current crop of young adults who comprise what might be called Canada's new post-nationalist literati. Above all, falling as they did in the midst of the literacy hysteria occasioned, for example, by the *Broken Words* report, these data provide a singular opportunity to test empirically the generalized claims of Robert Lecker and others that Canadian readers comprise a beleaguered minority awash in a culture of televisual narcotization. (It may well be the case, given the general stagnation of the Canadian book publishing sector throughout the 1990s, that these data reflect circumstances which obtained well into the decade and which, in turn, began to change only late in the decade under the pressure of globalization and technological change described above. This said, a comprehensive survey of Canadians' *current* reading and book buying habits would constitute a welcome supplement to the research literature.)

By its authors' own immodest admission, *Reading in Canada 1991* provided "a new benchmark readership survey in Canada," not least because it exposed the great gulf between the common belief that Canadians had little interest in reading and the seemingly incontrovertible evidence of their *bona fide* passion for it. Graves and Dugas specifically conceived their research as a longitudinal (comparative) complement to the last national survey of Canadians' reading and book purchasing habits, which had been commissioned in 1978.[15] Their work was based upon telephone interviews with 23 900 Canadians of all ages, of whom roughly 7 000 also completed a complementary written questionnaire. (Like many other researchers, Graves and Dugas admitted that their survey-based methodology almost certainly skewed their results by excluding non-readers, whom they estimated to comprise roughly ten percent of the general population; they also alluded to Canadians' tendency to exaggerate their reading prowess, a perennial problem arising from the fact that reading is regarded as a "socially desirable" behaviour.)[16]

Significantly, Graves and Dugas believed that it would come as a great shock to their readers that "[t]he vast majority of Canadians read for pleasure. Moreover, they read quite frequently and devote a very substantial chunk of their discretionary time to reading." Explicitly challenging the common belief that the habit of reading is in decline under the pressure of televisual media, they noted further, "Even considering all possible survey biases (it is most likely that) over 90 percent of Canadians read for pleasure—many of them with considerable appetite." Fully half of the sample group claimed to have read more than five hours in the past week, and more than one in six said they read for more than eleven hours in the same period. The greatest amount of this time was "devoted to book reading:" the sample average for book reading was 4.4 hours per week, for newspapers 3.6 hours per week, and for magazines 2.1 hours per week, for a total of ten hours per week. In general, asserted Graves and Dugas, "Reading occupies a central and impressive place in leisure time use. It is the third most time consuming activity, following television (conservatively underestimated at about 14.4 hours combining news and other TV programs) and listening to music. In fact, nearly one out of every six hours of discretionary time is devoted to reading." They also found, not surprisingly, given the public concern with children's literacy noted above, that older Canadians believe strongly in the need to teach younger Canadians reading skills. "The growing strategic importance of reading to Canadians is even more vividly revealed in their views on the importance of transmitting reading skills to the next generation. Only about one percent of Canadians disagree with the statement that 'it is important that a parent read to their young child.'"17

In an analysis of the materials that Canadians were reading for pleasure, Graves and Dugas showed that "the most spectacular growth [since 1978] has occurred in the area of book reading—presumably the most demanding of all types of reading materials." The number of Canadians reporting in 1978 that they had read from books in the past week was 43 percent, compared with 68 percent in 1991. Similarly, those reporting that they had read from books from the "past year" rose from 63 percent in 1978 to 84 percent in 1991. Contrary to the alarms about illiteracy then circulating widely in Canada, the authors asserted that "both the quantity and, quite plausibly, the quality of reading in Canada has improved dramatically in the past 13 years." What the data *did* reveal was that between 1978 and 1991, *newspaper reading* was "substantially lower, by half an hour," and that this relatively large decrease was "more than compensated for by a substantial increase in book reading." In retrospect, this was one of Graves' and Dugas' most suggestive claims, since it confirmed the findings of the newspaper industry that it has a serious succession problem, while bluntly refuting the contention that this decline in newspaper readership was the result of a rampant (and worsening) problem of illiteracy (see Figure 5.2).[18]

Among the most notable cohort-specific discoveries made by Graves and Dugas was that "groups over [the age of] 44 have the largest increases in book reading, especially the 65 to 69 age group"—a finding which raises questions about the IALS and other "functional" literacy studies purporting to show seniors to be the least literate Canadians. Graves' and Dugas' findings about the reading habits of young Canadians were equally striking. They found "an increase of 25 percent in book reading between 1978 and 1991 for Canadians 15 to 19 years of age." Moreover, the average time this cohort spent reading books "rose from an average of 2.8 hours to 3.5 hours in 1991." Taking sardonic aim at teachers' perennial complaints that their students' reading habits are in decline, Graves and Dugas editorialized: "Just as the apocryphal distance one walked to school increases with age, so teachers' nostalgic perceptions of the good old days exaggerated their former students' capabilities with the passage of time." One of the most surprising conclusions drawn by these researchers was that "[y]oung Canadians not only read a large number of books, [but] they read, on average, 5.3 Canadian-authored books in the past 12 months, *the*

**AVERAGE NUMBER OF HOURS SPENT IN THE PREVIOUS WEEK
READING NEWSPAPERS, MAGAZINES AND BOOKS, BY SEX, AGE,
MOTHER TONGUE AND PROVINCE: 1978 AND 1991 COMPARISONS**

	Newspapers		Magazines		Books	
	1978	1991	1978	1991	1978	1991
Age Group						
15-19	2.5	1.9	2.1	1.9	2.8	3.5
20-24	3.2	2.3	2.0	1.8	3.1	4.5
25-34	3.5	2.6	1.8	1.8	2.6	3.5
35-44	4.2	3.3	1.8	1.8	2.6	4.0
45-54	4.8	3.6	1.8	2.0	2.2	4.3
55-64	5.7	4.6	2.3	2.3	2.9	4.8
65-69	5.6	5.7	2.1	2.5	2.9	5.7
70 and Over	5.3	5.6	1.9	3.0	2.8	6.7

Figure 5.2
Source: Frank L. Graves & Timothy Dugas, Principal Authors, *Reading in Canada 1991* (Ottawa: Ekos Research Associates Inc., 1991), p. 18.

highest number of any segment in this analysis" (emphasis added). Though Canadians 65 and older were found to be the most voracious book readers, averaging 33.9 books per year, they were followed by the 15 to 19-year-olds, who read on average 25.4 books annually. The two groups least inclined to read books, interestingly, were those aged 25-34 and 55-64, both of which averaged only 21.3 books per year. Graves and Dugas offered no explanation for why Canadians in their late twenties were reading less for pleasure than teenagers; it may be speculated, however, that their commencement of post-secondary education and/or demanding entry-level jobs accounts in large measure for this variation.

Perhaps the most important trend discovered by Graves and Dugas—and this has enormous implications for the question of renewal in the Canadian book publishing sector—was that "[t]he characteristics of book *purchasers* stand in marked contrast to book *readers*." Specifically, while the youngest and oldest Canadians read the most books, *they accounted for "the lowest average number of books purchased."* The 35 to 44-year-old group, in contrast, showed the greatest propensity to purchase books, at an average of 7 per year (see Figure 5.3).[19] Given the rather dramatic stratification of Canadians' socio-economic status since the 1970s, in which "downwardly mobile" youth and young adults have fallen markedly behind the affluent baby boom cohort, this pattern should come as little surprise. At the very least, it confirms that little can be deduced about young Canadians' propensity for reading from their book purchasing habits alone; at worst, it bolsters Walter Kirn's and William Dowell's rather sardonic contention, noted in the Introduction, that books have become the latest yuppie lifestyle accessories.

All in all, Graves and Dugas were optimistic about the future of book publishing. Although they could not have anticipated the recession of 1992, the dramatic cuts in government funding that came in the mid–1990s or the widespread use of Net-based technologies—all of which conspired to stall the Canadian book publishing sector for much of the last decade—it remains significant that, on purely demographic grounds, these researchers predicted "a vibrant and growing market" for book publishers. Certainly one gets no sense whatsoever from these researchers that Canadian book publishing was in any way threatened by the defection of young Canadians; indeed, they repeatedly disabused their readers of indulging in this and any number of other stereotypes about Canadians' retreat from print culture. In the end, concluded Graves and Dugas, what Canadians believe about the decline of reading is simply not consistent with their lived experience: "It is evident that many Canadians are failing to appreciate the vibrancy and salience of reading in Canada. This may be a

AVERAGE NUMBER OF CANADIAN BOOKS PURCHASED IN THE LAST THREE MONTHS BY SELECTED SOCIODEMOGRAPHIC CHARACTERISTICS

	Average Number of Books Purchased	Average Number of Canadian Books Purchased	Average Per Cent of Books Purchased that were Canadian
Age Group			
15-19	5.0	1.1	18.0
20-24	6.5	1.4	20.5
25-34	6.7	1.2	20.9
35-44	7.2	1.4	21.0
45-54	6.7	1.5	25.1
55-64	4.8	1.6	28.0
65 and over	5.0	1.2	29.9

Figure 5.3
Source: Frank L. Graves & Timothy Dugas, Principal Authors, *Reading in Canada 1991* (Ottawa: Ekos Research Associates Inc., 1991), p. 28.

more particular expression of a disturbing general trend to over-state the problems in Canada while failing to celebrate, let alone recognize, our strengths and achievements."[20]

Nancy Duxbury's *The Reading and Purchasing Public*, published in 1995, constituted a reinterpretation of Graves' and Dugas' data pertaining to English Canada. It began by showing that, of a sample group of 4 842 English Canadians, 4 024 (or 83 percent) called themselves "book readers"—a figure more or less consistent with Graves' and Dugas' estimate that ten percent of Canadians may not read at all. With reference to specific age cohorts, Duxbury suggested that 90 percent of Canadians between the ages of 15 and 24 were book readers, compared with 80 percent of Canadians aged 25 to 34, 82 percent for those 35 to 54, and 83 percent for those 55 or older. She also found that formal education increases Canadians' propensity to read books, although not as dramatically as might be expected given the apparent correlation between educational attainment and basic literacy: 72 percent of English Canadians with primary school (or less) education were book readers, versus 80 percent who had "some" high school, 84 percent of high school graduates, 87 percent of Canadians with "some" postsecondary education, and 88 percent with "postgraduate" training (see Figure 5.4).[21]

As for the question of how much each cohort read on average, Duxbury took the total number of book readers as her sample (i.e. she excluded the non-book readers) and then calculated how much time in the "last week" they spent reading newspapers, magazines and books "for pleasure" (see Figure 5.5). Respondents' commitment to reading was divided into quintiles: no reading, light reading (1-2 hours), medium reading (3-5 hours), heavy reading (6-10 hours) and very heavy reading (11 hours or more). Here, as in Graves' and Dugas' study, the results confirmed that Canadian book readers are not big newspaper readers: the largest percentage of book readers were found to be light readers of newspapers at 37 percent, while 28 percent called themselves "medium" readers of newspapers. Significantly, only 20 percent of Canadian book readers called themselves heavy readers of newspapers, while only 7 percent called themselves "very heavy" newspaper readers. Interestingly, these data conformed exactly to the data for *all* English-speakers in the survey, meaning that the extent to which Canadians read newspapers is not appreciably affected by whether or not they are also reading books. Given the similarity of both Duxbury's and Graves' and Dugas' analyses of this issue, and the fact that both reports more or less coincided with the publication of the *Broken Words* survey, it may be confidently concluded that *nothing* whatsoever can be assumed about Canadians' ability or inclination to read on the basis of declining

PROFILE OF ALL BOOK READERS AND ENGLISH-SPEAKERS, BY SEX, AGE, EDUCATION, OCCUPATION, ANNUAL HOUSEHOLD INCOME AND REGION OF RESIDENCE

	ALL BOOK READERS	ALL ENGLISH SPEAKERS	% BK RDRS OF ALL ENGLISH SPKRS	
N	4024	4842	83%	
SEX				
FEMALE	2223	2512	88%	
	55%	52%	77%	
MALE	1785	2311	77%	
	44%	48%		
TOTAL	4008	4823	83%	
AGE				
15-24 YRS	573	634	90%	
	14%	13%		
25-34 YRS	723	906	80%	
	18%	19%		
35-54 YRS	1208	1479	82%	
	30%	31%		
55+	1502	1802	83%	
	37%	37%		
TOTAL	4006	4821	83%	
	100%	100%		
HIGHEST LEVEL OF FORMAL EDUCATION				
PRIM. OR LESS	458	632	72%	
	12%	14%		
SME H. SCHL	1084	1348	80%	
	28%	29%		
H. SCHL GRAD	595	706	84%	
	15%	15%		
SME P. SNDRY	653	748	87%	
	17%	18%		
P. SNDRY	1077	1226	88%	
	28%	26%		
TOTAL	3867	4660	83%	
	100%	100%		

Figure 5.4

Source: Nancy Duxbury, *The Reading and Purchasing Public: The Market for Trade Books in English Canada 1991* (Toronto: Association of Canadian Publishers, 1995), n.p.

newspaper readership alone. The relationship between magazine and book reading is similarly incongruous: 50 percent of book readers called themselves light readers of magazines, compared with 47 percent of the entire sample (book readers *and* non-book readers), while 20 percent of book readers were found to be medium readers of magazines, as compared to 19 percent of the entire sample group. Eight percent of book readers were heavy magazine readers, versus 7 percent of the general population; for very heavy magazine readers there was no difference, at 5 percent each. In short, the data for the most voracious magazine and newspaper readers in Canada do not vary *at all* with reference to whether or not they are also reading books.

Duxbury's breakdown of the relationship between the age of book readers and the number of hours per week during which they read for pleasure provides a somewhat more nuanced perspective on Graves' and Dugas' findings. On the one hand—and, again, in rather striking contrast with the IALS and other "functional literacy" data from the early 1990s—she corroborated Graves' and Dugas' discovery that elderly Canadians are the most voracious book readers: although Canadians 55 years of age or older comprised only 37 percent of her sample group, they represented fully 53 percent of English Canada's "very heavy" book readers (see Figure 5.6). In contrast with Graves and Dugas, on the other hand, Duxbury found that Canadians between the ages of 15 and 24 were disproportionately likely to be non-readers, light readers, or medium readers, and disproportionately less likely to be heavy readers or very heavy readers. She also found that 25 to 34-year-olds, who comprised 18 percent of her sample group, were disproportionately well represented in the no reading and light reading categories, at par with the national average for medium reading category, and lower than average in the heavy and very heavy categories. For Canadians between age 35 and 54, which constituted 30 percent of her sample, there were

TIME SPENT READING NEWSPAPERS, MAGAZINES, AND BOOKS LAST WEEK FOR PLEASURE BY BOOK READERS AND ALL ENGLISH-LANGUAGE SPEAKERS

	ALL BOOK READERS	ALL ENGLISH-SPEAKERS
N	4024	4842
ALL BOOK READERS:		
HOURS READING LAST WEEK		
Newspapers–		
Pleasure		
No Reading	247	369
	7%	8%
Light (1-2)	1337	1586
	37%	36%
Medium (3-5)	1026	1199
	28%	28%
Heavy (6-10)	737	879
	20%	20%
Very Heavy (11+)	266	321
	7%	7%
TOTAL	3613	4354
	100%	100%
Magazines–		
Pleasure		
No Reading	623	933
	17%	21%
Light (1-2)	1784	2061
	50%	47%
Medium (3-5)	736	822
	20%	19%
Heavy (6-10)	277	313
	8%	7%
Very Heavy (11+)	184	214
	5%	5%
TOTAL	3604	4343
	100%	100%
Books–		
Pleasure		
No Reading	604	1332
	15%	28%
Light (1-2)	855	923
	22%	19%
Medium (3-5)	930	917
	24%	19%
Heavy (6-10)	885	892
	23%	19%
Very Heavy (11+)	648	678
	17%	14%
TOTAL	3910	4742
	100%	100%

Figure 5.5
Source: Nancy Duxbury, *The Reading and Purchasing Public: The Market for Trade Books in English Canada 1991* (Toronto: Association of Canadian Publishers, 1995), n.p.

slightly more non-readers, disproportionately more medium and heavy readers, and disproportionately fewer very heavy readers.

Duxbury's analysis seems to challenge Graves' and Dugas' most strikingly in the realm of the literary *content* most favoured by English-Canadian book readers (even allowing for the considerably more nationalist literary predilections of Québec franco-phones represented in *Reading in Canada 1991*). She found that, in general, the older the reader, the more likely he or she will be reading Canadian-authored or Canadian-published books. Figure 5.7, for example, shows the nationality of the author of last book purchased according to demographic variables. In the 15 to 24-year-old age group, only 8 percent of the authors last read were Canadian (versus 92 percent foreign); for 25 to 34-year-olds, 12 percent were Canadian; for 35 to 54-year-olds, 15 percent were Canadian; and for Canadians 55 or older, fully 19 percent were Canadian. Similarly, Figure 5.8 shows the nationality of the publisher of the last book purchased, dividing publishers into "Canadian publishers," "Canadian agent," "foreign-owned Canadian base" and "direct import." Referenced against demographic criteria, the data reveal the same general pattern: only 7 percent of Canadian aged 15 to 24 purchased their last book from a Canadian publisher; for Canadians 25 to 34, the figure rose to 11 percent; for 35 to 54-year-olds, it rose again to 13 percent; and for Canadians 55 or older it peaked at 17 percent. Since the national average for all age groups was calculated to be 13 percent, Duxbury's analysis points to the rather dramatic conclusion that Canadian youth are not only far less likely than older Canadians to patronize Canadian publishers, but they are only about half as likely to do so as the *national average*.

Taken together, *Reading in Canada 1991* and *The Reading and Purchasing Public* affirm the following features of young Canadians' encounter with the culture of print: a) that, in the early 1990s at least, youth were highly disposed to read; b) that they were, at

AGE OF BOOK READERS BY HOURS READING BOOKS LAST WEEK FOR PLEASURE

	TOTAL		AGE							
			15-24 YRS		25-34 YRS		35-54 YRS		55+ YRS	
		%		%		%		%		%
N(4024)	4006		573	14%	723	18%	1208	30%	1502	37%
HOURS READING LAST WEEK										
No Reading	605	15%	88	15%	124	20%	189	31%	204	34%
				16%		18%		16%		14%
Light (1-2)	859	22%	136	16%	174	20%	252	29%	297	35%
				25%		25%		21%		20%
Medium (3-5)	920	23%	138	15%	169	18%	321	35%	292	32%
				26%		24%		27%		20%
Heavy (6-10)	886	23%	105	12%	147	17%	284	32%	350	40%
				19%		21%		24%		24%
Very Heavy (11+)	650	17%	72	11%	90	14%	143	22%	345	53%
				13%		13%		12%		23%
TOTAL	3920	100%	539	14%	704	18%	1189	30%	1488	38%
				100%		100%		100%		100%

Figure 5.6

Source: Nancy Duxbury, *The Reading and Purchasing Public: The Market for Trade Books in English Canada 1991* (Toronto: Association of Canadian Publishers, 1995), n.p.

NATIONALITY OF AUTHOR OF LAST BOOK PURCHASED, BY SEX, AGE, EDUCATION AND OCCUPATION OF BOOK PURCHASERS

	TOTAL	NATIONALITY OF AUTHOR			
		CANADIAN		FOREIGN	
			%		%
N (3661)	3629	525	14%	3104	86%
SEX					
FEMALE	1948	240	12%	1708	88%
	54%	46%		56%	
MALE	1646	279	17%	1367	83%
	46%	54%		44%	
TOTAL	3594	519	14%	3075	88%
	100%	100%		100%	
AGE					
15-24 YRS	529	44	8%	485	92%
	15%	33%		32%	
25-34 YRS	753	87	12%	666	88%
	21%	33%		32%	
35-54 YRS	1161	175	15%	986	85%
	32%	33%		32%	
55+	1169	218	19%	951	81%
	32%	33%		32%	
TOTAL	3612	524	15%	3088	85%
	100%	132%		128%	
HIGHEST LEVEL OF					
FORMAL EDUCATION					
PRIM. OR					
LESS	289	34	12%	255	88%
	8%	7%		9%	
SME H. SCHL	891	120	13%	771	87%
	26%	24%		26%	
H. SCHL GRAD	576	76	13%	500	87%
	17%	15%		17%	
SME P. SNDRY	665	97	15%	588	85%
	19%	19%		19%	
P. SNDRY DEGREE	1067	174	16%	893	84%
	31%	35%		30%	
TOTAL	3488	501	14%	2987	86%
	100%	100%		100%	
OCCUPATION					
STUDENT	472	46	10%	428	90%
	14%	9%		15%	
RETIRED	439	95	22%	344	78%
	13%	19%		12%	
HOMEMAKER	353	46	13%	307	87%
	10%	9%		11%	
S-SKILL/TRADE	661	97	15%	564	65%
	19%	19%		19%	
SLS/SER/CLER	552	73	13%	479	87%
	16%	15%		17%	
PROFESSIONAL	575	89	15%	486	85%
	17%	18%		17%	
MAN/ADMIN	340	53	16%	287	84%
	10%	11%		10%	
TOTAL	3392	499	15%	2893	85%
	100%	100%		100%	

Figure 5.7

Source: Nancy Duxbury, *The Reading and Purchasing Public: The Market for Trade Books in English Canada 1991* (Toronto: Association of Canadian Publishers, 1995), n.p.

90 percent, more likely than any other age group to identify themselves as book readers; and c) that, although they were not the most voracious book readers (a distinction consistently claimed by Canada's ostensibly illiterate seniors), they were spending approximately 25 percent more time in an average week reading books than the same age group had in 1978. Although there are minor variations in the analyses produced by these two studies, they nonetheless corroborate the finding of the IALS and subsequent national literacy studies that young people enjoy not only the greatest basic literacy skills but, indeed, the highest degree of comfort with the world of books and literature—something that should come as no surprise given their extraordinary exposure to high quality literature as children. With the extremely important exception of those youth who, for whatever reason, have found themselves forced to the margins of Canadian society—most notably those who have dropped out of school—it may be argued that young people in Canada have been disproportionately *advantaged* by the nation's "culture of literacy" as it has taken shape since the 1970s. Certainly young Canadians have been the primary beneficiaries of—as the *National Library News* put it—"the public awareness of the importance of literacy practices, opportunities for using literacy skills in the workplace to keep pace with technological advances, access to libraries, support for family literacy awareness and initiatives to foster good literacy practices as part of daily life." That more young Canadians than ever are both staying in school and pursuing postsecondary education suggests that the patterns documented by these researchers continue to obtain in Canada and that, indeed, the current Canadian youth cohort is, if anything, even *more* advantaged over older cohorts than its "Generation X" predecessors.

TYPE OF PUBLISHER OF LAST BOOK PURCHASED, BY SEX, AGE, EDUCATION AND OCCUPATION OF BOOK PURCHASERS

	TOTAL		PUBLISHER TYPE						
		CDN PUB	%	CDN AGNT	%	FRG OWNED CDN BASE	%	DIRECT IMPORT	%
N (3661)	3425	437	13%	878	25%	2054	60%	56	2%
SEX									
FEMALE	1849	217		477		1123		32	
	54%	50%	12%	55%	26%	55%	61%	57%	2%
MALE	1547	215		394		914		24	
	46%	50%	14%	45%	25%	45%	59%	43%	2%
TOTAL	3396	432		871		2037		56	
	100%	100%	13%	100%	26%	100%	60%	100%	2%
AGE									
15-24 YRS	518	37		141		331		9	
	15%	8%	7%	16%	27%	16%	64%	16%	2%
25-34 YRS	712	79		185		442		6	
	21%	18%	11%	21%	26%	22%	62%	11%	1%
35-54 YRS	1098	140		281		657		20	
	32%	32%	13%	32%	26%	32%	60%	35%	2%
55+	1088	181		270		615		22	
	32%	41%	17%	31%	25%	30%	57%	39%	2%
TOTAL	3416	437		877		2045		57	
	100%	100%	13%	100%	26%	100%	60%	100%	2%

Figure 5.8

Source: Nancy Duxbury, *The Reading and Purchasing Public: The Market for Trade Books in English Canada 1991* (Toronto: Association of Canadian Publishers, 1995), n.p.

Youth and the Canadian Canon

It is, of course, not easy to know what to make of the contradictory evidence about young people's inclination to "read Canadian." *Reading in Canada 1991* and *The Reading and Purchasing Public* were admittedly inconsistent on the question of the *content* of young Canadians' reading preferences, an ambiguity that is not inconsequential to renewal in Canada's literary/publishing culture. Taken at face value, if Graves and Dugas were correct in their finding that youth were the most voracious readers of Canadiana, the conclusion might be drawn that Canadian authors and publishers would be well favoured by the maturation into middle age of this strongly nationalist cohort; if, by contrast, Duxbury's interpretation of the data is accurate, and youth are only half as likely as the national average to pick up a Canadian book, then it might be presumed that unless young Canadians grow into a stronger appreciation for their national literature the Canadian-owned publishers' share of the domestic market could be seriously threatened.

To elucidate some of the nuances of this conflicting evidence —that is, to place it in the context of young Canadians' lived experience—it is worth returning to *Teen Trends* and especially to Reginald Bibby's and Donald Posterski's finding that, in general, reading was *not* at the top of Canadian teens' list of voluntary pastimes in the early 1990s and, moreover, that this "generation" appeared to be far more likely to be oriented towards the products of American mass media than any before it. "In contrast to [the enormous popularity of] television and videos," wrote Bibby and Posterski, "the number of teenagers who say they enjoy reading stands at only about 40 percent." These researchers emphasized, interestingly, that activities young people placed at the bottom of their "joy rankings" were those that tended to be promoted by adults, including school, jobs, youth groups and, "in last place," religious groups. At the top of the list of teens' preferred leisure activities were friends, music, one's stereo, dating, one's boyfriend or girlfriend, one's own room, sports, television, and one's VCR. Only 43 percent of Canadian teenagers indicated that they received a great deal or quite a bit of enjoyment from school, down from 54 percent in 1984. Reading, asserted Bibby and Posterski, was among those pastimes which were (negatively) identified with adult notions of discipline and self-improvement, a finding that corroborates my own impression that many young people—especially students—are inclined to identify extracurricular reading as "work."[22]

If, as suggested above, the Canadian Lit phenomenon was rooted in an historically specific nationalist project that achieved critical mass in the early 1970s, one that coincided with the formative years of the baby boom cohort, it would seem a matter of no small significance for Canada's literary/publishing culture that subsequent cohorts—the children of Free Trade, NAFTA and globalization—seem to be *far* less nationalist than their elders. Bibby and Posterski were so overwhelmed by their discovery that Canadian "[y]oung people have never been more . . . American" that they devoted whole chapters in *Teen Trends* to the matter. Adopting the McLuhanesque adage that media and their content are indivisible, these researchers attributed a declining sense of nationalism among young Canadians specifically to the influence of American *television*—a provocative notion for the purposes of this study since it seems to affirm that the simultaneous appearance of the post-centennial Canadian Lit boom and of nationalist fervour within the baby boom generation was not mere coincidence. Whatever one may say of the generalized impact of television on print culture (see the section Alarms about Mass Media in Chapter Four), according to this kind of analysis televisual media have been for Canadians a profoundly continentalizing and therefore de-nationalizing cultural force. Bibby and Posterski put the case emphatically: "If Canadian nationalists—in reflecting on books, films, music, and other art forms—have worried in the past about our being inundated by American culture, then American television should be bringing on total nervous breakdowns. For television does far more than merely inform and entertain. It shapes our very sense of what is. It creates reality." What bothered these researchers above all—and provided the critical subtext of *Teen Trends*—was that "Canadian young people, exposed as they are to American thought, complete with American self-confidence, power, and energy, are buying the idea that Canadians tend to rate behind Americans when it comes to a number of valued traits. We're not talking here about stars; we're talking about average people in the two countries." In general, they conclude bluntly, "The sense that 'American is best' is pervasive."[23]

Not surprisingly, young Canadians' lack of nationalism informs their sense of citizenship and their place in the nation's political life. Bibby and Posterski found that, with the exception of young Québecois (only 30 percent of whom said that Canada was "very important" to them), fewer than half of Canadian youth circa 1992 continued to "highly value being Canadian." Older Canadians' sense of nationalism remained relatively higher, though in the years 1985-90 the proportion of adults who said that "being a Canadian is 'very important' to them" declined from 68 percent to 61 percent. The implications of these data are twofold, namely that nationalism seems to be a declining force in Canadian life overall but nowhere more so than among young people: "Clearly morale has slipped somewhat in recent years. For many, the country is simply not as attractive as it was about a decade ago. The unity problems, a sluggish economy, and the preoccupation with constitutional reform appear to be wearing thin with many Canadians, young and old." Bibby and Posterski speculated on the causes of this decline, implying—paradoxically—

that the powerful left-nationalist consensus that characterized the Trudeau years in Canada failed young people: "Perhaps the fatal flaw in our post–60s social reconstruction efforts was our failure to lay out a national dream that would enable Canadians of all ages to pursue together what they have been saying they value the most: good relationships and economic prosperity. In opting to emphasize the 'just society' over the 'best society,' we left millions of young people and others with the message that our national objective is equitable co-existence."[24]

Evidence that young people are today less inclined than they have been since at least the 1950s to differentiate between Canada and the United States is ubiquitous: most of my Ontario under-graduate students have been to Florida but not to the Maritime or Western Canadian provinces; and, apart from school exchanges, astonishingly few have ever visited Québec. They have little inter-est in the products of Canadian media *per se*, and freely choose from among the myriad cultural offerings of the global entertain-ment industries (many of which, but certainly not all, are Ameri-can). They cannot relate to George Grant's *Lament for a Nation* or even Margaret Atwood's *Survival*, nor does the left-nationalist project that defined the nation's political mainstream in the Trudeau years inspire them in the least. (They seem incapable of even *conceiving* that "foreign investment" was once perceived as a threat to Canadian sovereignty, or that Canadians were ever anx-ious about the cultural, economic and military implications of continental integration.) The apparently dramatic decline in young Canadians' knowledge of their own country has itself reached fever pitch among older Canadians in recent years, to judge from books like J. L. Granatstein's *Who Killed Canadian History?* or from the founding of such organizations as the Dominion Institute, whose self-styled mission it is to acquaint "young Canadians" with "the links that exist between our history, civic traditions, and common identity."[25] Whether or not the

49th Parallel has ceased to carry the profound cultural and political meaning for Canadians that it once did, there can be little question but that the children of NAFTA, globalization and the Internet live in imaginative (perhaps even ideological) worlds in which the idea of "nation" is eroding apace.

This demonstrable decline in the strength of Canadian nationalism in recent years has profound implications for Canada's literary/publishing culture, notwithstanding the ambiguities in the reading survey data (nor the apparent strength of French-Canadian nationalism within Québec). However much contemporary Canadian youth read today—and, indeed, however much they may "read Canadian"—the evidence suggests that *they do so without reference to an expressly nationalist cultural or political agenda.* In stark contrast with the baby boomers, whose literary tastes were imprinted with the nationalist ethos of the post-Centennial period, youth in the 1980s and especially the 1990s appear not to harbour any such bias. Even in cases in which young people are choosing to read Canadian books, they tend to make such choices on the basis of literary merit rather than nationalist criteria and often are not even aware that the books they love have been written by Canadians (Douglas Coupland is perhaps the best exemplar of this phenomenon). Where the phrase "Canadian literature" does seem to carry a specific connotation, it is often negative. For the respondents to my questionnaire—not all of them in their teens or early twenties by any means—the word most often used to describe their experience of Canadian literature was "boring." Many told me that they had been "forced" to read Canadian-authored books in school and that this experience had effectively "killed" whatever interest they might otherwise have had in them. (Some older respondents admitted that when they ventured, years later, back into the realm of Canadian literature they were pleasantly surprised by what they found and have since made "catching up" on this literature a priority in their reading lives.)[26] Again, this is not to say that young Canadians are not interested in Canadian literature but, rather, that their interests tend to vary without reference to the traditional notion that literature somehow represents "the national." In short, young Canadians' taste for reading may be said to diverge widely—from indifference and outright hostility to genuine devotion—but it is no longer determined by the discourses of nationalism that gave rise to the Canadian Lit phenomenon in the 1970s and have since come to dominate Canada's literary/publishing culture.

Robert Lecker, the academic critic whose defence of the idea of a Canadian "canon" was noted above, tends to view young people's lack of interest in Canadian literature as a function of the growing divide between public and specialized academic approaches to book reading: "Ask a few well-read literate people who follow Canadian writing how they enjoyed such classics as *As For Me And My House, Roughing It In The Bush,* or *The Stud Horseman.* You will probably be told that they haven't heard of them. The industrialization of Canadian literature has created a whole world of Canadian literary classics that readers outside the academy (and many within it) know nothing about." For Lecker, the worry is that sooner or later—and probably sooner—this world will simply "disappear from public view." Teachers, he insists, must shoulder much of the blame for turning reading into a patriotic chore: "[S]tudents are seldom taught to see a connection between the Canadian literature they read and the Canadian space they inhabit, or, if they do, they are taught that the connection is so problematic and subjective that the ideas of collective action and community begin to seem worthless. In other words, the teaching of literature can provide no means of effective collective political change in the 'real' world because the nature of this world—in Canadian terms—has been radically called into question. The term 'Canadian' in the study of Canadian literature seldom forms part of discussions about the texts under study." This message, according to Lecker, is "fundamentally alienating" to young people; yet it is "the message many students take with them when they leave the university. . . ." He concludes provocatively, "There is little reason for students to invest in an invisible country. How can they be critical of it or contribute to its growth if they cannot see it or imagine it? If students find it difficult to be critical of their milieu it may be because, in many of their courses, so little attention has been devoted to examining the ways in which a specifically Canadian milieu does exist. Even to raise the issue of what a 'specifically Canadian milieu' might be seems dated, something one might have talked about in the late 1960s, but not today (when we need to talk about it more than ever)."[27]

Though well meaning, Lecker appears to me to have overstated the extent to which the "invisible country" he believes Canadians now inhabit could somehow be salvaged by a national literature well taught. Like the historians and other academics who now routinely bemoan what they see as young Canadians' wholesale ignorance of their native (or adopted) land, he has confused cause and effect. At the very least, to speak of the eclipse of the "specifically Canadian milieu" as a category of purely literary inquiry ignores the innovative ways in which many professors of English literature, himself included, do indeed attempt to place "the national" at the centre of their undergraduate course work. Worse yet, it fails to take into account the far more broadly cultural context within which so many young Canadians find the idea of "the national" anachronistic. Lecker, it would seem, cannot "imagine" himself living comfortably in a Canada that has been de-nationalized, hence he concludes that the young Canadians who do inhabit such an imaginative space are, at some deep level, as alienated as he would be in their place. In fact, there is very little evidence to suggest that Canadian youth—especially the most literate and literary—see things this way, and a good deal to suggest that they *resent* the efforts of the likes of Lecker to turn the clock back, as it were, and to restore "the national" as a defining literary (and especially personal) category. As author Andrew Pyper put it, "younger readers are feeling increasingly alienated from mainstream CanLit." It is entirely possible that young Canadians' defection from what Pyper calls the "quiet, earnest, uneventful, 'reaffirming,' morally obvious" texts of the Canadian canon preceded its critical eclipse, rather than vice versa.

One "young" Canadian writer who has been outspoken in his rejection of nationalist approaches to the literature written and read by Canadians is Russell Smith, the author of the best-selling novel *How Insensitive* and now a *Globe and Mail* columnist. I began corresponding with Smith after he and Peter Gzowski jousted on the Canadian Lit question at a round table hosted by Trent University in the fall of 1999. In this correspondence, Smith articulated what I believe is one of the finest—and bluntest—defences of young Canadians' "globalized" literary sensibilities, one which challenges not only the assumption that "the national" *ought* to take priority in literature but the implicit claim, made most forcefully by Lecker, that disposing of it is to live in a world of fundamental alienation. Because it constitutes such an important, powerful refutation of so many of the stereotypes under which young Canadian readers and writers labour, I have chosen to include it here as a single, only slightly abridged excerpt. The correspondence began with Smith's response to the questionnaire I sent to various Canadian publishers, in which I asked about the applicability of "targeting" young people as a market for Canadian literature.

> I object to the premises of your enquiry, namely that literature is a product like any other, and thus can be targeted at a particular market. The word "aimed" in your questionnaire makes me shudder. Any literature that is "aimed" at a particu-

lar social group, particularly a young one, is going to be crap. Literature is either good or bad, not good for a particular readership. Any writer with any kind of serious literary ambition is going to be writing for as wide an audience as possible, and wants to be read by young and old, in New York and Vladivostok. I would hate to be considered a "youth" author just because I write about young people. It makes me sound trivial. I recently received a letter from a 60-something woman in northern Ontario who said that one of my stories had made her cry—that is tremendously exciting for me.

Similarly, the subject matter is irrelevant to any serious reader of fiction or literary scholar. As a reader, I can be just as interested in a book about peasants in India—a place I have never been—as in a book about club-goers in Toronto. We read about foreign places so as to be taken there. What I'm interested in is the quality of the writing and the story—judged from a literary/technical standpoint, not by a political one. When I write about club-goers in Toronto, I am hoping to appeal to that woman in northern Ontario as much as to urban hipsters in my neighbourhood. I hope to make my place interesting to outsiders—just as Margaret Laurence didn't expect her audience to be limited to small-town people like her characters.

When we read about London and Cape Breton and about one day in June in Dublin in 1904 we want to learn about those places because they are foreign, we want to be given as much historical and surface detail about those places as to enable us to feel that we are there; it's this specificity, paradoxically, that makes the best books universal.

Nor are difficult and subtle books going to be lost on younger readers. Young readers are just as intelligent as any readers—indeed, when you are at university you are most excited by new ideas and experimental techniques and probably at your peak age for absorbing extremely difficult texts. When I look at the tomes I read in university I am baffled by how I could have done it; I certainly couldn't read most of them now. In other words, I don't think books need be about the internet and television for them to appeal to young readers. Young readers are more sophisticated than that.

Which is why your queries about e-books and e-publishing are irrelevant: young readers are just as interested in stimulating words as anyone else; they don't care about the delivery system. If you stress the delivery system you take attention away from the content, the quality of the writing and the innovation in the stories. It would be like focussing on the typography and the binding. Young readers aren't as superficial as that.

Now, having said all that, I do admit that there is a crisis, or at least a painful period in Canadian literature as it goes through a momentous change these days, and that there is something one could call an old school and a modern school and that the new school is probably more likely to appeal to younger readers. But the old school (a Canadian nationalist vision of literature which relies on rural settings and domestic themes) is not necessarily represented by older writers, and the new school (which is cosmopolitan, internationalist, more interested in literary style and innovative technique and tends towards urban or suburban settings) is not necessarily represented by younger writers. There are young writers writing sad tales of domestic abuse on Prairie farms, and there are old writers (like me—I'm 36, which has never before in human history been considered young) who are writing about advertising and body modification and transatlantic flights.

This new school—which I, being partisan, would call sophisticated and contemporary, but which the Peter Gzow-

ski Mentality, feeling threatened, might call merely hip and
therefore trivial—is perhaps best represented by Zsuzsi Gartner, whose book *All the Anxious Girls On Earth* is set in cities
and in the country, but reflects an urbane, modern consciousness: it is aware of popular culture, relentlessly contemporary in its references, caustic in its outlook, written in a
polished style and pervasively witty (which made it far too
difficult and threatening, of course, for it to be nominated for
any major literary awards, which is a travesty too embarrass-
ing to even contemplate; but I digress). Gartner is, I think, in
her late 30s or early 40s—and so cannot by any stretch of the
imagination be called young. Yes, I would think that her
book is more likely to appeal to university students than it is
to middle-aged CBC listeners, but the age thing is an accident:
what we're really talking about is sophistication.

Young people, having grown up in a prosperous, tech-
nologically advanced, internationally connected Canada,
saturated with international media and benefiting from university departments of post-colonial literature and media
studies and sports theory and whatever are more sophisticated than they ever have been. They are no longer happy
with didactic stories, or with simply uplifting ones.

But I would also say that one of the hippest writers in
Canada, who knows a great deal about contemporary urban
life, modern sexual relations, trends and mass culture, and
who always writes about it in a humorously satiric way, is
Margaret Atwood.

Let me give another example of the new school: Michael
Winter, in his book of short stories, *One Last Good Look* (The
Porcupine's Quill). Here, the setting is resolutely Canadian:
small-town Newfoundland. Nothing vaguely hip about that.
And yet the world-view and the style are utterly modern:
there is a self-reflexive quality, a fragmented and layered

consciousness in the narration, a view of relationships which is worldly—all of which would make this book of interest to literary scholars anywhere in the world. (Again, due to reasons too depressing to elucidate, this book was passed over by all literary awards.) And it would also make it of great interest to young people who want to feel excited by language and by new ideas. It is a highly modern book: that's where its youth appeal lies.

These books are not the exclusive domain of the small presses or the large presses. Winter's book was edited by John Metcalf, who is a white-bearded 60-year-old, and who has been part of a radical anti-establishment force in fiction for some 30 years. Gartner's book was edited by Patrick Crean (at Key Porter; not a small press), who is not exactly a teen raver either. McClelland and Stewart, the greying cornerstone of the Peter Gzowski Mentality, had the guts to publish a collection of experimental fictions by young people (*Concrete Forest*, edited by Hal Niedzviecki) which was supposed to be about urban themes but which was really about new styles of minimalism coming out of creative writing classes; this evolution of literary styles is at least a discussion that young people want to be a part of.

Meanwhile, the small presses that do consciously attempt to publish hip books by young writers for a hip audience— I'm thinking of Arsenal Pulp Press, Insomniac Press and Gutter Press—get all the mandatory hip themes right (drug abuse, violent sex, catatonic narrative tone, an importing of horror or fantasy genre elements), but unfortunately don't publish many good writers. They focus so much on the hipness of the subject matter they ignore literary skill, coherence, plausibility and universal appeal. It would be a mistake to privilege these publishers just because of the trendiness they embody. That too would be condescending to young people.

Certainly, I would be lying if I didn't admit that the most excited reaction I have had from readers of my fiction is from those under 30, who see themselves in my characters, and who do not see themselves anywhere else. (When I began work on my first novel, it was largely because I had never seen my life and environment and values, the kind of life all my friends and acquaintances lived, represented in any Canadian fiction.) I am constantly approached by university-age people in menial jobs—waiters, ticket takers, bookstore employees—who say they have read my work, where the very manager of the bookstore has never heard of me.

But I am also excoriated just as often in moralizing reviews by pious young people who have bought the old Canlit line that literature is something noble and uplifting and sad and therefore good for you, who feel that my subject matter—young people who live in cities—is not appropriate for fiction. (I was once scolded by a very young woman in the *Canadian Forum* because I did not have enough visible minorities in my fiction.)

And this, I think, is at the root of the disaffection among readers: our culture of literary evaluation, our book reviewers and our awards juries, are years behind our writers. The majority of book people in Canada are not really interested in literature as I am; they are interested in what is socially progressive or responsible, in what is good for you. There is a moral tone to the bulk of newspaper book reviews (did I like what happened in the story? Did I approve of what happened in the story?) that rewards dull, noble books and punishes clever, wicked ones. It rewards "important themes" but not innovative writing. (What did it teach me about homophobia? About racism?) It rewards niceness and not complexity. And the well reviewed books are the ones that end up on reading-club lists, which are the books that your Mom reads and which confirm in any young person's mind the utter boredom and banality of all literary endeavour.

By coincidence, this process does tend to reward older writers and not younger ones. It did not go unnoticed among my friends that of the combined nominees for this year's Giller Prize and Governor General's Award for English Fiction —10 writers in all—only one writer was under the age of 48.

But this is not really the fault of the publishers, who are all as desperate to get young, hip writers as they are desperate for young readers. It's the fault of our cautious, carefully representative, carefully nice systems of selecting prize juries, our unutterably bland reviewing establishment. Check the bio notes on most book reviews: "a. Reviewer is a librarian in Coburg . . . B. Reviewer is a schoolteacher in Moosejaw. . . ."

To sum up: what turns off young readers? A moral approach to literature. A lack of clever wickedness. And an outdated belief in an outdated vision of Canada. The Canada of the "garrison mentality", of *Survival*, of Peter Gzowski's interviews with brave and simple small town people. Books that are good for you. Canadian cultural nationalism is the literary equivalent of Sunday school, and young people won't sit through it.[28]

6

MARKETING
TO YOUTH

Dumbing Down,
Raising Up

RUSSELL SMITH'S INSISTENCE that young Canadians readers are "sophisticated" in their literary tastes rings absolutely true, and not only for the new literati comprised of writers like himself. Not all youth and young adults are avid readers, of course, but those who are—especially the university-educated—enjoy a truly enviable grounding in the skills and habits necessary for a lifelong relationship with literature (and with the printed word in general). That some Canadian students may temporarily lose the taste for pleasure reading while they are in school does not discount the possibility that, like Smith, they may be "absorbing extremely difficult texts" in class (though too onerous a reading regime in school does admittedly dampen some students' enthusiasm for books). Certainly nothing in the voluminous literacy research suggests that young people are at risk of "losing" their accumulated reading skills through neglect until late in adulthood, which means that most of those whose childhood encounter with books has undergone even a lengthy hiatus have the skills to re-enter the world of literature, quickly and comfortably, whenever the impulse strikes them. Bibby's and Posterski's finding that "only" 40 percent of teens claimed that reading gave them "joy" may, therefore, be interpreted optimistically, especially given the extent to which these researchers were interested in "ranking" pastimes that included friends, dating, music, television and movies—the staples of youth culture and, arguably, of adolescent social development. Cross-referenced against Graves' and Dugas's revelation that 90 percent of young Canadians call themselves "book readers," this statistic suggests that nearly half of the early 1990s youth cohort *never* lost their love of books and, moreover, that the remainder are well situated to rediscover literature later in life. Smith's eloquent testimony corroborates the statistical data powerfully on this question, suggesting that the children of the 1980s and the 1990s may surprise many of their critics by returning to the solid book reading habits with which they were reared as children and trained as students.

Two patterns in Canadians' "consumption" of the products of popular culture further buttress this optimistic prognostication. Firstly, as Paul Rutherford has suggested in his analysis of the impact of television viewing in Canada, Canadians have shown an historic tendency to "grow into" interest in their native land. The older Canadians become, it seems, the more intense becomes their interest in various form of self-discovery, of which "the national" is but one. Secondly, and far more importantly, it is also demonstrably true that the products of commercial mass culture—which by their very nature tend to be formulaic—have a limited capacity to enlighten or entertain over the long run. Magazines, pop songs, sitcoms, Hollywood movies—even for their most dedicated audiences, these products of the commercial entertainment industries characteristically begin to reveal their limitations in early middle-age, which explains why so many thirty-something Canadians inevitably seem to turn to jazz, classical and "world" music, live theatre and especially *literature* as pleasurable antidotes to the formulaic sameness of commercial pop culture. This pattern should not, I hasten to add, be taken as a veiled confirmation of the triumph of the "critique of mass culture" noted above. Many adults continue to enjoy the products of pop culture even as they broaden their pallets to include the more sophisticated pastimes traditionally identified with "high culture." One can now be a devotee of *both* Shakespeare and Oliver Stone movies, of Marilyn Manson and Mozart, of Dr. Seuss and Jane Austen without experiencing the contradictions (or guilt, should one also be reading Allan Bloom!) that such a range of interests might once have implied. This mix-and-match pattern of cultural consumption has, in fact, come to represent one of the salient features of "post-modernity"—and if the freedom implied by such a broad (indeed, global) cultural marketplace has been liberating for adults, it is simply taken for granted by youth today.

I placed Russell Smith's commentary prior to my remarks on book marketing because I tend to share his cynicism about the "superficial" strategies by which any number of youth-oriented products are promoted in the marketplace; more to the point, many young people themselves—having been targeted shamelessly by advertisers since the day they were born—have developed an acute sensitivity to the ways in which they are "positioned" by such corporate strategies (hence the emergence of culture jamming, ad busting and other subversive youth-based counter-strategies). The evidence that young people today are *far* more media savvy than their elders abounds in the marketing literature that has proliferated throughout the 1990s; indeed, in a curious cycle that seems to be an essential element in the post-fordist global capitalism of our era, the more discerning (or "fickle") young consumers' behaviour becomes, or the more fragmented their subcultural styles seem to be, the more youth-oriented consultants, demographers, "cool hunters" and marketing whizzes appear on the scene to sort them out. Given the overwhelming evidence of young Canadians' literacy skills, their exposure to high quality books as children and their high degree of comfort with literature generally, Smith's observation that *good writing* rather than hip advertising will cement their allegiance as book readers rings true as well. One may "outgrow" piercings, baggy pants, the Spice Girls and *Seventeen*—which is precisely why the marketing of such essentially disposable lifestyle accessories for young people is so blatantly mercenary. But, notwithstanding some of the admittedly mercenary means by which young readers have been targeted by the entertainment industries, books constitute a different kind of experience and, it follows, a different kind of commodity. One does not "outgrow" books as much as one grows *into* them—something which the purveyors of good children's literature have always understood. Book readers are made, not born. Thus a crucial element in the marketing of books— whether in Canada or elsewhere—must be the acknowledgement that young readers are not merely sojourning in literature—as they may be in a given subcultural scene—but preparing for a lifelong relationship with print culture.

This idea of young readers—not as a fleeting "niche" market to be seduced and exploited but as potential lifelong connoisseurs of books to be accorded respect—has been put forward passionately by Jean Baird, editor of the youth-oriented Canadian magazine *In 2 Print*. Writing in *Quill & Quire* in 1997, Baird asserted bluntly that youth (12 to 21-year-olds, in her estimation) are "the most underserved market in Canadian publishing." In contrast with children's and "young adult" publishing in Canada, she noted, which is not only growth-oriented and profitable but well served by marketing initiatives like books fairs, public readings and in-school promotions, publishers seem to believe that Canadians between their mid-teens and early twenties are a lost cause. There are few books available for those in this age range who are not quite ready for adult literature, she suggested; further, many publishers have incurred the wrath of parents and especially educational authorities when they have attempted to promote "controversial" materials for this age group (notably coming-of-age stories), thus they no longer have the nerve to put them out. According to Baird, the publishing industry in Canada has become so habituated to the notion that "schools are where the money is for this market" that they have simply ceased to consider alternative promotional sites and strategies: "For the most part, Canadian publishers do little to encourage the transition between children's/YA books and adult titles. Unlike CDs, clothing, and shoe manufacturers, publishing companies do not market directly to people between 12 and 18." She suggests that "[t]here needs to be more crossover between children's books and adult books—crossover in marketing and crossover in awareness. Books from adult lists can—and should—also be promoted in the teen market. In order to successfully market to this age group, publishers do need to target parents, teachers, and librarians, but more importantly, teens themselves. Although teens may not be technically or legally adults, they are sophisticated consumers and are able to think for themselves. With focused marketing the transition from reading children's books to reading adult books can mean increased sales, not decreased sales." Significantly, Baird is also attuned to the issue of readership succession: "Perhaps the most important consideration is that today's largely untapped market of teens is the consumer market of tomorrow. How can we expect people to turn 21 and suddenly start buying books if their interests and concerns have been virtually ignored by the publishing industry for the previous nine years? Marketing of children's books and YA titles has built the foundation. Don't abandon that energy. Investing in the teen market is investing in our future market."[1]

Parenthetically, Baird has quite literally put her money where her mouth is, launching *In 2 Print* in 1996 as a "national forum for emerging Canadian artists that publishes original works by young adults ages 12 to 21." Acknowledging that Canadians in this age group are highly likely to be reading adult books, she emphasizes that her magazine neither condescends to its contributors or readers, nor does it employ the cynical marketing jargon of youth trend-watchers (for example, "the teen market"). In stark contrast with other "teen magazines," moreover, *In 2 Print* refuses to compromise editorial and advertising content (there are no "advertorials"); it also refuses to run ads from cosmetics companies because this kind of marketing is "distasteful" to the magazine's readership. *In 2 Print* is thus explicitly non-formulaic, presenting "a teen's-eye view of everything from Canadian rock bands to first-year-university jitters." As Rona Maynard of *Chatelaine* has observed warmly, "For gifted teens, *In 2 Print* offers more than just a shot at publication. Many find their first mentor through the magazine—like the young cartoonist who had always worked in pencil until cartoonist Roddy Heading showed her how to use ink and brushes. Some build the confidence to pursue careers in the arts."[2]

Baird, having personally commissioned detailed research into the potential market for her magazine, knows of what she speaks. As any number of surveys (including my own) show, magazines are overwhelmingly the preferred media of high school-aged students, especially girls, and they thus constitute the most important *continuing* source of pleasure reading for young people who are "between" children's and adult literature.[3] This extremely important facet of young North Americans' reading lives has prompted myriad studies of youth magazines (including *zines*), in which critical questions of identity (gender, ethnic, national) and acculturation are explored. One of the most provocative of these is *Girl Talk* by Canadian sociologist Dawn H. Currie. Subtitled "Adolescent Magazines and their Readers," this study was based upon extensive interviews with teenaged magazine readers in British Columbia in the mid-1990s. Among Currie's most noteworthy (and arguably counter-intuitive) discoveries—one that directly informed her important theoretical contention that girls and academic researchers do not "read" the content of such magazines in even remotely similar ways—was that "'realism' rather than fantasy emerged as the most important characteristic in [girls'] descriptions of [their] favoured reading." Further, in contrast to the powerful stereotype of the teenaged girl thumbing distractedly through a "teenzine" merely to be tantalized by its images, this study found that "while the girls . . . claim to read 'for fun,' most reject the glossy ads and photo-spreads of magazines in favour of written texts." Although Currie, as a feminist researcher, is highly critical of the tendency of teenzines to foster "traditional femininity" among their young readers, she acknowledges the crucial role of magazine reading in "girls' exploration of Self and the social," a claim with suggestive implications for all publishers: "[T]he structure of everyday life organizes girls' agency around traditional feminine activities, such as reading, and away from non-traditional activities, including politics and sports. One consequence is that reading—whether magazines, books or television—can then become one of the few activities through which girls can explore and develop a sense of Self."[4]

In contrast with *In 2 Print*'s high-minded efforts to "raise up" the content of young people's magazines, virtually all commercial youth magazines are driven solely by profit-maximization and thus are characterized by an unabashed willingness to obfuscate distinctions between editorial and advertising content. Currie points out that the essential subtext of girls' magazines, for example, is not to be found in the publications themselves but in the rather extraordinary ways in which the publishers pitch them to advertisers. A *YM* ad in the trade publication *Media Week* exhorted:

> **The look: A real dazzler!** A full inch wider than *Seventeen.* More space, more impact, for ads and edit. A fashion and beauty showcase ... **The YM buy: It beats *Seventeen!* ...** Better edit-to-ad ratio. Less clutter. Great ad positioning. The new *YM*. Put it on your list. Finally, a real choice for change. **The Target: The Younger Woman!** The choice 14-to-20 reader. In college, or prepping to go. Career parents. High HHI. More money to spend. Big buyer of fashion and beauty. Smarter. More sophisticated. Nobody talks to her better than the new *YM. YM's* Younger Woman: Your target.[5]

The "advertorial" content which *In 2 Print* refuses to sanction is the stock in trade of such young people's magazines, obscuring any hard distinction between unbiased information and product promotion (most notably in matters of "health and beauty") and, in the process, "dumbing down" the reading process altogether. In the case of Dawn Currie's teenage subjects, this duplicity was openly acknowledged and, though it made few girls reject the magazines outright, it did have the effect of making them "cynical" readers. This pattern corroborated what was perhaps Currie's most striking finding: "[M]ost of the [girls] in this study claim to read magazines *just because they are readily available*" (emphasis added).[6]

In the 1990s, it is worth noting, print media began to once again challenge television as the advertising medium of choice for products aimed at children and young people. "Children are an elusive audience," announced *American Demographic* in 1992, "and the new wave of print media is the most efficient way to reach them." Television commercials were "rapidly growing more expensive and less efficient." Hence, in the search for "better ways to deliver messages to [North] American youth," advertisers were "turning to magazines, newspapers, and radio. Children's versions of *Sports Illustrated, National Geographic, Field And Stream,* and *Consumer Report* are already being thumbed by little hands. The number of periodicals for youngsters almost doubled between 1986 and 1991, with 81 new titles. . . ." Predictably, television/publishing "tie-ins" were (and are) the engine driving this trend: "The demographics are convincing enough that many established children's TV shows are now crossing over to print. The list of crossovers includes *Sesame Street Magazine,* the monthly *Nickelodeon,* Fox's *Kid's Club Magazine,* and Disney's *Duck Tales.*"[7] Susan Sachs, publisher of *Sports Illustrated For Kids,* admitted that pitching magazines towards children was part of a broader branding strategy: "We believe children make brand decisions very early that they will carry into their adult lives." She claimed, however, that one of her main missions at the magazine is "fighting illiteracy and creating long-term readers. Another [goal] is getting the magazine into the hands of those who couldn't otherwise afford it." Such altruistic ideals notwithstanding, the competitive edge of Sachs' magazine remains its allure for advertisers: "*Sports Illustrated For Kids* is a success because it offers advertisers a mix of flexibility and precision in reaching children. One advertiser, Wheaties, offered a free subscription on cereal boxes; another, McDonald's, co-produced a nutrition and fitness guide for teachers' use." In the end, she surmised, print is superior to television for advertisers because it is "easier to gauge children's use of print media. And fortunately for the producers of those media, it's easy to prove that children influence billions of dollars a year in consumer spending. As long as children remain a choice market segment, media options for them should grow more plentiful, more sophisticated, and more focused."[8]

If the idea of McDonald's producing a "nutrition and fitness guide" or even of *Sports Illustrated For Kids* promoting literacy sounds unlikely, such platitudes are nonetheless symptomatic of the triumph of the "tie-in"—a marketing strategy that is said to have revolutionized virtually all youth publishing in the 1990s. According to Karen Raugust of *Publishers Weekly*, "[t]he number of original book series inspired by television programming that targets teen and preteen girls has exploded since 1993. Much of the impetus has come from the licensors, who are more aggressively seeking publishing partners (often sister companies) for their properties." She notes that there have been more television programs over the last few years targeted toward teen and preteen female audiences, particularly on the American cable networks (Fox, WB Network and UPN) and that these viewers often seek "additional storylines about their favourite characters, which tie-in books can provide." (Echoing Sachs, Raugust adds happily that "[t]he series may even attract some girls to bookstores for the first time.") As of 1998, the major player in the youth tie-in market was Pocket Books, which publishes titles "inspired by a dozen different television shows" under the Minstrel Archway imprint, including *Buffy the Vampire Slayer, Clueless, Party of Five*, and *Sabrina the Teenage Witch*. Pocket Books also publishes *Star Trek* books, while Harper Collins publishes *X-Files* books and Random House publishes books based upon WB's *Seventh Heaven*.[9] As Nancy Pines, vice-president and publisher of Archway/Minstrel, puts it, the name of the book publishing game for the foreseeable future is tie-ins, since shows like *Sister, Sister, Moesha, Star Trek, Nickelodeon, Sabrina* and *Clueless* are "all owned by various components of the Viacom family . . . which has a big synergy mandate."[10]

Significantly, according to Sidney Jackson, an American "children's buyer" for book retailers, even the bestselling tie-ins for the teen and preteen age group "do not perform as well as non-licensed fiction series and titles such as *Nancy Drew* or *American Girls*. . . ."[11] It would seem, in fact, that apart from exploiting synergy within entertainment empires, such youth-oriented books have little "literary" appeal of any kind, either to the young people who presumably read them, or to the parents and grand-parents at whom they are primarily (and unabashedly) marketed. (Authorship of such works seems to carry little prestige, since presumably the writing of these books is also tied-in to television script-writing.) Significantly, whereas U.S.-based publishers of children's "literature" now seem to be preoccupied with tie-ins, there doesn't seem to be any enthusiasm for it in Canada—in spite of evidence that markets clearly exist for it.[12] The argument may be made that because of the unique circumstances of the "Kid Lit boom" in Canada—its surge in the 1970s, the fact that it was spearheaded by independent publishers and, above all, its commitment to high quality literature (see Chapter Five)—Canadians continue to harbour a somewhat elitist aversion to such openly exploitive marketing strategies. Large American (and now global) publishing houses regularly cloak their most mercenary "synergistic" strategies in the language of altruism, claiming, in the words of Pam Newton, vice-president of domestic licensing at Viacom Consumer Products, that books based on television series "get kids to read who otherwise wouldn't."[13] In Canada, it would appear that publishers are wary of such sanctimony and content with merely finding and printing great authors and great books.[14] The times may, however, be changing. As of 1997, McClelland and Stewart could claim the dubious distinction of having introduced the concept of "brand loyalty" into youth-oriented book promotion in Canada. In that year it launched two series of books aimed at "young readers," namely *True North Comics,* published in partnership with McDonald's, and the *Screech Owl* series of "hockey-mystery novels for 9–13 year olds." Said Ken Thompson, vice-president of sales and marketing for the publisher, "If we can hook young readers and get them reading McClelland & Stewart books, that bodes well for our future."[15] For "older readers," McClelland & Stewart has inaugurated "rebate" and "value-added" promotions, in which its customers receive either a cash kickback or a "free Canadian music CD on purchases over $40."[16]

As the example of children's and adolescent magazines suggests rather strikingly, much of the literature ostensibly aimed at a young readership is, in fact, targeted at their parents and grandparents, presumably in the belief that the latter are more apt to spend money in bookstores (or perhaps because a presumption exists that adults think they know what is best for youth). The recent Simon and Schuster ad noted in Chapter Four—"This Just In: Teens *Do* Read"—suggests rather bluntly, with its condescending third-person reference to young people, that adults are doing the book purchasing for teenagers (or at least that they *ought* to be). Like the ad itself, the titles being promoted there, most notably *Daily Reflections for Highly Effective Teens* and *Teens Can Make It Happen,* also distance themselves discursively from the lived experience of youth, indulging the "wholesome" quasi-evangelical discourses that are ubiquitous in advertising appeals designed to exploit the distance between parents and their sometimes troubled teens. *Chicken Soup for the Teenage Soul,* a 1997 spin-off of the successful "chicken soup" feel-good series aimed at a decidedly adult audience, epitomizes this syndrome.[17] Consumer reviews of the book posted at the Chapters.ca web site confirm that such books are often purchased—no doubt with the best of intentions—by parents or other adult relatives of young people who are thought to be adrift:

- This book, *Chicken Soup for the Teenage Soul,* can deffinatly [sic] help you in a time when you are in need of help. . . . It is such a great gift for the teenager in your family "Daffodil"
- My aunt and uncle sent me this book for my 13th birthday. For the first few days I had it, I admit I ignored it. I was too

busy with my new Sea-Doo and swimming in the new
pool my parents gave us, (my twin and I) to sit down and
read it. After a week, my Mum was cleaning my room and
found the book and asked me if I had read it yet. I said no
and she told me that she would appreciate it if I would read
it today. So I did. I was so surprised! I could not stop reading it. Each and every story touched me in some way. A
wonderful book for any teen to read "Ashley"[18]

The point is not that parents and their teenaged children should
not seek to improve their relationships or even to purchase books
for each other, but rather to show specifically how such advertising discourses can exacerbate young people's distance from the
presumed "normalcy" of the dominant culture instead of serving
as any kind of bridge to it. Such rather cynical promotional strategies, it may be argued, serve to maintain young people in a state
of alienation vis-à-vis the adult culture around them—something
to which even the least rebellious teens are keenly attuned—even
if the books themselves turn out to be beneficial.

Like Russell Smith and like many Canadian book publishers,
young Canadian readers are justifiably cynical about "tie-ins" and
corporate strategies aimed at their adult relatives (and so, too, it
is important to add, are many Canadian *adults*). The evidence
suggests rather strikingly, in fact, that many young readers in
Canada resent *any* effort to single them out as somehow beyond
the pale of serious adult literature and that, moreover, the parents, teachers, professors, librarians and other adults who seek to
influence their reading habits respect their growing intellectual
maturity and tend to treat them as literary equals. Further, in
direct contrast to the stereotype of youth as television- and Inter-
net-addicted, many young Canadians are less than enamoured
of new "gadgetry" commonly thought to be extending (or
enhancing) their reading pleasure—in part because they do not

regard computer-based technologies as novel and, hence, are quick to criticize exaggerated claims about their "revolutionary" potential. Like middle-aged and elderly book readers, young people get to know what is worth reading via various formal and informal channels that serve as literary filters—book reviews, award lists, library promotions and, above all, *word of mouth*. "Must-reads" are recommended by (and passed between) friends, family members, classmates and other personal acquaintances. "Literary" movies—very much in vogue in Hollywood at present, which is itself a sign that the ostensibly mass media-addicted youth cohort is interested in something more sophisticated than *Dumb and Dumber*—commonly inspire readers to seek out the novels on which they are based. Even MuchMusic's "Word for Word" clips, in which musicians discuss the book(s) they are currently reading, are couched in informal, word of mouth-styled discourses—yet another tacit acknowledgement that the hard sell does not appeal to youth when it comes to their reading tastes. (Whether publishers even *pay* for this publicity is impossible to tell from either the clips themselves or their positioning in Much's "video flow.") For those young Canadians who enjoy the more traditional fare of the Canadian Lit canon— and it is important to reiterate that, being as varied in their tastes as all Canadians, some most certainly *do*—these time-honoured channels of communication are entirely adequate to the task of spreading the word about books worth reading. In short, with the crucial exception of those young people whose literacy skills effectively exile them form the world of reading altogether, *there is no evidence that youth constitute an alien species of book reader* and, hence, there is no reason to market books to them as if they were.

Innovations

Although it remains a young, dynamic and even unpredictable medium, the Internet appears to many observers to be transforming young people's encounter with print culture. Catch phrases like "the Net Generation" have entered the North American vernacular, highlighting the ostensibly great technological divide between "digital" youth and all prior generations.[19] Among the myriad claims made about the Internet in the mid- and even the late 1990s was that it is an *essentially* text-based medium and, hence, a de facto literacy-enhancing medium. Now, however, given the profound commercialization of the Net and its inexorable "convergence" not only with traditional entertainment media but with the corporate giants that control their content, it would appear that the textual epoch in Internet history is rapidly giving way to the televisual. This is by no means to assert that the Internet will cease to be a text-based medium altogether, or even that it will cease to revolutionize the lives of people who work and create in text-based applications. It is merely to suggest that the *essence* of the Net—if it even has a single essence—may soon consist in the triumph of corporate multimedia rather than the printed word, and in the tyranny of the commercial "portal" rather than the democratic accessibility once heralded as the birthright of the Web. Internet-based textual literacy may well turn out to be merely an extension of traditional hierarchies of literacy, raising the economic, cultural and technological "haves" of the world even further above the impoverished and underprivileged "have-nots."

Whether "hypertext" constitutes a new form of literature requiring new "literacies" is one aspect of the Net upon which there has been a good deal of speculation. (Hypertext refers to the matrix of interconnected textual documents on the Internet which reference each other via on-screen "links.") Paul Levinson, the American scholar noted above for his "anthropotropic" theory of communications technology, embraces hypertext as a revolutionary new medium, one that has the power to literally "reconfigure the reader's world." He suggests that the activity of clicking one's way through various texts constitutes a blurring of the historic distinction between writer and reader, in which "the author's intentions quickly become irrelevant." He also intimates that hypertext represents a dramatic challenge to the "linear simplicity" of narrative insofar as it portends a new global culture in which "millions of readers make millions of jumps across thousands of documents daily." He enthuses:

> In the truly global, multiplex-of-multiplex movie theater that is the World Wide Web, not only is an endless series or simultaneity of productions showing—depending on whether we look at the links as sequences chosen by individuals, or as a collective of ever-changing links flashing in and out of being at any one time—but the productions vary radically in the texture, degree of original author expression, and internal-link possibilities within the constituent parts. To return to the montage analogy, we might say that in hypertext mounted on the Web there is no individual image, anywhere. Rather, we are dealing with images—texts which at their smallest linked component, by very virtue of that link, are themselves an image connected to another, a process already in motion.20

Given that young people are commonly thought to have abandoned print culture for cyberspace, it is not surprising to find a preoccupation among educators and cultural theorists with the implications of hypertext for pedagogy, and for reading and literacy.[21] Writing in the *Australian Journal of Language and*

Literacy in 1997, for example, James Garton argued that "the influence of information technology on the discourses of business, government and the media has reached the kind of critical mass where it is evident that new cyber-genres such as email and the World Wide Web cannot be ignored in a contemporary language and literacy curriculum." He observed that "[t]here is a strong identification of young people with the new media, including the Internet, which suggests that the new genres and new literacies that are being generated will shape our future information and knowledge cultures, whether or not they are accepted by the current older generation of print-oriented educators." Echoing Levinson, he speculated that hypertext construction as it appears on the Internet may constitute a new means of cognition: "This non-linear arrangement of information has led to new forms of knowledge production, with new rhetorical conventions, leading some observers to claim that it is now possible to dispense with linear, sequenced curriculum in schools and universities." Garton concluded ominously—and presciently— that, if schools did not make their peace with the Internet and with these new intertextual forms of cognition, the private sector would simply colonize pedagogy along with the technology itself. He asserted: "What is at stake here is the future shape of the new literacies. . . . Language and literacy educators must respond to the demands of the new cybergenres and the computer-mediated curriculum. . . . Otherwise, with the exception of a minority of schools on the Internet, the virtual curriculum for the new literacies will be dictated to the younger generation from outside the education system, by multinational media corporations."[22]

Henry A. Giroux, writing from a progressive cultural studies perspective, agrees. Learning, he argues, "is [now] located elsewhere—in popular spheres that shape [young people's] identities through forms of knowledge and desire that appear absent from what is taught in schools. The literacies of the post modern age are electronic, aural, and image based; and it is precisely within the diverse terrain of popular culture that pedagogical practices must be established as part of a broader politics of public life—practices that will aggressively subject dominant power to criticism, analysis, and transformation as part of a progressive reconstruction of democratic society." Youth today, Giroux argues, find themselves marginalized by this "dominant power" precisely because the literacy strategies that comprise their formal education have been antiquated at a pace that has left teachers (and other cultural mentors) reeling to keep up. He is therefore insistent that "educators, artists, and other cultural workers . . . address the challenge of developing pedagogies that teach kids how to use media as a mode of self-expression and social activism. We need to find new ways in which pedagogy can translate into an activist strategy that expands the opportunity for knowledge and skills that help young people to extend their participation into and control over those cultural, economic, and social spheres that shape daily life (mass media, schools, media, workplace, policy-making institutions, the arts)."[23] Reginald Bibby and Donald Posterski made much the same argument in *Teen Trends*, suggesting explicitly that young Canadians must now be taught to "read" well beyond mere text: "Profoundly important technological advances in the field of communications have transformed how information is disseminated. The written word has been supplemented by sight and sound. The world and all that is in it is being conveyed directly to the eye and the ear. With increasing frequency, even the words in a best-selling book are lifted off the printed pages and placed on audio cassettes." In short, they insisted, "[t]o read well but not view well, to write well but not hear well, to memorize formulas without knowing when to use the procedures, is to be less than literate in the 1990s."[24]

Whether or not hypertext will actually turn out to constitute a new form of literature or the myriad Net-based applications available to young people will erode the efficacy of traditional pedagogy—both of which are highly debatable claims—it is apparent that book publishers are experimenting widely with new digital technologies in their efforts to reach youth. Some of this experimentation seems destined to merely *reproduce* the experience of print, or perhaps to augment it with a little novelty. The e-book, and the even more promising e-paper, would seem to be examples of this tendency, since these technologies are likely to maintain the traditional (narrative) textual elements of the published book, albeit with greater dexterity (at least insofar as they may have many titles in memory simultaneously). Although e-books have been somewhat stigmatized to date as "toys for a small percentage of the population—typically males with disposable incomes," their growing storage capacity, improving user-friendliness and diminishing cost make them an extremely promising potential "mass" medium.[25] In addition, one assumes, they will before long have the capacity to interface with the Net and thus to reproduce the portable hyertextual capabilities of the "wireless" laptop computer. Whether e-books will ever usurp the practical expendability of the paperback—think of reading on the beach or in a crowded train car—remains an open question. Even more questionable will be readers' willingness to abandon the specifically *tactile* experience of the traditional book—not only the visual superiority of ink on paper (which even the best computer screens cannot approximate at present) but the ability to effortlessly highlight text or scribble marginalia. That the "book-as-object" has become a somewhat fetishistic preoccupation of some publishers and their readers is further evidence of the long road new electronic media may have to travel to seduce traditional book-lovers.

A second publishing innovation, one that is more directly applicable to young people acculturated to Net-based media, is MP3—a digital compression technology that allows for fast and easy downloading of audio files (something which is, even now, wreaking havoc on the recording industry). Pioneering the application of MP3 to literature and publishing is Gary Hustwit, the publisher of Incommunicado Press and founder of MP3Lit.com, a web site featuring "audio excerpts" read by a broad range of established and underground authors. With the right computer gear, readers can log on to MP3Lit and listen to clips by A.M. Holmes, Jonathan Lethen, Henry Rollins, and Nick Cave. (Hustwit, who is at the centre of the independent press scene in the U.S., claims defiantly that his web site "is something that actually has a purpose. It is not just some pointless e-commerce site.") At present, MP3 technology allows up to 20 minutes of audio, which means an entire short story can be posted in this format. Hustwit says enthusiastically of this medium: "It is more engaging than trying to read something off the screen. And it doesn't replace the paper product like MP3 in the music business." Significantly, his site is specifically "designed to market younger and mid-list authors who usually don't get audio book deals to a twentysomething audience, or to those with a twentysomething mindset." Hustwit asks pointedly: "People are always complaining how 20-year-olds are not reading books. Has anyone tried to do audio books that are geared to that market by authors in that age group?" His plans for the future include producing "unabridged audio books in MP3 format, again with an eye toward a young demographic." Says Hustwit of MP3, "There's no limit to what you can do with it."[26]

Yet another Web-derived publishing innovation is "telepoetics," a California-based movement in which the virtual conferencing capabilities of the Net are used to hold "poetry readings across several cities simultaneously." As *Globe and Mail* culture critic Val Ross noted in 1999, telepoetics represents a unique opportunity to reach young writers who "work outside books and magazines—the dub poets, rappers, performance poets, storytellers, and writers who publish in on-line magazines."[27]

In Canada, the organization at the forefront of the telepoetics movement is the non-profit, Vancouver-based Edgewise Electrolit Centre (EEC), which runs regular "Teen Telepoetics" workshops linking young Canadians with each other and with their US counterparts. With support from the Canada Council's Spoken and Electronic Word Program, the EEC has an explicit mandate to reach youth, as the following workshop agenda, posted in February 2000, attests:

> This three session workshop will take youth through the process of preparing to perform their own creative writing, event planning and marketing, the use of video-conferencing technology, and holding the event itself. Youth will gain communication, organizational, technical, and marketing skills. Teen Telepoetics offers the opportunity for youth to develop their creativity in the context of performing for an audience and gain self-esteem.28

Related to youth telepoetics, at least in the sense of pushing serious literature well beyond its traditional enclaves, is the movement of drama, poetry and authors' readings from "traditional theatres and into the urban night." In a lengthy analysis of the Toronto street theatre scene in late 1999, *Globe and Mail* columnist Leah McLaren observed that clubs rather than traditional venues now "play host to a rotating selection of gallery nights, performance pieces, fashion shows and reading series, in addition to the usual club grind of drinking, dancing, and recreational drugging." She describes Keith Wyatt's play *Ecstasy*, for example, as a "play about club kids, performed by club kids, primarily for club kids." Club-based theatre has spread to Canadian cities from New York, where "the theatrical roots of night life run deep in the traditions of cabaret and street-based performance art," and it is designed specifically to appeal to youth. Says McLaren: "Not surprisingly, club performances are attracting a younger crowd to theatre. At a time when established Canadian companies like Tarragon, Stratford, and Soul Pepper are cooking up complicated programs to lure even a few young bums into seats, *Ecstasy* is being performed to under-30s crowds of anywhere from 60 to 160 people." The moral of the story is clear: "Don't bring kids to the theatre; bring theatre to the kids."[29] Rebecca Brown, the 25-year-old head of an experimental drama company in Toronto, believes that club-based theatre now constitutes the *avant-garde*: "We are like rats running from a sinking ship to a floating one. Our goal as theatre artists is not to revitalize the Factory or Tarragon, but to create a new thing entirely."[30] Brown is explicit in her dismissal of the stereotype of youth as "restless or distracted," noting that at a recent performance in Toronto the young audience "howled and held its breath through [an] entire 2-hour show." She concludes bluntly: "The old models of theatre fail to engage my peers. We are trying to create a non-verbal symbology to tell the stories of a generation."[31]

Notwithstanding the introduction of various Web-based innovations to book publishers' youth-oriented marketing strategies, it is *far* too early in the evolution of the Internet (and its related electronic technologies) to predict with any certainty how it will diminish or enhance the viability of print culture. Contrary to the powerful myth of "revolutionary" technological change, the transition towards new media rarely occurs quickly or seamlessly, since "unlearning" the ways of older media is usually a prior condition of habituating oneself to their successors. Typically, new and old media tend to coexist and even to "interface" for a long while before the one is superseded by the next. Moreover, if the centuries of cultural change since Gutenberg have proved anything, it is that print culture is extremely resilient. The demise of reading, it is worth recalling, was variously predicted with the onset of radio, recording, film, and especially television. In the nineteenth century, it was thought that public libraries would mark the end of book purchasing and thus the eventual demise of book publishing—a familiar claim in our own time because it is now a commonplace in prognostications about the future of the Internet. Even in the twenty-first century, as we witness the massive, seemingly inexorable shift to new digital technologies—the driving force of what is now called the "new economy"—the rather more prosaic book remains, in fact, an extraordinarily sophisticated, practical and pleasurable *technology*.[32] We remain, despite the hyperbole or our age, a long way from dispensing with the printed word.

NOTES
FROM THE
UNDERGROUND

Zine Culture

F IT IS TRUE that some young people in Canada have acquired
a taste for what might be called the mainstream "classics" of
Canadian literature—Russell Smith's praise for Margaret Atwood speaks to this point—it is also true that others would prefer
to seek out alternatives to the canon and even to the conventional
book. Indeed, young people's sometimes obsessive interest in
new authors, challenging literary experiences and especially the
act of writing itself have produced an important "underground
scene" in Canada, one which has only recently begun to register
in the established channels of book publishing and promotion
(and may well be invisible to many mainstream book readers even
now). This scene is relevant to the question of renewal in Canadian publishing because it *explicitly* embodies a critique of the

dominant baby boom-oriented literary culture in Canada and, even more importantly, it seeks to represent young people's lived experience as culturally marginal and downwardly mobile outsiders vis-à-vis that culture. Although this scene is, predictably, comprised of a highly diverse, amorphous and sometimes fractious collection of writers and publishers, their pursuits are characterized by a number of common elements. The most notable of these is their rather fierce determination to remain "independent," that is, to publish works in which they have a great personal commitment, and to do so largely without reference to the "commercial" criteria of mainstream publishing. Like other manifestations of "alternative" culture—most notably "alternative music" in the days before its discovery by the major record labels—this scene has its roots in a shared progressive, often radical, conception of the political and also, perhaps most importantly, in a shared enthusiasm for the subversive (or "counterhegemonic") possibilities of contemporary youth culture. Notwithstanding its deep commitment to "the local," underground culture is an *international* phenomenon, in which the common experiences of the culturally marginal throughout the industrialized world are emphasized, usually in explicit opposition to the dominant global *corporate* culture and often, though not always, at the expense of "the national." The (self-)importance of this alternative scene for book publishing throughout North America and Europe is thus to be found in its bold assertion of the priorities of the young and the marginal in a world increasingly dominated by commercial mass culture. In particular—and this point can hardly be exaggerated—the works published by many of the alternative zines and book presses arise directly out of—and thus speak directly to—the *lived experience* of contemporary Western youth.

American zine scholar Stephen Duncombe has described the politics of the "underground" as follows (and much of what he says of zines may equally be said of the myriad chapbooks, comics, journals, spoken-word and Net-based works of the alternative presses in North America):

> Zines and underground culture constitute a free space where people can experiment with possibility. . . . Reading each zine is delving into the author's idiosyncratic world, and taken as a whole the underground culture maps out an unfamiliar and multiform universe. Knowing it you identify possibility, undermining the most powerful hegemonic tool that the powerful have at their disposal: the justification of the current order as "natural. . . ." [T]he world of zines is not entirely imaginary—it is built, and in the building of this culture political lessons are learned. Initially ignored by mainstream culture, zine writers have created vast networks of independent communication in order to share the ideas and thoughts they feel are not being expressed elsewhere. These networks make up a distinct material infrastructure of communication that uses the technology of mass commercial society—computers, copy machines, mail system—but steers the use of these technologies towards nonprofit, communitarian ends. . . . [Z]ines also function to raise the consciousness of individuals who do not belong to any set group. Reading the range of opinions and lifestyles, the probing search for authenticity, and the depth of the rage against society in zines encourages readers to think about who they are and what they believe in. Such testimony from regular people—fellow losers—can also lend them the courage to stand up and profess their own opinions, and then, perhaps, to act upon them.[1]

Generally speaking, *zine culture is the product of highly literate, literary and politically engaged young people,* hence it stands as a singular, powerful refutation of the stereotype of youth as illiterate, depoliticized and lazy. Corey Frost of the Canadian micro-publisher ga press has poignantly observed, "I think that young people are natural producers of literature. There are few young people who aren't excited by the idea of producing an anthology lit-zine if the possibility is presented to them."[2]

As Duncombe's characterization of underground publishing suggests—and as the voluminous literature on youth subcultures attests—there is a constant "threat" that the element of *subversion* which alternative culture seeks to embody will be co-opted by mainstream (corporate) culture and sold back to young people in the form of "hip" lifestyle accessories.[3] This co-optation strategy has been a crucial ingredient in marketing to youth since at least the 1960s, when "hippy" music and fashion entered the mainstream; in the 1990s, however, the success of multinational corporations in co-opting and commodifying the styles of the "streets" was truly astounding, as Nike, Tommy Hilfiger, Fubu and myriad other "brand names" commodified the very hip-hop, rave and alternative styles young people had pioneered to *challenge* the status quo. The relationship of alternative culture to the mainstream has thus become a defining element in underground politics and a subject of almost continuous debate among its most passionate practitioners. Where book publishing is concerned, wariness of the power of large corporations to co-opt the credibility of the small presses can occasionally take the form of a siege mentality among the latter, as well as a tendency to define the two in explicitly antithetical terms. Practically, however, there is widespread acknowledgement within the publishing industry—at least in Canada—that small and large presses are not competitors as much as they are complements to one another.

Hal Niedzviecki, the editor of *Concrete Forest,* is also an acclaimed novelist, the founding editor of *Broken Pencil* (a periodical for zine and micro-publishers in Canada), and coordinator of the annual Canzine festival for independent Canadian presses.

He is a tireless promoter of the "alternative" publishing scene in Canada, and one of its most thoughtful advocates. In a recent article entitled "It's Hip to Buy," Niedzviecki assessed the current state of the relationship between mainstream and alternative culture in Canada, arguing that, in this age of government downsizing and waning state support for culture, the two seem to be collapsing into a single market-driven hybrid. The crucial subtext of the article is that young Canadians have the most to lose as this hybridization intensifies, even though they themselves constitute its leading edge. Niedzviecki begins by characterizing "independent Canadian culture" as an historic collection of "dogged and distinctive cultural enterprises pursued by artists of all disciplines and publishers of every format for no profit and very little recognition." Now, however, "with the Liberal government in Ottawa and the Conservatives in Ontario leading the charge to dismantle the grant system, what little money there is tends to go to middle-class projects of no interest to younger generations." Observing that "corporate arts organizations" are today "eating up the cash," Niedzviecki asserts that we have entered an era of "corporate distrust" in which the credibility of the independent cultural producers is taking the upper hand. "Corporate distrust might be nothing more than a trend," he speculates, "but in Canada it is driving buyers toward that spot where independent culture is poking its ugly nose out of the back-roads." Young people, he maintains, are at the centre of this cultural shift: "Leading the consumer revolution in underground Can-con are the kids. The reason ads are suddenly post-modern, the CBC is programming inner city angst and 'rock' radio stations have gone 'alternative' is because that's what the kids are buying. . . . Do-it-yourself is sweeping the country—or should we call it sell-it-yourself? Whatever implications one wants to attach to this shift in cultural mores, there's no denying that the god of industry, the market-place, is being affected."

Niedzviecki puts forward a carefully nuanced argument concerning the transformation of cultural production in Canada, as state involvement is displaced by market forces:

> Old-style Canadian culture was grant based, which meant it was not for profit, which meant it didn't have to sell, which meant that it didn't immediately eliminate most kinds of artistic endeavours and anything too damn complicated. In contrast, the kind of product being produced by the independent Canadian culture industry of the nineties is the saleable kind. If it doesn't have a hook, if it can't be explained in less than five minutes, it isn't worth doing. Generic angst, violence and bad attitude effectively replace location specific projects that either can't be marketed, or wouldn't have a market outside of Canada. The selling of the Canadian underground to the U.S. plays a big role in this shift away from grant based culture. While Canada might be able to sustain some radical culture, the real money is in reaching that huge audience of U.S. hipster consumers.

Referring specifically to Canadian publishing, Niedzviecki argues that, until recently, "there has been very little published for the hipster generation." Now, however, newer independent Canadian publishing houses—Insomniac, Gutter Press and Arsenal Pulp, for example—are all "looking for that elusive nose-ring population." While this trend might once have been cause for celebration, Niedzviecki now tends to see it as evidence that even the Canadian indies have been seduced by the lure of American "hipster consumers." He cites Insomniac as an example of a Canadian publisher that has begun to increase its output of "generic but visually enticing books with titles like *Angels and Amphetamines*." Says Niedzviecki sardonically of this strategy:

These are anthologies of writers grouped together in a pack-agable theme. If you didn't already know that these were all Canadian writers, nothing in the writing would ground these anthologies in place or time period. These are perfect books for export. While the quality of the writing varies, the pack-age remains constant and, hopefully young and oh so sexy.

Significantly, Niedzviecki does not indict the publishers them-selves for acceding to the demands of the marketplace, since the circumstances that have forced them to do so, especially the ero-sion of state funding, are beyond their control:

> No one can blame [Mike] O'Connor [of Insomniac] for his marketing techniques. He knows that Canadian bookstores are less and less willing to support their own, and increasingly reluctant to take chances. He's banking on the grants cut killing off many medium-sized Canadian publishing houses and leaving a gaping hole waiting to be filled by new, more aggressive publishers. These publishers, not hindered by any state sentiments about culture, will be sales-oriented and ulti-mately, like the indie record labels, will force corporate con-cerns to react to a younger market.

Niedzviecki points out that "multinational corporations are anx-ious to imitate independent culture," citing the now common phenomena of "major" record labels which promote their new releases as if they are "independent," and soft drink companies which produce their own zines and "youth culture magazines." That such duplicitous strategies appear to be working is, for Niedzviecki, profoundly disillusioning: "Most kids don't want revolution, they aren't interested in developing a radical lifestyle and don't intend to carry a boycott short-list of companies who exploit their workers in the third world. Underground culture for younger generations has to be like a toothless mouth, warm, moist and womb-like."

Niedzviecki closes his meditation by placing the question of youth and alternative culture in the context of much broader discourses about nation and identity: "A country's culture is the marker of its past, its present, and its future. If specialization and generic pseudo-underground teen stuff is all that's left of Canadian alternative culture, then the past looks proud, the present looks ugly and Canada's future looks dumb and dumber." He concludes provocatively: "Canada is a country that refuses to support its true talents, and rewards mediocrity. That this is the result of a culture corrupted both by a visionless grant system and an obsession with creating a U.S.–style culture of consumption is both a starting and ending point of this article. The global economy is all well and good, but only a grass-roots local economy can stop underground culture from trail-blazing a path straight to the high-way of consumerism."

That Niedzviecki overstated the case in "It's Hip to Buy" for polemical effect is suggested by evidence of his deep loyalty to the underground scene in Canada. (He has put his own fiction on the line for this cause, in fact, by allowing Coach House to publish his most recent book, *Smell It.*)[4] Writing for the trade publication *Canadian Bookseller* in 1999, Niedzviecki sang the praises for what he called the "relatively new movement of Canadian independent micro-publishers," demanding that intransigent Canadian book retailers "take note of [their] endeavours." Differentiating the micro-presses not only from "the big publishers" but also "the established small presses," he asserted that they "come to publishing not as a job, but as a passion. Halfway between the peripatetic world of zines (eccentric photocopied periodicals) and the world of the small press, buoyed by accessible technology and a young reading public hungry to hear their voices scribbled in the margins of a new generation's prose,

Canada suddenly has more micro-publishers than ever before." Niedzviecki was especially insistent that Canadian book retailers begin to consider stocking the "chapbooks" put out by the independents, which, he claimed, have the twin advantages of being inexpensive to produce in small runs and of appealing to "younger audiences who seem to feel more comfortable with literature that has the slim girth of a magazine as opposed to the heft of a book."[5] He was not, however, overly optimistic about this prospect, noting that retail bookbuyers—under the same sorts of competitive pressure as the presses themselves—increasingly take the view that "[t]he days of the worthy little books that look like crap are over."[6] Niedzviecki thus characterizes the Canadian micro-publishers as inhabiting an ambiguous, even paradoxical cultural space—one that has evolved in large measure out of the paradoxical cultural condition of contemporary youth: "As an industry, it's an incongruous one. It's an industry that produces 'books' that aren't always supposed to look like books for a generation that isn't supposed to have the attention span to read them. It's an industry that has responded to the overall indifference of bookstores by, for the most part, appealing directly to their audience—launching titles and holding events in clubs more used to the deafening feedback of amplified instruments than the quiet murmur of a single voice." Though increasingly compromised by the demands of the marketplace, the greatest virtue of the micro-presses for Niedzviecki, one which has potentially profound implications for the renewal of Canadian publishing, is their commitment to the particular: "In an age of what many see as mass-produced, cookie-cutter books filling giant, faceless bookstores, personality may be a more vital commodity in publishing than ever before. . . . [It is] the personal touch that will help make this next wave of micro-presses an indispensable addition to the Canadian publishing landscape."

The Role of the Independent Presses

The many small Canadian presses and micro-publishers with whom I corresponded during my research confirmed Hal Niedzviecki's sympathetic characterization of the underground scene in Canada, its relationship to the larger publishers and especially its determination to represent (and reach out to) young people. Although they do not always agree with one another, there is sufficient common ground and especially practical collaboration between them to warrant a generalized review of their role in Canadian publishing, particularly as it pertains to youth.

It is extremely important to preface this review, however, by noting that *the micro-presses in Canada do not have a monopoly on literary independence, or risk-taking, or receptivity to new voices.* (That McClelland and Stewart published *Concrete Forest: The New Fiction of Urban Canada* under Niedzviecki's general editorship in 1998 is a case in point.) Although it is true that the small presses bear much of the responsibility for breaking new talent and especially for pushing forward the frontiers of literary technique, it is also true that without renewal the large Canadian presses, and even the multinationals, risk their own extinction. As in the other popular arts, a high degree of risk is, in fact, built into book publishing, at least in the sense that one can never know exactly which titles are going to succeed or fail in the marketplace. Given the statistical probability that seven Canadian books in ten will "stiff" (see Chapter Two), this means that for any given firm the best-sellers inevitably subsidize the weaker titles, that author "development" over several books remains the only practical strategy for amortizing risk over the long run and, above all, that even the most conservative publishers must at least occasionally test the relatively unknown and the untried in the marketplace. This said, it is true that a kind of "division of labour" has grown up in publishing, one which is analogous to the well established relationship between the "major" record labels and the "indies." Smaller cultural producers serve to seek out and nurture new talent, and also to test its commercial viability, most often in a highly localized marketplace. Once they have proven themselves successful—measured at least in part against the criteria of commercial profitability— the artists in question (and sometimes even the firms that "discovered" them) are absorbed by larger companies which then seek to market them to a far larger, often international audience. That most of the writers published by the small presses in Canada are first-time authors attests to the persistence of this division of labour. Even so, as Andy Brown of the fiercely independent Conundrum Press has observed, the micro-publishers cannot lay exclusive claim to the literary cutting edge nor, in particular, do they alone seek to appeal to the young:

> Presumably if a book is published with McClelland and Stewart it must always be *less* radical, due to the immense cost of printing thousands of copies and promoting and distributing the book. Interestingly, this is not always the case. Mainstream publishers are becoming somewhat aware that the young readers searching out independent press material will one day grow up and become the reading public they will need to buy their books. Some of these publishers are responding by trying to bridge the gap between supposedly radical content and the ability of this content to reach a wider audience. The anthology of new urban fiction *Concrete Forest*, recently published by M & S, shared a handful of contributors with the anthology of short stories *Burning Revisions* put out by maverick Toronto publisher Rush Hour Revisions.

> HarperCollins Canada is publishing the second novel by zine guy Jim Munroe. His first novel was self published.[7]

Unfortunately, as noted above, there is a tendency among some advocates of underground culture to overstate this division of labour and to simply assume, as Lance Blongren of Intrepid Tourist Press puts it, that "[t]he publishing industry is at the opposite side of the spectrum from small presses. Everyone knows what happens when their favourite band or writer gets 'discovered.' The work, once innovative, becomes commodified and soon the things that excited you are being labelled and sold and soon you're bored with the whole damn thing and nodding off in the corner."[8] In some cases, this tendency appears to have hardened into dogma, complete with a "zero-sum" attitude which, among its other unfortunate consequences, can produce a penchant for deriding the most commercially successful literature. Blain Kyllo, for example, marketing director of Arsenal Pulp Press, has said:

> The quirky reality about the big publishers is their inability to take risks. They want to take advantage of changes in the marketplace, but they aren't willing to establish or develop those changes. I guess it isn't the fact that big publishers capitalize on what we've established that bothers me. What bothers me it is the way big publishers try to take all the credit for something they had nothing to do with. Regardless, without us, writing would never change, never develop, never advance. We'd all be reading Atwood and Davies forever.[9]

Most of the small and micro-publishers with whom I corresponded were, in fact, far more nuanced in their understanding of their relationship vis-à-vis the "big" presses, acknowledging that they have made their peace with playing what Judith Isherwood of Shoreline Press has called "an ancillary role in the literary world."[10] Simon Dardick of Véhicule Press, for example, likens small presses to the "farm teams" of professional sport:

> The small presses take most of the risks and through effective management of their modest resources, manage to stay in business. This is not to say the large publishers do not publish important, quality writing. Of course they do. But there is no question that the independent presses publish most of the first-time authors in all genres. The reality is that we sometimes fill the role of farm team for the large publishers. Small presses are indispensable players in the infrastructure that is Canadian publishing—regionally and nationally. The fact that so many independent publishers' authors win national prizes is telling.[11]

Beth Follett of Pedlar Press agrees: "Independent presses are often the ones to spot emerging talent. . . . I do believe that small presses fill very unique markets, and the big houses could never replicate the efforts of the small. Yes, we take the risks."[12] Corey Frost, in contrast, tends to see small publishers as occupying more discreet "marginal" cultural spaces that are simply not practical for larger presses to stake out:

> I don't think micro and large presses are or ever will be competitors, but I think that large presses dominate the distribution and publicity networks (chain bookstores, newspaper book sections) to the detriment of micro-presses (of course this is not always the fault of the publishing companies). Micro-presses definitely produce things that major companies would never touch, and so are indispensable to literature/art. It's not usually a question of "breaking new talent" to prepare them for larger-scale publication, it's more about publishing alternatives.[13]

All of this is not to say that there is no resentment among small Canadian presses for having repeatedly done the reconnaissance work for the larger publishers. As Brian Kaufman has said: "We take great risk and often are poached by larger publishers (who can dangle large advances) once we have worked to establish a writer in the market."[14] Adds Mike O'Connor: "There really isn't much of relationship between the [small and large presses]. We're very different animals with very different readers. Occasionally, they'll pick up one of our authors and when that the author doesn't earn out their advances they will turf the author."[15] Tim Inkster of Porcupine's Quill Press (PQL), notable for having launched the careers of both Andrew Pyper and Russell Smith, was especially candid on this question in my lengthy correspondence with him:

> PQL published Russell [Smith]'s first novel, *How Insensitive*, and it was a huge (8000 copy) hit. We also published his second, *Noise*, which was a much better book, better promoted &c &c and it didn't sell. Now Russell [has] published his most recent book with Doubleday/Bertelsmann. Russell is a big success, but PQL shared in no way in the financial rewards of that success. PQL [also] published Andrew Pyper's first collection of stories, *Kiss Me*. It did very well—it sold 2000 copies. Andrew Pyper sold his second book, a mystery novel, to HarperCollins/Dell (NYC) and Macmillan (London) for a combined unearned advance in excess of half a million dollars, Canadian. This is more money than I have made, cumulatively, in 30 years of publishing the likes of Andrew Pyper.

Pyper and Russell, insisted Inkster, were not isolated examples: "Russell Smith has signed with Doubleday/Bertelsmann; Andrew Pyper signed with HarperCollins/Dell (U.S.) and Macmillian (U.K.) for over $500 000, advance; Stephen Heighton signed with Knopf, for $65 000; Elizabeth Hay has jumped to McClelland & Stewart; Jane Urquhart published with PQL before she got famous; Caroline Adderson, Cynthia Holz and Elise Levine have all signed with Key Porter; Michael Winter has just recently jumped to Anansi, for a $12 000 advance." He concludes resignedly that, given the enormous talent of Canadian writers and the limited opportunity to publish in this country, doing reconnaissance for the big presses seems to be the lot of the small houses: "In general, any author good enough to be published by PQL is already too good to be published by PQL. It would be nice if (as is the case with Junior hockey) we could be compensated for the development work we do on behalf of the larger trade houses, but this has been a dream for over 25 years."[16]

As Tim Inkster's comments suggest, the people behind most of the small and micro-publishers in Canada persevere in the world of publishing—against great odds and often without recognition—as a labour of love. In a recent survey of some of his small press allies, for example, Andy Brown observed: "Although the publishers I've talked to . . . produce a wide spectrum of books with varying levels of production costs, they all share in the small (or independent) press philosophy of making quality objects considered deserving simply because they contain something interesting and worthwhile. Some are bitter, some are optimistic for the future, but all are committed to the making of books, not money." He asserted, moreover, that this kind of thinking is "antithetical to the principles of a larger press," where commercial considerations figure more prominently and "the division of labour resembles an assembly line."[17] Mike O'Connor concurs: "We publish, primarily, new and experimental fiction. . . . *We publish it, because we like it.*"[18] Many independent press owners, who have emerged out of the zine scene in Canada, or who identify themselves explicitly with the ethos of the underground noted above, claim that they are *solely* interested in literature that is considered too "edgy" or "experimental" for the mainstream. Darren Wershler-Henry of Coach House put it this way: "What [we] have to offer is Oprah-free literature. I guess by that you could say things that haven't been sanitized for people who think that they are doing the world a favour by reading books the same way they do aerobics."[19] Vern Smith of Rush Hour Revisions agrees: "Traditional Canadian literature doesn't leave a lot of room for punk and porn. The stuff we are putting out there is a whole lot edgier than what even the established small presses are doing. We're not just putting something out there, we're putting something out that stands for something."[20] Adds David Lester of Vancouver's Get To The Point, "More and more people are doing it. This is a genuine underground movement, it's a reaction to the corporate world. It's a real radical reaction—to produce something small. . . . We're saying: there's room for experimental work and for pushing the boundaries of literature, and that's how you develop culture in this country."[21]

There is a sense among many of these publishers, moreover, that the form and content of the works they produce are inextricable—not least because in many cases the publishers are artists in their own right. As Corey Frost has said of ga press: "We've published chapbooks and anthologies by young experimental writers, often spoken-word texts. Our motivation stems mostly from direct involvement as writers and performers, the desire to promote the work, and also the inherent creative satisfaction of the publishing process (i.e., creating and manufacturing the books is an artistic not a commercial activity)."[22] Many of the micro-publishers extend this dedication to an "organic" correlation of form and content to a quasi-fetishistic preoccupation with the book-as-object. This is, perhaps ironically, a profoundly *conservative* impulse, one that is often rooted explicitly in a kind of artisan's pride in the work of printing and binding, and also in the tactile pleasure (appearance, texture, even scent) in which generations of book lovers have indulged themselves. (This interest in the craft of book production may also be seen as a backlash against the limitations of the "assembly line" process noted above, i.e. shoddy book design, flimsy construction, inadequate copy editing, excessive errata, etc.) Writes Andy Brown: "[T]he move toward renewing the sense of the book itself as a singular, valuable and beautiful item is fraught with difficulty. Indie presses must create and publish within a system that devalues the book as an object, that makes no distinctions between a mass paperback and a hand-bound limited edition. Additionally, books must fight against video games and video recordings."[23] Adds Corey Frost: "The mass-production of books and the assumption that text conveys meaning transparently makes U.S. forget about the physicality of books."[24] Mike O'Connor is even more blunt: "The concept of a book is such bullshit. The problem comes from the U.S. where books are considered a product." Referring to his work at Insomniac, O'Connor adds: "I do all my own graphic design, it is an integral part of the book. There is a graphic literacy that isn't really addressed in traditional books. I think that people now, especially the younger readership, are much more attuned to that. Design is everywhere, and it should be in the literature as well."[25]

Like zine culture and the underground generally, many independent Canadian publishers have made the inclusion of young writers and readers a top priority in their work. Interestingly, however, virtually all of the people to whom I spoke—many of whom were themselves in their twenties or early thirties—rejected the notion that young people somehow constitute a special literary case or a "niche" market. Rather, as they told me repeatedly (and often rather aggressively), they tend to consider young writers and readers to be part of the general adult audience for literature—and often its most *sophisticated* element. Joe Blades of Broken Jaw Press, for example, told me pointedly: "What youth?

They're not all one entity!"[26] Judith Isherwood concurs: "We [at Shoreline] feel that there are as many different types of young readers as older readers. . . . We try to produce eclectic books for eclectic readers."[27] For her part, Beth Follett suggests that, in such instances where youth appear to have lost the taste for reading, the dominant culture itself is to blame; otherwise young people are apt to be as passionate about reading as anyone: "I think some youth are as eager for literature as youth have ever been; but I think many have been lost to capital E Entertainment—T.V., THE WEB, T.V., THE WEB. . . . I think we live in a philistine culture that promotes addictions and dumbing-down processes. To this end, many youth (and adults) only want the thrill of an endless unabsorbed stream of information (read noise). The smart ones, though, still want the incredible and beautiful private experience of the book."[28] Adds Heather Haley, Executive Director of the Edgewise Electrolit Centre, with characteristic understatement: "I can only speak for the [young people] I've encountered. They are very interested in literature and quite well read."[29]

Although their views on the literary tastes and reading habits of young Canadians vary, one finds in the opinions and especially the marketing strategies of the small presses virtually *none* of the condescension evident in the advertising discourses of much mainstream youth publishing. (Indeed, in contrast with the alarmism of *Broken Words* and the pervasive stereotype of print culture as alien to youth, there is in the commentary of many independent publishers a refreshing casualness about their working assumption that young readers are *not* exceptional.) Says Corey Frost: "Young people are of course interested in texts produced—I mean written and published—by young people. There's less interest in traditional forms like the novel if they have been artificially imposed on the material (i.e. the story), and a great interest in cross-genre, loosely structured texts, such as

collage, comics, text-based art, spoken-word, etc . . ."[30] Joe Blades
is characteristically blunt: "Most really small Canadian presses
don't even know or care what a 'niche market' is and they don't
call themselves or their friends 'new talent'. . . . Some titles are *by*
so-called 'youth' authors. So some certainly do appeal to that age
range (& people of other age ranges I hope)."[31] Even when publishers have a well developed sense of the cultural capital their
readers bring to their publications—and most do—this has far
less to do with age than with levels of educational attainment,
place of residence and degree of intellectual curiosity. Says Beth
Follett of Pedlar's readers: "[They] tend to be 23-55, urban, hip
intelligentsia, the curious, those who adore beautiful books and
will purchase them almost indiscriminately, those looking for
an alternative to the mainstream/conventional narrative."[32]
Mike O'Connor said of Insomniac: "Our readership tends to be
younger, between 20 and 35. They are well educated and tend to
live in large urban centres." O'Connor added, in response to my
query about his sense of young people's reading skills: "I think the
age this study is inquiring about reads as much if not more than
previous generations, but they do not read books or mainstream
newspapers. They read zines, a lot of stuff on the web and magazines. They're interested in cultural marginalia."[33] Similarly,
Brian Kaufman says of Anvil Press: "We publish for the inquisi-
tive, hungry reader who is looking for material that is taking
chances in some manner—form, content etc. We presume most
of our readers to have some post-secondary education and to
consider the world of books as an integral part of their life."[34]
In striking contrast with the common view that books must be
"dumbed down" for young persons with literacy problems, Judith
Isherwood, a former reading teacher and consultant, told me:
"I am well aware of the need for 'high interest/low reading level'
books for students with literacy problems, and of 'young adult'
novels. We [at Shoreline] do not believe in watering down text,

but rather in giving young people reasonable reading goals to strive for."[35] Adds Corey Frost: "I think visual literacy is much more important for young readers. The use of graphic elements in the text, and the design of the book in general, play a big role in the appreciation of a zine or chapbook. I think it's important to think of this as a new kind of literacy, not as a loss of interest in reading text. It's an evolution of the way people interpret text."[36]

Like their favourable responses to my queries about the reading proclivities of young people, the independents' critique of the notion that youth somehow constitute a "market" that can be isolated, targeted and exploited reflected their long and often intimate experience with sophisticated young readers. Some, like Corey Frost, suggested politely that marketing was irrelevant: "This question does not really apply because for me it's not about attracting a certain market. (The "market" is dictated by the work.) However, I'd say that I'm conscious of certain things that will make the book more appealing to a younger crowd: first of all, we try to keep the prices low (in the zine and chapbook world, $5 is a high price). If we charge a price that is fully commensurate to the value of the writing and the design, we know a different group of people—and a different age group—will be buying the books."[37] Others emphasized inexpensive and innovative sites of book promotion, virtually all of which privileged intimate, word-of-mouth discourses rather than any kind of hard sell. Simon Dardick, for example, one of many small Canadian presses putting the Internet to good use, emphasizes "content" over novelty: "Our web site receives about 24 000 visitors a year. In addition to our catalogue, we include interesting editorial material. We believe it is essential to provide content if you want people to return to your site." Dardick added: "We try to stay current with various zines. And keep an eye on what my daughters read!"[38] Another popular strategy is the author's tour. Says Judith Isher-wood: "[O]nce the book is in print, our authors are the most wonderful salesmen, giving talks and interviews, signing books, and suggesting possible readers and reviewers. We have a very personal, productive working relationship, which I hope makes up for the lack of marketing money available to the big presses."39 Mike O'Connor admits that Insomniac has "tried everything from the web to mammoth author tours to voodoo charms. The three most successful elements of campaigns have been author tours, a strong web presence and having booths at small press books fairs."40 Of course, not all small presses are averse to mass-mediated publicity but, as Tim Inkster's wry commentary suggests, even the most successful ventures into "mass" marketing do not come without irony: "Russell Smith's *How Insensitive* was short-listed for the Governor General's Award, the Trillium Prize, and the Chapters/Books in Canada First Novel Award. The prizes were pleasant, but what *really* sold the book was a seven-minute video made for MuchMusic in which a young woman displayed her garters in public, on camera. Russell Smith's second novel, *Noise* (1998), sold less than 2 000 copies. No video."41

Having made it clear in my initial correspondence with the small presses that I was interested in hearing from them on the matter of the impediments they face in their efforts to reach young readers, I am particularly at pains to allow them to speak for themselves on the question. Not surprisingly, the most critical problem facing the small and especially micro-presses in Canada is lack of access to working capital—something which nearly all of my correspondents stressed. Michael Harrison of Broadview Press summarized their general situation: "The main point is that Canadian publishers are so poorly capitalized that they simply cannot afford to do more than play in the market place [in which] they find themselves. The money needed to really be involved (think of the $ millions or billions being spent by the multinationals) is simply beyond the scope of Canadian independent publishers—*all of them* (unless you consider Harlequin and Nelson/Thomson International to be Canadian)![42] Harrison, who is also the president of the Association of Canadian Publishers (ACP), is spearheading a lobbying campaign in Ottawa to restore government funding and to "address our undercapitalization problem." At present the ACP is promoting the idea of a "publishing equity investment tax credit." This would constitute "a tax break for investors in qualified Canadian-owned publishing houses" designed to "facilitate some valuable structural changes." In particular, according to Harrison, "[it] would have a positive effect with the banks, which are much more willing to grant or extend lines of credit to houses with significant shareholder equity." (The ACP is especially worried about renewal in the Canadian-owned sector. Says Harrison: "We also need to find a mechanism that would help publishers who want to retire and pass their companies on to fresh blood, existing employees or new people. Many of the people responsible for the dramatic expansion of the Canadian industry in the 1960s and 1970s are now at or near retirement age. An investment tax credit would help them, and at the same time make sure their houses continue to thrive.")[43]

Another prominent item on the small publishers' agenda is the need for improved book distribution channels—itself a biproduct of the chronic undercapitalization of independent distributors. Said Joe Blades: "[M]any small, indie publishers have no means to reach the coast-to-coast Canadian 'market'—that requires distributors, wholesalers, sales reps, etc. Many small presses only sell locally in their own community, or at readings and small press fairs which they organize, without marketing resources, for themselves. Or they go on the road with a car (if they have one), backpack and boxes of books, selling as they travel (or simply trading for a meal, beer, whatever) the same way unknown indie musicians travel. They are taking huge risks, with zero support or back-up."[44] Corey Frost argues explicitly for some kind of public distribution/publicity subsidy for smaller presses, placing his comments in the context of federal policies that tend to privilege larger presses:

> If you want to encourage young people's interest in literature, then find a way to distribute youth-produced zines to youth. What would be vastly more beneficial than grants to publishers is a subsidized (and appropriately publicized) distribution system for zines and chapbooks. The system would have to be free to the book producers—they would send in copies of their book to be distributed to bookstores and participating high schools or colleges across the country. It could be juried, as long as it was young people and zine producers on the jury, and as long as the parameters were wide open in terms of format/genre/content. A government-funded distributor would be hugely beneficial not just to young people but to all kinds of new self-published writers and artists and zine-publishers.
>
> I'm concerned that no matter how broad the criteria, there will still be publishers who are "under the radar." So much micro-publishing happens sporadically and on a very small scale, which means even getting together a grant proposal might be more trouble than it's worth. I'd encourage you to consider those publishers who might produce one chapbook every year or two, or even only one or two chapbooks ever, and who spend maybe 100 dollars total on the production. They would definitely be helped by distribution and publicity assistance. (Toronto mag *Broken Pencil* has been very helpful in this way.) For example, one really useful thing would be a web-based chapbook clearing house. Or a national chapbook/micro-press awards. I'd just like to see the profile of small-publishing raised, in order to a) attract more people to get involved, and b) to broaden the potential audience.45

If Frost speaks for the "low output" publishers on the need for distribution assistance, Judith Isherwood insists that the problems small publishers have in reaching their markets do not necessarily diminish even as their catalogues grow: "We feel that small presses can provide well-written memoirs and enjoyable reading for young people today. We hope that after the young adult novels are packed away, our books, being more timeless, would remain. . . . When [Shoreline] had only a few books to publish and market, it was manageable and we could work with the marketing available. Now that we have 27 books to market, plus trying to master the new technology, things are much more difficult. Help would be Very Much appreciated!"[46] Other responses included Beth Follett's important observation that young people's purchasing patterns are dictated by the affordability of books: "Spend federal money on the indie presses. Help them lower the costs of their products so that youth can afford them."[47] Joe Blades spoke for many when he observed that there is also a great need among the smaller presses for "some sort of funding and resource structure (training, technology acquisition or access, book publisher accounting and inventory software)."[48]

In the end, as Hal Niedzviecki told me rather bluntly, there remains a good deal of suspicion in the small press community— and certainly in underground publishing in particular—that the heavy hand of "top-down" bureaucracy is not good for literature and that, though a system of grants would be welcomed by capital-starved publishers, it would have to respect the democratic, independent ethos of the movement:

> I'm in favour of funding and subsidies for small and indie presses and creators, but I am wary of the kind of entrenchment you get when presses depend on those subsidies year after year and no longer get out there and reach the audience anyway possible. But I can tell you that a little seed money

goes a long way. We need the money, but we also need to avoid complacency and getting into a situation where outside bodies evaluate and determine content by approving or disapproving a certain project. Those decisions need to be made at the grass roots level not by committee.49

Clearly, despite their many common goals and strategies, there is a great gulf between the small presses in Canada—which *are* eligible for stable state funding, most notably via BPIDP operating grants—and the micro-presses which tend, as Frost put it, to remain "under the radar" of granting agencies. The traditional criteria for federal funding—including a minimum number of annual publications, a traditional (usually UNESCO-based) definition of a "book" and a certain level of sales—serve to exclude most underground publishers from state subsidy, even as they may abet conservative tendencies in some of the so-called "traditional" small presses. This is not, by any means, to be taken as a critique of the latter (or as a valorization of the former). Small presses, faced with fierce competition in an increasingly globalized marketplace and especially the likelihood that their most commercially successful authors are apt to be "poached" by the large presses must, willy nilly, play by the rules of the market or perish. That the micro-presses are chronically under-capitalized, unprofitable and typically operated on a hand-to-mouth basis may be frustrating for their devotees; but, perhaps ironically, it is precisely their detachment from the demands of the marketplace that allow them the luxury of publishing whatever and whenever they might like. Suspicious of government funding, resistant to the conformist standards of conventional book retailing, and often wedded ideologically to a radical political or aesthetic ethos that prevents compromise with mainstream culture, underground publishers are, to an extent that many openly acknowledge, sleeping in the beds they have themselves made.

As for young people and their relationship with literature (and print culture in general), it is clear that the existing hierarchical structure of the Canadian publishing industry serves them well at virtually every level. For the subversive, "counterhegemonic" or highly experimental young writer, the micro-publishers serve as an extension of (or adjunct to) a well established underground zine culture that celebrates autonomy and artistic freedom and openly refuses any sort of compromise with the dominant culture (whether it is thought to be represented by "corporate" mass culture or the state). Zine and underground press readers have become habituated to the "marginal" distribution channels available to their favourite publications, while zine and micro-publishers, long advantaged by inexpensive desktop publishing and photocopying technology, have positioned themselves to take full advantage of the marketing and distribution potential of the Internet. The micro-publishers' essential problem, it would seem, is the difficulty of finding *new* audiences for their work, either because traditional book distribution channels are largely closed to them or because booksellers are growing more and more reluctant to stock their unconventional publications. Insofar as both of these impediments are inherent in the relationship between book publishers, wholesalers and retailers—that is, they are the result of "voluntary" relationships common to all buyers and sellers in a given marketplace—there is little in the way of public policy that might rectify this problem. Simply stated, booksellers, bound by their own tastes and experience (if not by their own profit-maximization strategies) will stock whatever they believe will sell. It is thus incumbent upon the zine and micro-publishers to concentrate their efforts on stimulating *demand* for their publications rather than in persuading intransigent booksellers and other retailers to stock works for which there is no demonstrated market.

The small Canadian presses labour under a different set of constraints. They enjoy comparatively easy access to the conventional channels of retail distribution and sales, at least insofar as they are producing conventional "books" (and with the important proviso that they feel themselves to be increasingly at the mercy of capricious retailers who now command enormous clout in the marketplace). They also continue to enjoy access to stable state funding. Lastly, they are advantaged—at least by comparison with zine and micro-publishers—by their willingness to compromise ideologically and hence to publish works in a broad range of styles, from the most commercial to the most experimental (or to embrace marketing strategies in which the former effectively subsidize the latter). They acknowledge that they are bound by the rules of the marketplace, and although they can be highly critical of its rigidity and especially of its tendency towards conformity, they are prepared to make pragmatic concessions to these demands. Indeed, they are not averse to making money in the process! (Toronto's Insomniac Press is a striking example of a small Canadian publisher attempting to straddle the line between the underground and the mainstream, producing a good deal of work that is novel, exciting and unconventional while adopting a rather conventional marketing strategy centring on increased domestic retail visibility and export growth.) The essential problem for the small presses appears to consist in a more or less chronic shortage of capital, the reasons for which range from poor revenue-generation, to shrinking margins, to the vicissitudes of public taste (in a market in which the great majority of books are destined to be money-losers). Above all, small presses must accept the fact that their most promising new authors are apt to be lost to larger presses the moment they become profitable. (The experience of Porcupine's Quill Press is exemplary in this respect; over the years they have "discovered" and nurtured an extraordinary stable of Canadian writers but, owing to the prevailing hierarchical structure of the publishing industry, they have realised very little profit from sales of their work.) In short, where the zine and micro-publishers need readers, the small presses need capital.

Though these constraints limit the growth (and sometimes even the *survival*) potential of small Canadian publishers—which may alone constitute sufficient grounds for a review of public policy pertinent to their activities—these factors do not in themselves constitute impediments for young readers or, more obviously, for young writers. With the exception of the zine and chapbook readership associated with the underground micro-publishers—a readership that tends to be openly averse to mainstream culture—young Canadians' literary tastes range over an extraordinarily broad spectrum, from the traditional to the experimental and beyond. Small presses, in fact, tend to work from the assumption that young readers are simply included in the various audiences that coalesce around their various authors, and that targeting them (or any other age-based demographic) is a fool's errand. (So, too, do the large Canadian-owned presses, for that matter, which helps to explain why "edgy" and "urban" fiction is showing up at virtually all levels of the publishing hierarchy in this country.) As for "young" writers, many of whom aspire quite reasonably to make a career of writing and thus conceive of themselves as upwardly mobile in the publishing world, the publishers' loss is often the authors' gain. That a Russell Smith or an Andrew Pyper might well "graduate" from a small Canadian press to a six-figure deal with a multinational is acknowledged by publisher and author alike to be a likely consequence of their successful collaboration—even if this prospect does not seem particularly "fair."

In short, *the various problems facing the small and micro-presses in Canada do not constitute impediments to young Canadians' encounter with reading or with Canadian literature.* The very fact that an hierarchical structure exists in the world of Canadian publishing—from the most conservative defenders of traditional

Canadiana at the top to the anarchistic subversion of the punk zinesters at the bottom—speaks to the extraordinarily broad range of literary experiences available to young Canadian readers. Little wonder, perhaps, that many independent publishers in Canada are perplexed when, with so much great literature before them, young Canadians *opt* for a literary experience that is, in Hal Niedzviecki's words, "toothless mouth, warm, moist and womb-like." The truth is that placing great books in front of young readers is not the problem. The trick is getting them to bite.

CONCLUSION

T IS ALWAYS A PLEASURE to investigate an area of appre-
hended crisis in a cultural industry and then to be able to
announce that things are not as bad as they appear. Less re-
warding is the task of challenging casual stereotypes, since these
can be tenacious, emotionally charged and all too easily deployed
in support of narrow political agendas.

Among the common beliefs I encountered during the preparation of this book were that aging baby boomers had a hammer
lock on Canadian literary culture; that the publishing industry
had hitched its star, without much regard for its future, to this
lucrative demographic; that Canada, along with the rest of the
industrialized West, is pioneering a "post-literate" culture characterized by the "death of print," the triumph of the televisual, and
the hegemony of corporate mass media; that an appalling number of Canadians are illiterate; that the Internet is usurping traditional print culture (including the corollary that hypertext is
superseding conventional narrative); and, above all, that young
people in Canada are fundamentally alienated from books (either
because their literacy skills are declining, they are too lazy to read,
or they have become irredeemably distracted by video games,

movies and the Internet). Though there may be kernels of truth here—none of them unambiguous or beyond the realm of political manipulation—these generalizations do not fare well in the light of the overwhelming evidence to the contrary. In truth, the Canadian publishing industry is remarkably diverse, dynamic and flexible entity, one that has persevered through the myriad challenges of recession, globalization and technological innovation to position itself admirably for a future in which print culture may be expected not merely to survive but to thrive. Far from overthrowing print culture, the Internet has thus far had the net effect of increasing book sales, even as it has made billionaires of the first wave of online booksellers. Canadians are, in general, far better educated today—and far more literate—than they have ever been. Above all, young Canadians are more comfortable with the world of print than any of their forebears, even if it is also true that they are the most comfortable with new digital media.

At the risk of over-generalizing about various "generations" of Canadians, it is apparent that Canadian publishing—and in particular its role in the lives of successive cohorts of young people —has been coloured greatly by the circumstances of the "Canadian Lit" project as it was conceived in the late 1960s and the 1970s. Canadian literature, along with myriad other nationalist cultural pursuits, contributed to the growth and ultimately the dominance of a broadly based left-nationalist ideology in this period which, in turn, buttressed state support for culture. Great Canadian literature from the historic and also from the more recent past was sought and found (the New Canadian Library series became its primary medium); uniquely Canadian modes of literary criticism were explored; the Canadian "small press movement" was launched; and, most dramatically of all, an unabashedly nationalist literary bias appeared, not only in the high-brow circles of the universities but among "ordinary" Canadian readers (those who made Pierre Berton, Farley Mowat and

Margaret Atwood, for example, household names). At every step of the way, prodding this symbiotic cultural and political process towards critical mass were the "early" baby boomers, those born in the late 1940s and the 1950s. Though they were in many important respects inspired by older intellectual visionaries— Harold Innis, George Grant and Northrop Frye, most notably— for many youths and young adults of the post-Centennial era these phenomena coalesced into a profound impulse to "read Canadian," cementing the inextricable correlation of literature, nation, citizenship and identity that has obtained for many members of this generation right up to the present.

Though affluent and flush with disposable income at every stage of their life cycle, the boomers' advantages have not been merely economic. Consider, for example, the extraordinary cultural capital they initially brought to the Canadian Lit project. They were *far* better educated than earlier cohorts, which meant, among other things, that they were also, in relative terms, far more literate. (It is worth recalling in this connection Garnett Picot's observation that the marked "educational advantage" the baby boom enjoyed vis-à-vis its parents has not been even remotely approximated by subsequent youth cohorts). Baby boomers also enjoyed the advantage of sheer numbers, utterly dominating the educational systems through which they were passing—first as a deluge of students and then as a wave of exceptionally young teachers and professors. To an extent that is all the more striking in retrospect, students and young university faculty collaborated, particularly within the new liberal arts universities that were springing up all over Canada in the 1960s, on the institutionalization of the Canadian Lit project, while their young friends and alumni worked to build up the independent presses, journals and bookstores that anchored it. Moreover, because their formative years coincided with the civil rights, anti-war, feminist, gay rights and other "anti-establishment" movements in the United States—the Sixties "counterculture" was only the most obvious offspring of this political crucible—the early baby boomers happen to have been highly politicized and hence, as some older Canadians will not have to be reminded, *noisy*. In contrast with the depoliticized and largely silent youth of the 1990s, boomers were able to persuade (or goad) the dominant culture into heeding their views in the 1960s, eliciting from it an extraordinary degree of latitude, cooperation, even empathy. It was their great good fortune to inherit a world in which, comparatively speaking, anything seemed possible (hence their reputed "idealism"). This world offered them—on top of inexpensive higher education, decent wages and upward mobility—a relatively untried and untested publishing environment, as well as a highly supportive system of state subsidies designed to encourage "creative" young people to follow their muses. Little wonder that they—along with their more senior collaborators—were sufficiently inspired and later disciplined to cement the Canadian Lit project as the dominant strain in Canada's nascent literary/publishing culture.

Though *individual* young people are today far better positioned even than the baby boomers to develop a lifelong love of books, they have enjoyed none of the *collective* demographic advantages with which the boomers were so uniquely favoured. On the one hand, not only are youth and young adults today better educated and more literate than any prior cohort, but they are far more *worldly*. Polling evidence suggests that young people read substantially more now than the same age group did even at the height of the Canadian Lit boom, and that an astonishing 90 percent call themselves "book readers." Clearly, contemporary youth have been extremely well served by increasing access to education, by the extraordinary movement within Canada to make reading part of every family's home environment, and by the "high-brow" children's literature tradition that has taken shape in Canada since the 1970s. Taken as a whole, on the other hand, Canadians born in the wake of the baby boom are far less affluent, which has meant increased poverty for working class youth and increased economic dependency for the children of the middle class. Young people's real wages have been declining more or less continuously since the 1970s, while the costs of higher education have soared by over 100 percent in the 1990s alone. Canadians who came of age in the late 1980s and the 1990s have inherited a world in which very little is possible—a world of low wages, high unemployment, and downward mobility. In this world, the state, far from being a principal source of inspiration and support for young people's aspirations, has contributed greatly to their demonization. Predictably, with the significant exception of young Québecois, the children of NAFTA and of globalization have little of the nationalist fervour with which so many of their forebears were imprinted. They are, in general, far less politically engaged (hence their declining inclination to read newspapers or even to vote); they are also far less *noisy*, more inclined to internalize their struggles and to shrug them off with a characteristic "Whatever . . ." than to collectivize or politicize them. In short, youth *are* alienated—not from books, but from a culture of extraordinary opulence in which they have been largely marginalized, stigmatized and silenced. That there is a youth underground *at all* these days is itself in some ways remarkable.

Though largely silent, 1990s youth have provided the pretext for any number of recent moral panics and civic crusades; and, as per *Beavis and Butt-head*, young people's supposed alienation from print culture is commonly seen as a defining element of their more general cultural and political impoverishment. As noted in Chapter Two, for example, since the late 1980s the North American newspaper industry has been spearheading a broadly based campaign to fund—and thereby to sensational-ize—"literacy research," heightening the public perception that illiteracy is a rampant problem, especially among the young. The evidence suggests that newspapers do indeed have a readership succession problem. Young people simply do not gravitate towards newspapers the way older people do, and in the age of the Internet—with its virtually unlimited supply of news-styled information—it is possible that they will never acquire the traditional newspaper habit. (That the Thompson Corporation is abandoning print in favour of electronic information services attests to this broader trend in the sector.) The newspaper industry cannot be faulted for worrying about its declining readership base, but it can (and must) be taken to task for having exaggerated the magnitude of the literacy "crisis" in North America. Although the tenacity of the stereotype of youth as alien, deviant, apathetic and illiterate is somewhat disheartening, the evidence that even in the worst socio-economic circumstances Canadian families continue to inculcate literacy skills and good reading habits is truly extraordinary.

Whither book publishing? It is curious, but not surprising perhaps, that the most affluent Canadians, notably the baby boomers, are more likely to purchase books than to read them, while the least affluent cohorts, namely the elderly and the young, are more likely to read books than to purchase them. This pattern has arguably de-centred Canada's mainstream literary/publishing culture because, as Philip Marchand and Andrew Pyper have noted, the industry *status quo*, with its infrastructure of grants, academic chairs, awards and other distinctions, may not be edifying the books and authors favoured by Canada's most voracious book readers. Obviously, publishers must conduct their business with some sensitivity to this tension because, while they are most certainly interested in promoting good literature, they are also interested in selling books. In the increasingly globalized marketplace in which Canadian publishers must now compete, it has admittedly become expedient—for some at least—

to adopt more mercenary marketing strategies. Whether Canadian publishers will follow the example of their foreign competitors and adopt the kinds of "synergistic" strategies that now prevail in the international marketplace remains to be seen. Suffice it to say that, for the present at least, young people's disinclination (or inability) to purchase books cannot be taken as evidence that they are not interested in reading, nor can it be interpreted to mean that publishers are indifferent to youth. The hierarchical structure of the Canadian publishing industry—with large, Canadian-owned and multinational publishers at the top and cash-starved zinesters and micro-publishers at the bottom—presents many challenges for public policy, but there is very little evidence to suggest that the problems facing the industry are having a detrimental effect on either the literacy skills or the reading habits of young people. Although some micro-publishers and small, independent Canadian publishers may occasionally grumble about the thanklessness of the work they do, very few of those with whom I spoke attempted to persuade me that their survival was linked directly to the quality of young Canadians' literary lives. Even some of the most radical micro-publishers and zinesters affirmed rather charitably that Canadian publishing, even as it is presently structured, delivers the goods, maintaining an environment of extraordinary diversity in which virtually all youth, no matter what their tastes or reading proclivities, can find a place. The very fact that in 1996–97—the most recent year for which Statistics Canada has published comprehensive data on the Canadian publishing industry—321 Canadian-owned publishers put out a total of 10 497 books is an extraordinary affirmation of the strength and the diversity of Canadian publishing in an era in which it had been severely tested.

The turn of the millennium would appear to be a propitious time for writing about youth and Canadian literature for any number of reasons, as this book has suggested, but one of the most striking is that young writers, publishers and readers now appear to have achieved the kind of critical mass not only to voice their objections to the hegemony of the traditional canon but, in fact, to nudge the mainstream in new directions. This point can hardly be overstated. While some of the more outspoken of the young literati have been quite critical of the publishing *status quo* in Canada, it is also true that they are themselves—often with the support of the biggest names in publishing—prodding Canadian literature squarely in the direction of their own post-nationalist, cosmopolitan visions. Young Canadians now and in the future may well gravitate towards the classics of Canadian Lit—after all, there are some wonderful books to be found there—but they are no longer apt to do so out of any sense of ideological obligation. In contrast with some older critics' anxiety about the disjunction of literature and citizenship, youth do not feel the least bit compromised for selecting books and authors from among the *world* of choices available to them. Indeed, in the brave new world of post-nationalist, postmodern identity formation, one may reject the Canadian canon out of hand and not feel any less Canadian. Although these circumstances may mystify the keepers of the canon, some of whom cannot imagine a sense of place without reference to "national identities," it is quite clear that young Canadians—and indeed a good number of older ones—are finding this ideological dissolution enormously liberating. This does not, by any means, imply that Canadians will cease to be interested in the literature of their native land, or that they will necessarily stop locating themselves imaginatively within it. But in a postmodern, globalized world of seemingly infinite choice, the idea of *the national* as the defining element in Canadian Lit appears to have had its day.

NOTES

Introduction

1. Robert Wright, "Reading Canadian: Youth, Book Publishing and the National Question" (Ottawa: Department of Heritage, 2000).

2. Ray Conlogue, "CanLit Gets Shot in the Arm as Thomas Allen Shows It Cares," *Globe and Mail* (14 February 2000). American novelist Philip Roth speaks for many, it would seem: "The evidence is everywhere that the literary era has come to an end. The evidence is the culture, the evidence is the society, the evidence is the screen, the progression from the movie screen, to the television screen, to the computer. . . . Literature takes a habit of mind that has disappeared. It requires silence, some form of isolation, and sustained concentration in the presence of an enigmatic thing." Cited in David Macfarlane, "This Generation—My Generation—is Losing Something More Than Youth. It's Losing the Places of Summer" *Globe and Mail* (15 May 2000).

3. See, for example, Lisa See, "Appealing to Urban Teens," *Publishers Weekly* 230:21 (November 1986); Ellen A. Seay, "Opulence to Decadence: The Outsiders and Less Than Zero," *The English Journal* 76:69 (October 1987); Paula S. Berger, "Teaching About Teen Suicide Using Young-Adult Novels," *Education Digest* 52:48 (April 1987); and Robert E. Probst, "Adolescent Literature and the English Curriculum," *English Journal* 76:26 (March 1987). A related concern beginning in the 1980s was the worry that public libraries, once the cornerstone of young people's encounter with print culture, had grown too staid and

thus had to be rejuvenated for the benefit contemporary youth—a precursor of the general crisis of relevance libraries now face in the information age. See, for example, Fay Blostein, *Invitations, Celebrations: A Handbook of Ideas And Techniques For Promoting Reading in Junior and Senior High Schools* (Toronto: Ontario Library Association, 1980); and especially Patrick Jones, *Connecting Young Adults and Libraries: A How-to-do-it Manual* (New York: Neal-Schuman Inc., 1992).

4. See, for example, Beverly Claunch and Patricia Nutt, "Non-Readers Are Made, Not Born: Sixteen Ways to Turn Off A Reader," *English Journal* 76 (January 1987); Leonard A. Wood, "How Teenage Book Tastes Change," *Publishers Weekly* 230:22 (August 1986); and Leonard A. Wood, "Teenage Book Buying Matches Adult Purchasing," *Publishers Weekly* 230:25 (July 1986).

5. See John Neale, "Betting On An E-book Future," *Quill & Quire* 66:4 (April 2000), p. 21.

6. See, for example, Mark Evans, "Webcasting To Shake Up Internet, Study Says," *Globe and Mail* (1 May 2000); and Donald Gutstein, *E.con: How the Internet Undermines Democracy* (Toronto: Stoddart, 1999).

7. See Darren Wershler-Henry, "A Manifesto for Electronic Publishing in Canada," *Quill & Quire* 66:3 (March 2000), p. 17; see also www.chbooks.com.

8. Jim Allen, cited in Conlogue, "CanLit Gets Shot in the Arm." See also Derek Weiler, "An Elusive Gold Mine: Online Book Marketing Still Shows More Promise Than Return," *Quill & Quire* 66:4 (April 2000), p. 36; and David Olive, "The Best Days of the Web are Yet to Come: And the Net Mania has Given Print a New Vitality," *Financial Post* (14 April 2000).

9. Rowland Lorimer, *Book Publishing in Canada* (Vancouver: Canadian Centre For Studies and Publishing, 1995), posted at www.harbour.sfu.ca.

10. Walter Kirn and William Dowell, "Rediscovering the Joy of Text," *Time Canada* 149:16 (21 April 1997), pp. 56-60. See also Jonathan Gatehouse, "Pamela Wallin Offers Between-the-Covers Advice," *National Post* (8 March 2000).

11. Frank L. Graves and Timothy Dugas, *Reading in Canada 1991* (Ottawa: Ekos Research Associates Inc., 1992), pp. 29-31.

12. Philip Marchand, "What I Really Think about Margaret Laurence, Michael Ondaatje, Margaret Atwood, Timothy Findley, and the Rest of the CanLit Crowd," *Saturday Night* 112:8 (October 1997), pp. 52-6, 58.

13. Graham Knight, review of Sarah Course, *Nationalism and Literature, Canadian Review of Sociology and Anthropology* 36:1 (February 1999), pp. 129-31.

14. Robert Lecker, *Making it Real: The Canonization of English-Canadian Literature.* (Toronto: House of Anansi, 1995), p. 12. See also Bill Reading, *The University in Ruins* (Cambridge: Harvard University Press, 1996).

15. Niedzviecki explicitly links this new "urban" movement in Canadian fiction to the lived experience of Canadian youth: "Many will encounter in *Concrete Forest* a brash sensibility that embodies the attitudes of young people in Canada—the TV generations (anyone born after 1965). This sensibility, however, is not so much a matter of age as much as it is a consequence of diminishing opportunity in a changing country. . . . [This] collective understanding allows writers of the TV-generations to refer to shared circumstances without having to allude to them explicitly. Emerging writers like Golda Fried, Matthew Firth, Jonathan Goldstein, Derek McCormack, and Elise Levine cut in and out of the collective imaginative space of their peers. In their stories, a pop song, a movie, a seedy apartment building, and a doctor's office can all be speedily invoked by a single word or phrase. It's as if just a glimpse is enough to call upon the bank of universal images deposited in our minds, a giant video store of pre-fab moments that need only be referenced to be instantly recalled." See *Concrete Forest: The New Fiction of Urban Canada* (Toronto: McClelland and Stewart, 1998), "Introduction."

16. See Robert Wright, "Historical Underdosing: Pop Demography and the Crisis in Canadian History," *Canadian Historical Review* 81:1 (December 2000).

17. Allan Hepburn, "Urban Kink: Canadian Fiction Shakes Off Its Rural Roots," *Quill & Quire* 66:4 (April 2000), pp. 30-1. See also Devin Crawley, "Poetry Month Courts New Image" in *ibid.,* p. 7.

18. "Survey Reads Canadian Adults," *National Library News* 29:9 (September 1996).

Chapter One: Background

1. Rowland Lorimer, *Book Publishing in Canada.* (Vancouver: Canadian Centre For Studies and Publishing, 1995), posted at www.harbour.sfu.ca.

2. *Ibid.*

3. Paul Audley, *Canada's Cultural Industries: Broadcasting, Publishing, Records and Film* (Toronto: Lorimer, 1983), pp. 87, 103.

4. *Ibid.*, p. 101.

5. Robert Lecker, *Making it Real: The Canonization of English-Canadian Literature* (Toronto: House of Anansi, 1995), pp. 1-4.

6. *Ibid.*, pp. 4-6.

7. *Ibid., pp.* 8-9. Lecker makes the important point that this critical myopia is hardly unique to Canada. See also Edward Said, "Opponents, Audiences, Constituencies, and Community" *Critical Inquiry* 9 (1982), pp. 1-26.

8. *Ibid.*, pp. 9-10, 232-3.

9. See, for example, Robert Wright, "Dream, Comfort, Memory, Despair: Canadian Popular Musicians and the Dilemma of Nationalism, 1968-72," *Journal of Canadian Studies* 22:4 (Winter 1987-8), reprinted in Diamond and Witmer, eds., *Canadian Music: Issues and Identity* (Toronto: Canadian Scholars' Press, 1994).

10. Margaret Atwood, *Survival: A Thematic Guide to Canadian Literature* (Toronto: Anansi, 1972).

11. Robert Fulford, David Godfrey, Abraham Rotstein, eds., *Read Canadian: A Book About Canadian Books.* (Toronto: James, Lewis & Samuel, 1972).

12. *Ibid.*, pp. vii-ix.

13. *Ibid.*, pp. 264-5.

14. *Ibid.*, pp. 265-6.

15. *Ibid.*, p. 267.

16. *Ibid.*, p. 270.

17. *Ibid.*, pp. 272-3.

18. Philip Marchand, "What I really think about Margaret Laurence, Michael Ondaatje, Margaret Atwood, Timothy Findley, and the rest of the CanLit crowd," *Saturday Night* 112:8 (October 1997), pp. 52-6, 58.

19. *Ibid.*, pp. 52-6, 58.

20. *Ibid.*, pp. 52-6, 58.

21. *Ibid.*, pp. 52-6, 58.

22. Andrew Pyper, personal correspondence (December 1999). According to the *Globe and Mail's* "National List Fiction" for 4 December 1999, the ten best selling authors in Canada were Bonnie Bernard, Michael Crichton, Stephen King, Danielle Steel, Alaistair MacCleod, Matt Cohen, Timothy Findley, Dick Francis, Thomas Harris and Scott

Turow. Though anecdotal, the tone of the trade press coverage of Canadian publishing in the late 1990s suggests that Pyper's observations about generational bias are correct. As recently as the spring of 1999, *Publishers Weekly* noted that Penguin Canada's foremost authors were popular historians Pierre Berton and Peter C. Newman, and fiction writers Pauline Gedge, Jack White, and Stuart Maclean. See John F. Baker, "Northern Lights" *Publishers Weekly* 246:22 (31 May 1999), p. 52. The Fall 1996 season roster from McClelland & Stewart, as reported in *Publishers Weekly*, celebrated works by Margaret Atwood, Alice Munro, Mavis Gallant, Guy Vanderhaeghe, Anne Michaels, and Michael Ondaatje. See Beverley Slopen, "Brighter Times Ahead For Canada?" *Publishers Weekly* 245:21 (25 May 1998). Similarly, Iris Tupholme, editor-in-chief of HarperCollins Canada, was quoted as saying that fall 1998 would see "the finest Canadian list since I've been here. We should own the bookstores this fall!" The reason for this enthusiasm was the appearance of new titles by Barbara Gowdy and Greg Hollingshead, a new biography of Margaret Atwood, a new collection by Timothy Findley, and a "true-crime thriller about a Canadian swindler and maybe murderer whose trial in England this summer should be a sensation." Cited in John F. Baker, "Canada: If You Can Make It Here, You'll Make It Anywhere" *Publishers Weekly* 245:21 (25 May 1998), p. 41. See also "Canada's Major National Literary Awards," posted on the web site of the National Library of Canada (www.nlc-bnc.ca).

23. Andrew Pyper, personal correspondence (December 1999).
24. Andrew Pyper, personal correspondence (December 1999).
25. Guy Vanderhaeghe, cited in Diane Turbide, "Increasing Their Word Power: Authors and Readers Flock to Literary Love-ins," *Maclean's* 110:44 (3 November 1997), p. 68.
26. John Pearce, cited in John F. Baker, "Canada: If You Can Make It Here, You'll Make It Anywhere," *Publishers Weekly* 245:21 (25 May 1998), p. 41.
27. Jack Stoddart, cited in Beverley Slopen, "Brighter Times Ahead For Canada?" *Publishers Weekly* 245:21 (25 May 1998).
28. John F. Baker, "Canada: If You Can Make It Here, You'll Make It Anywhere," *Publishers Weekly* 245:21 (25 May 1998), p. 41.
29. *Ibid.,* p. 41.
30. *Ibid.,* p. 41.
31. Turbide, "Increasing Their Word Power," p. 68.
32. Tom Henighan, cited in *ibid.,* p. 68.

33. *Ibid.*, p. 68.
34. Greg Gatenby, cited in *ibid.*, p. 68.

Chapter Two: Publishing in Canada

1. n.a., "Profile of Book Publishing and Executive Agency in Canada, 1991-92 to 1994-95 and 1996-97," (Ottawa: Statistics Canada, n.d.). Given that, according to trade press sources, there had been virtually no growth in the Canadian industry up to 1999, these figures will suffice for the purposes a generalized review of the state of Canadian publishing.
1. Anita Elash, "An Industry in Bloom: Canadian Publishers Prepare to Put an End to Hard Times," *Maclean's* 110:36 (8 September 1997), pp. 82–3.
3. *Ibid.*, pp. 82-3.
4. Paul Audley, *Canada's Cultural Industries: Broadcasting, Publishing, Records and Film* (Toronto: Lorimer, 1983).
5. John F. Baker, "Canada: If You Can Make It Here, You'll Make It Anywhere," *Publishers Weekly* 245:21 (25 May 1998), p. 41.
6. *Government Expenditures on Culture* (Ottawa: Statistics Canada, October 1999).
7. Elash, "An Industry in Bloom," pp. 82-3.
8. Bridget Kinsella, "Coach House Closes, Blames Government Cuts," *Publisher's Weekly* (22 July 1996), p. 138.
9. David Kent, paraphrased in John F. Baker, "Canada: If You Can Make It Here, You'll Make It Anywhere," *Publishers Weekly* 245:21 (25 May 1998), p. 41.
10. Beverley Slopen, "Brighter Times Ahead For Canada?" *Publishers Weekly* 245:21 (25 May 1998).
11. Robert Lecker, *Making it Real: The Canonization of English-Canadian Literature* (Toronto: House of Anansi, 1995), p. 230.
12. Baker, "Canada," p. 41.
13. John F. Baker, "Northern Lights," *Publishers Weekly* 246:22 (31 May 1999), p. 52.
14. Jack Stoddart, cited in Slopen, "Brighter Times Ahead For Canada?"
15. Paul Davidson, cited in Baker, "Northern Lights," p. 52.
16. Bridget Kinsella, "Publishing 2000," *Fiction Writer* (February 2000).
17. *Ibid.*

18. See Baker, "Northern Lights," p. 52.

19. *Ibid.,* p. 52.

20. John Neale, cited in Baker, "Northern Lights," p. 52.

21. Paul Davidson, cited in *ibid.,* p. 52.

22. Baker, "Canada," p. 41.

23. "Canadian Publishing Surprised By M&S Transfer to University of Toronto, Sale to Random House," *Just The Fax* 10:25 (29 June 2000).

24. Kinsella, "Publishing 2000."

25. Morgan Entrekin, cited in *ibid.*

26. *Ibid.*

27. *Ibid.* See also Karen Hammond, "Indie Author Goes It Alone For Second Novel," *Quill & Quire* 66:4 (April 2000), p. 14.

28. Avie Bennett, cited in Baker, "Northern Lights," p. 52.

29. Jackie Hushion, cited in Baker, "Canada," p. 41.

30. Cynthia Good, cited in Baker, "Northern Lights," p. 52.

31. Judy Stoffman, "Children's Bookstore: The Final Chapter," *Toronto Star* (15 January 2000), pp. K1, K17. See also John Lorinc, "Children's Bookstore Closes After 25 Years," *Quill & Quire* (February 2000), p. 4; and Derek Weiler, "Pegasus Buys Children's Wholesaler," *Quill & Quire* 6:2 (February 2000), p. 5.

32. Ian Jack, "Chapters Investigated on Book Marketing Share," *National Post* (25 February 2000).

33. See *ibid.;* Rowland Lorimer, "Opening New Chapters in the Book Wars," *Globe and Mail* (28 February 2000); Zena Olijnyk, "This Is What It Must Fell Like To Be Operated On," *National Post* (7 March 2000); Ian Jack, "Bound and Gagged: Small Fry Scared to Squeal on Chapters," *National Post* (8 March 2000); Zena Olijnyk, "Indie Bookseller Takes on Book Chains," *Financial Post* (13 March 2000); and Ann Gibbon, "The Catch-22 of Working with Chapters," *Globe and Mail* (24 April 2000).

34. Jean Baird, personal correspondence (December 1999–January 2000).

35. Danya Ruttenberg, "Taming The Paper Tiger: The Book Industry Roars Online," *E Business Magazine* (November 1998). (This e-publication is the property of Hewlett-Packard.)

36. "Former Premier to Lobby Ottawa for Amazon.com," *National Post* (23 June 2000); see also Ian Jack, "Ottawa Should Consider Letting U.S. Book Superstores into Canada, Liberal Says," *National Post* (14 April 2000); and "Amazon.com Knocking on Ottawa's Door," *Just The Fax* 10:25 (29 June 2000).

37. *Ibid.*

38. *Ibid.*

39. *Ibid.* See also Kim Askew, "I'd Buy That for a Dollar: Thousands Download Stephen King's *The Plant*," *Quill & Quire Insiders' Report* 1:26 (25 July 2000).

40. *Ibid.* Canadian journalist John Lorinc describes the big chains' "multi-channel promotional blitz" over Christmas 1999, which featured "radio, billboard, and Web advertising." He noted that Chapters has also begun selling from its Internet site "a range of other non-book items, such as MP3 players and palm pilots." He estimates that Chapters.ca did $12.2 million for the quarter ending 1 January 2000, or 20 times more than the site's inaugural Christmas season (1998). See "Internet Sales Skyrocket," *Quill & Quire* 6:2 (February 2000), p. 10.

41. Ruttenberg, "Taming The Paper Tiger." See also Peter Foster, "E Canada, Our Home and Native LAN," *National Post* (19 January 2000).

42. *Ibid.*

43. Baker, "Northern Lights," p. 52.

44. Kevin G. Barnhurst and Ellen Wartella, "Newspapers and Citizenship: Young Adults' Subjective Experience of Newspapers," *Critical Studies in Mass Communication* 8:2 (June 1991), pp. 195-210.

45. *Ibid.*, pp. 195-210.

46. Diane McFarlin, "Young People Don't See Themselves as Part of the Newspaper Reading 'Club,'" *Bulletin of the American Society of Newspaper Editors* 757 (March 1994), pp. 5-8.

47. David Astor, "More Features for Younger Readers," *Publisher & Editor* 125:47 (21 November 1992), pp. 46-7.

48. Lee Salem, cited in Astor, "More Features for Younger Readers," pp. 46-7.

49. Bruce Gaultney, "'Totally Teen' Can Be Totally a Turn-Off," *Bulletin of the American Society of Newspaper Editors* 766 (March 1995), pp. 8-9. See also Hallgeir Halvari and Cheryl White, "Effects of Reading Motivation on the Belief in and Consumption of Newspapers Among Youth," *Psychological Reports* 81:3 (December 1997), pp 899-915.

50. Andy Aleff, "Research Finds Kids Do Read Newspapers: But They Have as Many Complaints About Them as Adults," *Bulletin of the American Society of Newspaper Editors* 766 (March 1995), pp. 5-8.

51. William B. Ketter, "Market-driven Editorial Content—How Viable?" *Editor & Publisher* 127:42 (15 October 1994), pp. 13-14.

52. *Ibid.*, pp. 13-14. See also Bruce Gaultney, "Young Writers May Help Reach Young Readers—But They Require Special Handling," *Bulletin*

of the American Society of Newspaper Editors 766 (March 1995), pp. 10-11; and Brian Cooper, "Just Give Them What They Want (How Newspapers Can Attract Young People)," *Bulletin of the American Society of Newspaper Editors* 768 (May-June 1995), pp. 16-17.

53. Mark Fitzgerald, "Connecting With Kids (Newspapers Reach Children Through Online Editions)," *Editor & Publisher* 130:12 (22 March 1997), pp. 20-22.

54. Bill Schiller, "Extra! War Heats Up For Newspaper Readers," *Toronto Star* (23 October 1999). See also Susanne Craig, "Black Plans Newspaper Sell-off," *Globe and Mail* (26 April 2000).

55. Elash, "An Industry in Bloom," pp. 82-3.

Chapter Three: Youth Culture in Canada

1. See Robert Wright, "Historical Underdosing: Pop Demography and the Crisis in Canadian History" *Canadian Historical Review* 81:1 (December 2000).

2. Don Kerr, *et al.*, *Children and Youth: An Overview* (Ottawa: Statistics Canada/Prentice Hall Canada, 1994), pp. 5-8. See also Colin Lindsay, *et al.*, *Youth in Canada*, second edition (Ottawa: Statistics Canada, 1994).

3. Kerr, *et al.*, *Children and Youth*, p. 8.

4. *Ibid.*, p. 4.

5. This is not to say that Canadians currently in their late twenties or early thirties are "youths" but, rather, that their experience of youth in the late 1980s and the 1990s accords with those Canadians now in their teens and early twenties.

6. The socio-economic plight of young Canadians in the 1990s has been described in Marlene Webber, *Street Kids: The Tragedy of Canada's Runaways* (Toronto: University of Toronto Press, 1991); Paul Anisef and Paul Axelrod, eds., *Transitions: Schooling and Employment in Canada* (Toronto: Thompson, 1993); John F. Conway, *The Canadian Family in Crisis* (Toronto: Lorimer, 1993); Anthony N. Doob, *et. al.*, *Youth Crime and the Youth Justice System in Canada: A Research Perspective* (Toronto: University of Toronto Centre of Criminology, 1995); and Burt Gallaway and Joe Hudson, eds., *Youth in Transition: Perspectives on Research and Policy* (Toronto: Thompson, 1996).

7. Lindsay, *et al.*, *Youth in Canada*.

8. Mark Stevenson, "Youth Unemployment Lowest in Almost 10 Years,

Labour Market Survey Shows More Living at Home," *National Post* (24 December 1999).

9. Garnett Picot, *What is Happening to Earnings Inequalities and Youth Wages in the 1990s?* (Ottawa: Statistics Canada, July 1998), pp. 7-10.

10. Picot, *What is Happening to Earnings Inequalities?* See also "Labour Market Polarization . . . What's Going On?" HRDC *Applied Research Bulletin* 2:2 (Summer-Fall 1998).

11. Picot, *What is Happening to Earnings Inequalities?*, p. 25.

12. *Ibid.*, p. 25.

13. Myles Corack, paraphrased in Elaine Carey, "Poor Economy Hits Young Hard, Analysis Says," *Toronto Star* (22 January 1999).

14. Cited in Elaine Carey, "Jobs Elude Most Teens, Report Says," *Toronto Star* (19 January 1999).

15. Anne Cira, cited in Dana Flavelle, "Firms Ignore Jobless Youth," *Toronto Star* (25 June 1999). See also Ross Laver, "The 'Lost Generation,'" *Maclean's* 110:22 (2 June 1997), p. 47, in which Holger Kluge, the "president of personal and commercial banking" at the CIBC is quoted as saying that youth unemployment is "Canada's single most important social issue."

16. Kerr, *et al.*, *Children and Youth.*

17. G. Taylor, "The Serene Teens," *Maclean's* (15 April 1991), p. 52. In a provocative article entitled "A Politics for Generation X," Ted Halstead has distilled Americans' views of young people into two competing stereotypes—both of which apply to Canadian youth. His observations imply that the very category "youth" now tells us far less about young people than it does about the anxieties and aspirations of adults: "The 1990s opened with a frenzy of negative stereotyping of the roughly 50 million Americans born from 1965 to 1978: they were slackers, cynics, whiners, drifters, malcontents. A *Washington Post* headline captured the patronizing attitude that Baby Boomers apparently hold toward their successors: 'The Boring Twenties: Grow Up, Crybabies.' Then books and articles began to recast young Americans as ambitious, savvy, independent, pragmatic, and self-sufficient. For instance, *Time Magazine* described a 1997 article titled 'Great Xpectations' this way: 'Slackers? Hardly. The so-called Generation X turns out to be full of go-getters who are just doing it—but their way.'" See Ted Halstead, "A Politics For Generation X," *Atlantic Monthly* (August 1999).

18. J. L. Granatstein, *Who Killed Canadian History?* (Toronto: HarperCollins, 1998), p. 14.

19. See Robert Wright, "I'd Sell You Suicide: Pop Music and Moral Panic in the Age of Marilyn Manson," *Popular Music* 19:3 (Autumn, 2000); and Wright, "Historical Underdosing."

20. "The Year for Kids," *Maclean's* (21 December 1992), p. 58.

21. Taylor, "The Serene Teens," p. 52. The poll on which this article was centred was "jointly commissioned" by Health and Welfare Canada, Pepsi-Cola Ltd. and YTV.

22. Lawrence Grossberg, *We Gotta Get Out of This Place: Popular Conservatism and Postmodern Culture* (New York and London: Routledge, 1992), p. 185.

23. Henry A. Giroux, "Teenage Sexuality, Body Politics, and the Pedagogy of Display," in Jonathon S. Epstein, ed., *Youth Culture: Identity In A Post-Modern World* (Oxford: Blackwell, 1998), p. 25-6. Giroux concludes with an impassioned plea for what might be done by progressive people for youth: "Pedagogically and politically, young people need to be given the opportunity to narrate themselves, to speak from the actual places where their experiences are shaped and mediated. This suggests more than letting kids have the opportunity to voice their concerns, it means providing the conditions—institutional, economic, spiritual, and cultural—that allow them to reconceptualize themselves as citizens and develop a sense of what it means to fight for important social and political issues that effect [sic] their lives, bodies, and society." See also, from the same anthology, Jonathon S. Epstein, "Introduction: Generation X, Youth Culture, and Identity," pp. 4-19.

24. Mike A. Males, *The Scapegoat Generation: America's War on Adolescents* (Maine: Common Courage Press, 1996), pp. 265-6.

25. See Bernard Schissel, *Blaming Children: Youth Crime, Moral Panics and the Politics of Hate* (Halifax: Fernwood, 1997); and Elliott Leyton, "A Generation No Better, No Worse," *Globe and Mail* (21 April 2000).

26. See Wright, "I'd Sell You Suicide."

27. Mitch Potter and Betsy Powell, "Agonizing over Ecstasy," *Toronto Star* (20 November 1999). For a balanced and thoroughgoing history of raves, in contrast, see Simon Reynolds, *Generation Ecstasy: Into the World of Techno and Rave Culture* (New York: Routledge, 1999).

28. Virginia Galt, "Alarm Raised Over Students Behaving Badly," *Globe and Mail* (15 September 1999).

29. Reginald W. Bibby, *The Bibby Report: Social Trends Canadian Style* (Toronto: Stoddart, 1995), p. 101.

30. See "Eric Beauchesne, "School Costs More, Pays Less, Study Says," *National Post* (22 February 2000).

31. Bibby and Posterski, *Teen Trends,* pp. v, 3-4.

32. *Ibid.,* pp. 11-14.

33. *Ibid.,* p. 73.

34. *Ibid.,* p. 283.

35. *Ibid.,* p. 301.

36. Roger Tonkin, cited in Andre Picard, "B.C. Teenagers Defy Reckless Stereotype," *Globe and Mail* (28 September 1999).

37. Statistics Canada, *National Longitudinal Survey of Children and Youth: Transition into Adolescence* (Ottawa: Statistics Canada, 6 July 1999). The National Longitudinal Survey of Children and Youth (NLSCY), a joint project of Human Resources Development Canada (HRDC) and Statistics Canada, is a "comprehensive survey which follows the development of children in Canada and paints a picture of their lives." The "first cycle" of the NLSCY was conducted in late 1994 and early 1995 and consisted of interviews with parents of approximately 23 000 children up to the age of 11.

38. See, for example, Suzanne Kingsmill and Benjamin Schlesinger, *The Family Squeeze: Surviving the Sandwich Generation* (Toronto: University of Toronto Press, 1998).

39. Elaine Carey, "More Adult Offspring Live at Parents' Homes," *Toronto Star* (12 March 1999).

40. Bob Glossop, cited in *ibid.*

41. "Canada's Children Deserve Better," *Toronto Star* (20 November 1999).

42. Michael Adams, *Sex in the Snow: Canadian Social Values at the End of the Millennium* (Toronto: Viking/Penguin, 1997), pp. 105-8.

43. See, for example, Doob, *et al., Youth Crime and the Youth Justice System in Canada;* and Webber, *Street Kids.*

Chapter Four: Media/Literacy

1. See, for example, Chris Morris, "The Dumbing Down of Canada's Universities," *Toronto Star* (26 February 2000).

2. The ad appeared in the *Quill & Quire* 6:2 (February 2000), pp. 26-7. Significantly, the four books advertised in this ad were Sean Covey's *Daily Reflections for Highly Effective Teens,* Stedman Graham's *Teens Can*

Make It Happen, Francine Pascal's *Fearless* and Catherine Ryan Hyde's *Pay It Forward.* The latter featured the caption "believe in your power to change the world. Soon to be a major motion picture starring Kevin Spacey."

3. Allan Bloom, *The Closing of the American Mind* (New York: Simon and Schuster, 1987), pp. 61-4.

4. Steven Best and Douglas Kellner, "*Beavis and Butt-Head*: No Future for Post Modern Youth," in Jonathon S. Epstein, ed., *Youth Culture: Identity In A Post-Modern World* (Oxford: Blackwell, 1998), pp. 81-5.

5. Robert Fulford, "The Young in History's Stream: Generation X and the Survival of Tradition" (Lecture presented at the University of Chicago, 16-18 May 1997), posted at robertfulford.com.

6. Virginia Davis, cited in "Ben Wicks' Born to Read: Literacy Begins at Home," *Maclean's* 108:17 (24 April 1995), pp. S1-4.

7. Roch Carrier, cited in *ibid.,* pp. S1-4.

8. Peter C. Emberley, *Zero Tolerance: Hot Button Politics in Canada's Universities* (Toronto: Penguin, 1996), pp. 39-40.

9. *Ibid.,* pp. 41-2.

10. Paul Rutherford, *When Television Was Young: Prime Time Canada 1952-1967* (Toronto: University of Toronto Press, 1990), pp. 9, 470.

11. Reginald W. Bibby and Donald C. Posterski, *Teen Trends: A Nation in Motion* (Toronto: Stoddart, 1992), pp. 60-2.

12. *Ibid.,* pp. 279-80.

13. Paul Litt, *The Muses, The Masses and The Massey Commission* (Toronto: University of Toronto Press, 1992), p. 252. See also Mary Vipond, *The Mass Media in Canada* (Toronto: Lorimer, 1992), esp. Chapter 2 "The Media and Canadian Nationalism: 1920-1950."

14. Rutherford, *When Television Was Young,* pp. 450-1.

15. A research study entitled *A Leisure Study—Canada* (1972) found that "[r]etirement often left people with a lot of time on their hands, too much time, which given the problems of frail health or limited resources meant that they spent more hours with television than did other adults." Paraphrased in *ibid.,* p. 463.

16. Kirsten Drotner, "Youthful Media Cultures: Challenges and Chances for Librarians," *Papers of the 64th IFLA General Conference* (16-21 August 1998), posted at www.ifla.org.

17. Paul Levinson, *The Soft Edge: A Natural History and Future of the Information Revolution* (New York and London: Routledge, 1997), pp. 60-1.

18. *Ibid.,* p. 152.

19. Motheread is "a non-profit organization that uses children's books to improve adult reading skills." Clinton gave Gaj a National Humanities Medal in November 1998. See Sophfronia Scott Gregory, "Page Turners," *People* 51:11 (29 March 1999), p. 157.

20. John Wandell, paraphrased in Simon Tuck, "*AutoSkills* Reads Into Future of Educational Software," *Globe and Mail* (16 December 1999).

21. Peter Calamai, ed., *Broken Words: Why Five Million Canadians Are Illiterate* (Ottawa: Southam News, 1987), posted at www.nald.ca.

22. *Ibid.*

23. *Ibid.*

24. *Ibid.*

25. *Ibid.*

26. *Ibid.*

27. Predictably, *Broken Words* found that illiterate Canadians were much poorer than literate Canadians: "The personal income of literates is 44 percent more than that reported by illiterates."

28. See, for example, Andrew Nikiforuk and Deborrah Howes, "Why Schools Can't Teach," *Saturday Night* 110:7 (September 1995), pp. 22-7; and James Collins and S.C. Gwynne, "How Johnny Should Read," *Time Canada* 150:17 (27 October 1997), p. 56.

29. Candis McLean, "Why Johnny's Reading is Getting Even Worse: A Hidebound Education Monopoly is Blamed for the Rising Tide of Illiteracy," *Alberta Report* 25:29 (6 July 1998), p. 48.

30. Michael Coren, cited in Michael Jenkinson, "The Young and the Illiterate," *Alberta Report* 23:2 (25 December 1995).

31. Robert Lecker, *Making it Real: The Canonization of English-Canadian Literature* (Toronto: House of Anansi, 1995), p. 232. See also "Ben Wicks' Born to Read: Literacy Begins at Home," *Maclean's* 108:17 (24 April 1995), pp. S1-4; and Gwynneth Evans, "From Author to Reader: Trends in Literacy and Reading in Canada and Internationally," *National Library News* 31:1 (January 1999), posted at www.nlc-bnc.ca.

32. J. Douglas Willms, *Literacy Skills Of Canadian Youth* (Ottawa: Statistics Canada, September 1997), pp. 6-7.

33. n.a., "Survey Reads Canadian Adults" *National Library News* 29:9 (September 1996). Posted at www.nlc-bnc.ca

34. Willms, *Literacy Skills Of Canadian Youth*, pp. 11-13.

35. Calamai, ed., *Broken Words.*

36. Willms, *Literacy Skills Of Canadian Youth*, pp. 4-7, 22-7.

37. *Ibid.*, p. 24. See also Human Resources Development Canada, "Liter-

acy Skills of Canadian Youth," *HRDC Bulletin* 4:1 (Winter–Spring 1998), posted at hrdc-drhc.gc.ca.

38. Statistics Canada, *Inequalities in Literacy Skills Among Youth in Canada and the United States* (Ottawa: Statistics Canada, 22 September 1999). This report also confirmed that recent immigrant youth in Canada scored "considerably lower" on the IALS than Canadian-born youth—a finding that earlier researchers had deployed in their critique of the *Broken Words* report. See also Douglas Willms, *International Adult Literacy Survey: Inequalities in Literacy Skills Among Youth in Canada and the United States* (Ottawa: Statistics Canada, September 1999).

39. Burt Perrin, *How to Engage Youth in Literacy: Lessons Learned from an Evaluation of a Cluster of Youth and Literacy Projects* (presented to The Literacy And Youth Cluster Steering Committee, 12 October 1998), pp. iii-vi.

40. Vivian Shalla and Grant Schellenberg, *The Value of Words: Literacy and Economic Security in Canada* (Ottawa: Statistics Canada, May 1998).

41. *Ibid.,* pp. 11-12, 43-4.

42. *Ibid.,* pp. 46-8. See also Adele Thomas, ed., *Family Literacy in Canada: Profiles of Effective Practices* (Welland: Editions Soleil, 1998).

Chapter Five: Reading Youth

1. Wendy Cole, "How to Make a Better Student," *Time Canada* (19 October 1998).

2. *Ibid.*

3. See Devin Crawley, "Canada Book Day Gives Book Buyers a Break," *Quill & Quire* 66:3 (March 2000), p. 8; and John F. Baker, "Northern Lights," *Publishers Weekly* 246:22 (31 May 1999), p. 52.

4. "Ben Wicks' Born to Read: Literacy Begins at Home," *Maclean's* 108:17 (24 April 1995), pp. s1-4. Sponsors of Born to Read Day include celebrities—David Crombie and Margaret Atwood, most notably—as well as corporate sponsors, such as Canada Post, the Bank of Montreal, Honda Canada, Bell, Sears Canada, Smithbooks, Kellogg Canada, Southam Inc., Noranda, ReMax, Wrigley, Syncrude Canada, MacMillan Bloedel and the Edmonton Oilers. Supporting children's literacy would appear to be a central element in good corporate citizenship in Canada.

5. Brian Bethune and Diane Turbide, "The Kidlit Boom," *Maclean's* 108:50 (11 December 1995), pp. 44-8.

6. Valerie Hussey, cited in *ibid.*, pp. 44-8.
7. Rick Wilkes, cited in *ibid.*, pp. 44-8.
8. Michele Landsberg, cited in *ibid.*, pp. 44-8.
9. Judy Sarick, cited in Judy Stoffman, "Children's Bookstore: The Final Chapter," *Toronto Star* (15 January 2000), pp. KI, KI7. See also Alberta Graham, "Should Kids Read *Goosebumps*? No," *NEA Today* 16:3 (October 1997), p. 43.
10. National Library of Canada, "Young Authors Add to Canada's Published Heritage," *National Library News* 29:3/4 (March/ April 1997). One hundred and twenty-one authors between the ages of 9 and 12, worked on this project for three weeks, "learning how to express their thoughts, feelings and visions in various poetic forms." Co-coordinator Sharon Katz also "introduced them to the art and technology of book production, and discussed the place of literature in society and the role of creativity in communication." The students learned to use "professional computer design to illustrate and lay out the book." And as part of the "pre-publication process" they saw it receive an ISBN number from the National Library.
11. Dale Simmons, "Read Up On It: Looking Forward to the Next Ten Years," *National Library News* 30:9 (September 1998), posted at www.nlc-bnc.ca.
12. *Ibid.*
13. In 1994, a Statistics Canada study found that "[p]eople aged 15-19 devote less time than the overall population aged 15 and over to productive activities, while they have more free time and spend more time sleeping." "Productive activities" were defined as "paid work and related activities such as travel to and from work, and meal and other breaks; unpaid work activities such as domestic work, child care, shopping and services, and organizational and volunteer work; and educational activities." Further, "Young people spend most of their free time socializing or watching television. In 1992, people aged 15–19 averaged over two hours per day on each of these activities. But while 15–19-year-olds spent a half an hour more per day socializing than the overall adult population, *they watched about the same amount of television*" (emphasis added). See Colin Lindsay, *et al.*, *Youth in Canada*, second edition (Ottawa: Statistics Canada, 1994), p. 35. American scholar Arthea J. S. Reed has observed: "The peak of reading interest often occurs around age 12; that is also the age when many readers lose interest in books. This happens for several reasons. Young readers are required by schools

or pushed by parents to read books for which they are not emotionally and intellectually ready. Many adolescents have difficulty finding books with young characters who face the problems of adolescents. Some parents, teachers, and librarians are unaware of appropriate books to recommend. Some adults discourage adolescents from selecting books on certain topics or themes of interest. . . . For some adolescents, reading is not accepted by their peer group." See *Comics to Classics: A Parent's Guide to Books for Teens and Preteens* (Delaware: International Reading Association, 1988), pp. 13-14.

14. Given the importance of "summer reading lists" as a promotional tool of the publishing trade in Canada, it would appear that book publishers are fully aware of Canadians' good literary intentions.

15. See *Report of a Survey of Book Reading Among Canadians* (Montreal: Data Laboratories Research Consultants, 1978). See also *Survey of Young People's Reading Interests* (Toronto: Toronto Public Libraries, 1976); Michel Ben-Gera and Brian L. Kinsley, *Library and Bookstore Use in Canada* (Ottawa: Secretary of State, 1980); Kenneth F. Watson, *Leisure Reading Habits* (Ottawa: Infoscan, 1980); L.J. Amey, "Information Seeking Activities of Adolescents of Different Socio-economic Classes in a Canadian Urban Centre," (Ph.D. dissertation, University of Toronto, 1981); and Douglas E. Angus and Owen A. Charlebois, *Consumer Sensitivity to Increases in Book Prices* (Ottawa: Coopers and Lybrand, 1986).

16. Frank L. Graves and Timothy Dugas, *Reading in Canada 1991* (Ottawa: Ekos Research Associates Inc. 1992), pp. 2-5.

17. *Ibid.*, pp. 6-10.

18. *Ibid.*, pp. 15-17.

19. *Ibid.*, pp. 18-27. Two other interesting demographic patterns also emerged: although women read nearly twice as much as men, they purchase only slightly more; and although francophones in Québec were found to read fewer books that both allophones and anglophones in that province, they tended to buy more, at an average of over 8 books annually. Francophones also tended to purchase more Canadian authored books—at a rate of more than double the anglophone average.

In 1997 a *Publisher's Weekly* survey of American readers and book shoppers explicitly challenged the conventional wisdom that "readership and book-buying [are] on the decline, characterizing heavy readers and hard-core book buyers as older rather than younger." It found that "[y]ounger book buyers are more likely to buy an increasing number of books, with more than half the respondents under 35 . . . saying they purchased more books now than they did two years ago." The survey also found that younger people inclined to purchase books "overwhelmingly by word of mouth." See John F. Baker, "Younger Book Customers Buying More: *PW* Survey," *Publishers Weekly* (2 June 1997), p. 24.

20. Graves and Dugas, *Reading in Canada 1991*, p. 37.

21. Nancy Duxbury, *The Reading and Purchasing Public: The Market for Trade Books in English Canada 1991* (Toronto: Association of Canadian Publishers, 1995), n.p. (Volume II of this document was comprised of a vast collection of tables, none of which was paginated; my analysis of the data are drawn exclusively from this volume).

22. Bibby and Posterski, *Teen Trends,* pp. 22-4.

23. *Ibid.,* pp 68-9.

24. *Ibid.,* pp. 159-60, 185.

25. See Wright, "Historical Underdosing."

26. There is evidence that some young Canadians' literary choices are influenced by this traditional strain of literary nationalism, though it is not unambiguous. A poster contest for Canada Book Day 1999 was held by the youth magazine *In 2 Print*, in which readers' favourite Canadian books were described. Their choices, according to editor Jean Baird, revealed "an eclectic mix ranging from hockey books and history texts to Farley Mowat and Franklin. Some of the most popular authors included Kit Pearson, Dennis Lee, Jean Little, Paul Kropp, Monica Hughes, Janet Lunn, Paulette Bourgeois, Barbara Reid, Phoebe Gilman, and classic Canadian fav, Lucy Maud Montgomery. The all-time, out-and-out author of choice for them was Robert Munsch—everybody's favourite funnyman!" Letters accompanying the poster submissions seem to reflect at least the possibility that adult coaching had influenced these young Canadians' choices—or at least the language with which they described them. Wrote one contestant: "I have read the work of many wonderful Canadian authors—everyone from Margaret Atwood and Alice Munro to Timothy Findley, Robertson Davies and the writings and poetry of Leonard Cohen. When I read *The English Patient* [by Michael Ondaatje]—I was captivated by the novel's poetic language. Although I have read many books, I have never come across one as descriptive or as moving." Another wrote: ""I enjoyed [Margaret Laurence's *The Diviners*] because it embodies the emotional strength and courage a woman exerts during her tough life. I admired the way the main character, Morag, pulled through as an inde-

pendent woman. She is a naturally-described heroine and role model for everyone."

27. Lecker, *Making it Real,* pp. 12-14. One of the most interesting themes that runs throughout this analysis is Lecker's obsession with the New Canadian Library series (NCL), conceived by fiction writer Malcolm Ross in the early 1950s. By the beginning of the 1960s, according to Lecker, the NCL had become "the major vehicle through which Canadian literature reached the high-school and college market in paperback form." He claims that the NCL ushered Canadian literature into "its industrial phase" and then "provided the texts on which the industry would be based." Books printed in the NCL series which had formerly been bedside reading for ordinary Canadians now became literary texts that "required professional interpretation"—as signified by the fact that Ross had the academic critics produce "critical introductions" to each volume. Thus, according to Lecker, "[b]y reinforcing the idea that the books in this series were serious enough to explain to the reader (who is not sophisticated enough to understand them without help), the New Canadian Library paradoxically undercut the public's ability to feel comfortable with its literature." The message to the general reader was clear: "you need special knowledge to understand the literature we are talking about. . . ." See pp. 16, 77. See also William Riggan, "Of Obstacles, Survival, And Identity: On Contemporary Canadian Literature," *World Literature Today* 73:2 (Spring 1999); and Cyril Dabydeen, "Places We Come From: Voices of Caribbean Canadian Writers (In English) and Multicultural Contexts," *World Literature Today* 73:2 (Spring 1999).

28. Russell Smith, personal correspondence (November–December 1999).

Chapter Six: Marketing to Youth

1. Jean Baird, "Send More Shoes," *Quill & Quire* (February 1997), p. 24.
2. Rona Maynard, "A Forum For Teens," *Chatelaine* 69:4 (April 1996), p. 6.
3. Canadian writer Naomi Klein has argued that the popularity of magazines among the "slacker" generation more generally is itself a bi-product of the early stereotyping (and commodification) of Generation X: "The demographic was clearly defined and it was just too easy to cash in on." See "Why Slacker Mags Suck: Because They're Editorially

Vapid," *Ryerson Review of Journalism* (Spring 1996), pp. 76-7. For an interesting perspective on women's and girls' book clubs in the U.S., see H.J. Cummins "'Girls Wind Up Seeing Their Mothers as Real People: Book Clubs Give Mothers, Daughters a Conversational Starting Point," *Minneapolis-St. Paul Star Tribune* (12 April 2000).

4. Dawn H. Currie, *Girl Talk: Adolescent Magazines and their Readers* (Toronto: University of Toronto Press, 1998), pp. 156-9, 281.
5. *MediaWeek* ad (1989), cited in *ibid.*, pp. 302-3.
6. *Ibid.*, pp. 147.
7. S. K. List, "The Right Place To Find Children," *American Demographic* 14:2 (February 1992), pp. 44-48.
8. Susan Sachs, cited in *ibid.*, pp. 44-48.
9. Karen Raugust, "TV Tie-Ins Target Teen and Preteen Girls," *Publishers Weekly* 245:3 (19 January 1998), pp. 243-44.
10. Nancy Pines, cited in *ibid.*, pp. 243-44.
11. *Ibid.*, pp. 243-44.
12. See Derek Weiler, "Toy Story: In the Lucrative Licensing Business, Canadian Publishers are Mostly Stuck on the Sidelines," *Quill & Quire* 65:10 (October 1999), pp. 18-19.
13. Pam Newton, cited in Raugust, "TV Tie-Ins," pp. 243-44.
14. See Valerie Hussey, "TV, Toys and Other Tie-ins," *Quill & Quire* 66:4 (April 2000), p. 20.
15. Ken Thompson, cited in Anita Elash, "An Industry in Bloom: Canadian Publishers Prepare to Put an End to Hard Times," *Maclean's* 110:36 (8 September 1997), pp. 82-83.
16. Elash, "An Industry in Bloom," pp. 82-83.
17. Mark Victor Hansen, Kimberly Kirberger, Jack Canfield, *Chicken Soup for the Teenage Soul: 101 Stories of Life, Love & Learning* (New York: Health Communications, 1997).
18. Consumer reviews of *Chicken Soup for the Teenage Soul,* posted at http://www.chapters.ca (March 2000).
19. See Don Tapscott, *Growing up Digital: The Rise of the Net Generation* (New York: McGraw-Hill, 1998).
20. Paul Levinson, *The Soft Edge: A Natural History and Future of the Information Revolution* (New York and London: Routledge, 1997), pp. 139-45.
21. Statistics Canada tracks the use of the Internet in Canadian households. It found that, in 1998, 4.3 million households (or 36 percent) had "at least one member [who] used computer communications regu-

larly," compared with 3.5 million households in 1997. The use of computer communications in Canada increases with socio-economic status in the household. "In 1998, the highest regular Internet use (65 percent) was among individuals living in households in the top income quartile and among households where the head had a university degree (68 percent). In contrast, Internet use was far lower in the bottom quartile (13 percent), and in households where the head had not graduated from high school (13 percent)." After accounting for "income differences, young households and households with children under 18 were more likely to be users of computer communications than older or childless households." Further, "research shows that the biggest computer and Internet user in a family is most likely to be a teenager." See Paul Dickinson and Jonathan Ellison, "Plugged in into the Internet," *Canadian Social Trends* 55 (Ottawa: Statistics Canada, Winter 1999).

22. James Garton, "New Genres and New Literacies: The Challenge of the Virtual Curriculum," *Australian Journal of Language and Literacy* 20:3 (August 1997).

23. Henry A. Giroux, "Teenage Sexuality, Body Politics, and the Pedagogy of Display," in Jonathon S. Epstein, ed., *Youth Culture: Identity In A Post-Modern World* (Oxford: Blackwell, 1998), pp. 49–50.

24. Reginald W. Bibby and Donald C. Posterski, *Teen Trends: A Nation in Motion* (Toronto: Stoddart, 1992), p. 71.

25. Bridget Kinsella, "Publishing 2000," *Fiction Writer* (February 2000). See also Zena Olijnyk, "Digital Book to Make Debut at Chapters," *Financial Post* (17 February 2000); and Carol Toller, "Chapters Launches Digital Delivery," *Quill & Quire* 66:4 (April 2000).

26. n.a., "Borrowing Technology from the Music World," *Fiction Writer* (February 2000), p. 17. See also Sarah Ferguson, "The Punks of Publishing," *Village Voice* (30 June–6 July 1999).

27. Val Ross, "Canada Council Finally Tuning Into The New Media: Goodbye Gutenberg," *Globe and Mail* (2 March 1999).

28. "Teen Telepoetics," cited in Gordon Platt, personal correspondence (February 2000).

29. Leah McLaren, "A Change of Scene," *Globe and Mail* (6 November 1999).

30. *Ibid.*

31. Rebecca Brown, cited in *ibid.*

32. See Cynthia Good, "The Triumph of Ideas," *Quill & Quire* 66:4 (April 2000), p. 22.

Chapter Seven: Notes from the Underground

1. Stephen Duncombe, *Notes From Underground: Zines and the Politics of Alternative Culture* (New York: Verso, 1997), pp. 174-181.
2. Corey Frost, personal correspondence (December 1999–January 2000).
3. On subcultures, see Stanley Cohen, *Folk Devils and Moral Panics: The Creation of the Mods and Rockers* (London: Basil Blackwell, 1972); and especially Dick Hebdige, *Subculture: The Meaning of Style* (London: Methuen, 1979).
4. Hal Niedzviecki, *Smell It* (Toronto: Coach House Books, 1998).
5. Hal Niedzviecki, "Independent Minds," *Canadian Bookseller* (February 1999), pp. 8-11.
6. Nick Pashley, trade bookbuyer for the University of Toronto Bookstore, cited in *ibid.,* pp. 8-11.
7. Andy Brown, "Uncovering the Book," *Broken Pencil* 8 (Winter, 1999), pp. 14-17.
8. Lance Blongren, cited in *ibid.,* pp. 14-17.
9. Blain Kyllo, cited in *Ibid.,* pp. 14-17.
10. Judith Isherwood, personal correspondence (December 1999–January 2000).
11. Simon Dardick, personal correspondence (December 1999–January 2000).
12. Beth Follett, personal correspondence (December 1999–January 2000).
13. Corey Frost, personal correspondence (December 1999–January 2000).
14. Brian Kaufman, personal correspondence (December 1999–January 2000).
15. Mike O'Connor, personal correspondence (December 1999–January 2000).
16. Tim Inkster, personal correspondence (December 1999–January 2000).
17. Brown, "Uncovering the Book," pp. 14-17.
18. Mike O'Connor, personal correspondence (December 1999–January 2000).
19. Darren Wershler-Henry, cited in Hal Niedzviecki, "Independent Minds," pp. 8-11.
20. Vern Smith, cited in *ibid.,* pp. 8-11.
21. David Lester, cited in *ibid.,* pp. 8-11.
22. Corey Frost, personal correspondence (December 1999–January 2000).
23. Brown, "Uncovering the Book," pp. 14-17.
24. Corey Frost, cited in *ibid.,* pp. 14-17.

25. Mike O'Connor, cited in *ibid.*, pp. 14-17. This theme ran through much of my correspondence with small presses. Andy Brown: "For me it has to do with the love of the object of the book, wanting to explore what a book is besides just pages and binding. We publish people, not books." Brian Kaufman: "But pleasure reading, to me, is bound up (literally) in the tactile (paper/ink) and the visual (type/design) form of The Book." Beth Follett: "The world turns, let there be novelty, but for my money, and I mean this rather literally, give me the artifact called *book*."

26. Joe Blades, personal correspondence (December 1999–January 2000).

27. Judith Isherwood, personal correspondence (December 1999–January 2000).

28. Beth Follett , personal correspondence (December 1999–January 2000).

29. Heather Haley, personal correspondence (December 1999–January 2000).

30. Corey Frost, personal correspondence (December 1999–January 2000).

31. Joe Blades, personal correspondence (December 1999–January 2000).

32. Beth Follett, personal correspondence (December 1999–January 2000).

33. Mike O'Connor, personal correspondence (December 1999–January 2000).

34. Brian Kaufman, personal correspondence (December 1999–January 2000). Kaufman adds: "My opinion (and I hope I'm wrong) is that all the new e-world products (video games/Internet etc.) have captivated [young people] with the splashy graphics, the apparent sexiness of it all. Though my take on most web-zines I have looked at is that there may be pizazz, but very little good content. Personally, I think school curriculums have to have some major overhauls, updating, to make literature relevant to the current youth generation. My feeling it is that it is the educational institutions who have to take this challenge on. They have to emphasize the importance of literature and art as much as any other subject. We as publishers work hard and long hours to put inspiring, evocative, challenging, educational work into the market, but there it is much work to be done to create and enhance the appetite for the work of Canadian authors."

35. Judith Isherwood, personal correspondence (December 1999–January 2000).

36. Corey Frost, personal correspondence (December 1999–January 2000).

37. Corey Frost, personal correspondence (December 1999–January 2000). Frost adds: "Our print runs are very small—usually no more than

200—and the books are sold at performance events (launches, spoken word shows), in independent bookstores that have special sections for chapbooks, or at small-press exhibitions. The people who buy them are usually writers, spoken word audiences (young, urban, artsy types, needless to say), or chapbook collectors."

38. Simon Dardick, personal correspondence (December 1999–January 2000).

39. Judith Isherwood, personal correspondence (December 1999–January 2000).

40. Mike O'Connor, personal correspondence (December 1999–January 2000).

41. Tim Inkster, personal correspondence (December 1999–January 2000).

42. Michael Harrison, personal correspondence (January 2000). Harrison added: "The best way to foster Canadian literature would be massively support education in the humanities and social sciences at all levels. Given the almost universal view that education is something that you fill students up with and that it needs to lead directly to a job, I very much doubt to see this anytime soon."

43. Michael Harrison, cited in Carol Toller, "Seeking Allies for the ACP" *Quill & Quire* 6:2 (February 2000), p. 20.

44. Joe Blades, personal correspondence (December 1999–January 2000).

45. Corey Frost, personal correspondence (December 1999–January 2000).

46. Judith Isherwood, personal correspondence (December 1999–January 2000).

47. Beth Follett, personal correspondence (December 1999–January 2000).

48. Joe Blades, personal correspondence (December 1999–January 2000).

49. Hal Niedzviecki, personal correspondence (December 1999–January 2000).

BIBLIOGRAPHY

Adams, Michael. *Sex in the Snow: Canadian Social Values at the End of the Millennium*. Toronto: Viking/Penguin, 1997.

Aleff, Andy. "Research Finds Kids Do Read Newspapers: But They Have As Many Complaints About Them As Adults," *Bulletin of the American Society of Newspaper Editors* 766 (March 1995).

"Amazon.com Knocking on Ottawa's Door," *Just The Fax* (Association of Canadian Publishers) 10:25 (29 June 2000).

Amey, L. J. "Information Seeking Activities of Adolescents of Different Socio-Economic Classes in a Canadian Urban Centre." Ph.D. dissertation, University of Toronto, 1981.

Angus, Douglas E. and Owen A. Charlebois. *Consumer Sensitivity to Increases in Book Prices*. Ottawa: Coopers and Lybrand, 1986.

Anisef, Paul and Paul Axelrod, eds. *Transitions: Schooling and Employment in Canada*. Toronto: Thompson, 1993.

Askew, Kim. "I'd Buy That for a Dollar: Thousands Download Stephen King's *The Plant*," *Quill & Quire Insiders' Report* 1:26 (25 July 2000).

Astor, David. "More Features For Younger Readers," *Publisher & Editor* 125:47 (21 November 1992).

Atwood, Margaret. *Survival: A Thematic Guide to Canadian Literature*. Toronto: Anansi, 1972.

Audley, Paul. *Canada's Cultural Industries: Broadcasting, Publishing, Records and Film*. Toronto: Lorimer, 1983.

Baird, Jean. "Send More Shoes," *Quill & Quire* (February 1997).

Baker, John F. "Canada: If You Can Make It Here, You'll Make It Anywhere," *Publishers Weekly* 245:21 (25 May 1998).

_____. "Northern Lights," *Publishers Weekly* 246:22 (31 May 1999).

_____. "Younger Book Customers Buying More: PW Survey," *Publishers Weekly* (2 June 1998).

Barnhurst, Kevin G. and Ellen Wartella, "Newspapers and Citizenship: Young Adults' Subjective Experience of Newspapers," *Critical Studies in Mass Communication* 8:2 (June 1991).

Beauchesne, Eric. "School Costs More, Pays Less, Study Says," *National Post* (22 February 2000).

Ben-Gera, Michel and Brian L. Kinsley. *Library and Bookstore Use in Canada.* Ottawa: Secretary of State, 1980.

"Ben Wicks' Born to Read: Literacy Begins at Home," *Maclean's* 108:17 (24 April 1995).

Berger, Paula S. "Teaching About Teen Suicide Using Young-Adult Novels," *Education Digest* 52:48 (April 1987).

Bethune, Brian and Diane Turbide. "The Kidlit Boom," *Maclean's* 108:50 (11 December 1995).

Bibby, Reginald W. *The Bibby Report: Social Trends Canadian Style.* Toronto: Stoddart, 1995.

Bibby, Reginald W. and Donald C. Posterski. *Teen Trends: A Nation in Motion.* Toronto: Stoddart, 1992.

Bloom, Allan. *The Closing of the American Mind.* New York: Simon and Schuster, 1987.

Blostein, Fay. *Invitations, Celebrations: A Handbook of Ideas and Techniques for Promoting Reading in Junior and Senior High Schools.* Toronto: Ontario Library Association, 1980.

"Borrowing Technology from the Music World," *Fiction Writer* (February 2000).

Brown, Andy. "Uncovering the Book," *Broken Pencil* 8 (Winter, 1999).

Calamai, Peter, ed. *Broken Words: Why Five Million Canadians are Illiterate.* Ottawa: Southam News, 1987. Posted at www.nald.ca.

"Canada's Children Deserve Better," *Toronto Star* (20 November 1999).

"Canadian Publishing Surprised by M&S Transfer to University of Toronto, Sale to Random House," *Just The Fax* (Association of Canadian Publishers) 10:25 (29 June 2000).

Carey, Elaine. "More Adult Offspring Live at Parents' Homes," *Toronto Star* (12 March 1999).

Claunch, Beverley and Patricia Nutt. "Non-Readers are Made, Not Born: Sixteen Ways to Turn Off a Reader," *English Journal* 76 (January 1987).

Cohen, Stanley. *Folk Devils and Moral Panics: The Creation of the Mods and Rockers*. London: Basil Blackwell, 1972.

Cole, Wendy. "How to Make a Better Student," *Time Canada* (19 October 1998).

Collins, James and S.C. Gwynne. "How Johnny Should Read," *Time Canada* 150:17 (27 October 1997).

Conlogue, Ray. "CanLit Gets Shot in the Arm as Thomas Allen Shows It Cares," *Globe and Mail* (14 February 2000).

Conway, John F. *The Canadian Family in Crisis*. Toronto: Lorimer, 1993.

Cooper, Brian. "Just Give Them What They Want (How Newspapers Can Attract Young People)," *Bulletin of the American Society of Newspaper Editors* 768 (May-June 1995).

Craig, Susanne. "Black Plans Newspaper Sell-off," *Globe and Mail* (26 April 2000).

Crawley, Devin. "Canada Book Day Gives Book Buyers a Break," *Quill & Quire* 66:3 (March 2000).

_____ . "Poetry Month Courts New Image," *Quill & Quire* 66:4 (April 2000).

Currie, Dawn H. *Girl Talk: Adolescent Magazines and their Readers*. Toronto: University of Toronto Press, 1998.

Dabydeen, Cyril. "Places We Come From: Voices of Caribbean Canadian Writers (In English) and Multicultural Contexts," *World Literature Today* 73:2 (Spring 1999).

Danesi, Marcel. *Cool: The Signs and Meanings of Adolescence*. Toronto: University of Toronto Press, 1994.

Dickinson, Paul and Jonathan Ellison. "Plugged in into the Internet," *Canadian Social Trends* 55 (Ottawa: Statistics Canada, Winter 1999).

Doob, Anthony N., *et al. Youth Crime and the Youth Justice System in Canada: A Research Perspective*. Toronto: University of Toronto Centre of Criminology, 1995.

Drotner, Kirsten. "Youthful Media Cultures: Challenges and Chances for Librarians," *Papers of the 64th IFLA General Conference* (16-21 August 1998).

Duncombe, Stephen. *Notes From Underground: Zines and the Politics of Alternative Culture*. New York: Verso, 1997.

Duxbury, Nancy. *The Reading and Purchasing Public: The Market for Trade Books in English Canada 1991.* Toronto: Association of Canadian Publishers, 1995.

Elash, Anita. "An Industry in Bloom: Canadian Publishers Prepare to Put an End to Hard Times," *Maclean's* 110:36 (8 September 1997).

Emberley, Peter C. *Zero Tolerance: Hot Button Politics in Canada's Universities.* Toronto: Penguin, 1996.

Epstein, Jonathon S., ed. *Youth Culture: Identity in a Post-Modern World.* Oxford: Blackwell, 1998.

Evans, Gwynneth. "From Author to Reader: Trends in Literacy and Reading in Canada and Internationally," *National Library News* 31:1 (January 1999).

Evans, Mark. "Webcasting to Shake Up Internet, Study Says," *Globe and Mail* (1 May 2000).

Ferguson, Sarah. "The Punks of Publishing," *Village Voice* (30 June–6 July 1999).

Fitzgerald, Mark. "Connecting with Kids (Newspapers Reach Children through Online Editions)," *Editor & Publisher* 130:12 (22 March 1997).

"Former premier to lobby Ottawa for Amazon.com" *National Post* (23 June 2000).

Foster, Peter. "E Canada, Our Home and Native LAN," *National Post* (19 Januray 2000).

Fulford, Robert, David Godfrey, Abraham Rotstein, eds. *Read Canadian: A Book about Canadian Books.* Toronto: James, Lewis & Samuel, 1972.

Fulford, Robert. "The Young in History's Stream: Generation X and the Survival of Tradition," (Lecture presented at the University of Chicago, 16–18 May 1997. Typescript posted at www.robertfulford.com.)

Gallaway, Burt and Joe Hudson, eds. *Youth in Transition: Perspectives on Research and Policy.* Toronto: Thompson, 1996.

Galt, Virginia. "Alarm Raised Over Students Behaving Badly," *Globe and Mail* (15 September 1999).

Garton, James. "New Genres and New Literacies: The Challenge of the Virtual Curriculum." *Australian Journal of Language and Literacy* 20:3 (August 1997).

Gatehouse, Jonathan. "Pamela Wallin Offers Between-the-Covers Advice," *National Post* (8 March 2000).

Gaultney, Bruce. "'Totally Teen' Can Be Totally a Turn-Off," *Bulletin of the American Society of Newspaper Editors* 766 (March 1995).

_____. "Young Writers May Help Reach Young Readers—But They Require Special Handling," *Bulletin of the American Society of Newspaper Editors* 766 (March 1995).

Gibbon, Ann. "The Catch-22 of Working with Chapters," *Globe and Mail* (24 April 2000).

Good, Cynthia. "The Triumph of Ideas," *Quill & Quire* 66:4 (April 2000).

Government Expenditures on Culture. Ottawa: Statistics Canada, October 1999.

Graham, Alberta. "Should Kids Read Goosebumps? No," NEA *Today* 16:3 (October 1997).

Granatstein, J. L. *Who Killed Canadian History?* Toronto: HarperCollins, 1998.

Graves, Frank L. and Timothy Dugas. *Reading in Canada 1991.* Ottawa: Ekos Research Associates Inc., 1991.

Gregory, Sophfronia Scott. "Page Turners," *People* 51:11 (29 March 1999).

Grossberg, Lawrence. *We Gotta Get Out of This Place: Popular Conservatism and Postmodern Culture.* New York and London: Routledge, 1992.

Gutstein, Donald. *E.con: How the Internet Undermines Democracy.* Toronto: Stoddart, 1999.

Halstead, Ted. "A Politics For Generation X," *Atlantic Monthly* (August 1999).

Halvari, Hallgeir and Cheryl White, "Effects of Reading Motivation on the Belief in and Consumption of Newspapers Among Youth," *Psychological Reports* 81:3 (December 1997).

Hammond, Karen. "Indie Author Goes It Alone for Second Novel," *Quill & Quire* 66:4 (April 2000).

Hansen, Mark Victor, Kimberly Kirberger, Jack Canfield. *Chicken Soup for the Teenage Soul: 101 Stories of Life, Love & Learning.* New York: Health Communications, 1997. (Also reviews of *Chicken Soup for the Teenage Soul.* Posted at www.chapters.ca, March 2000.)

Hebdige, Dick. *Subculture: The Meaning of Style.* London: Methuen, 1979.

Hepburn, Allan. "Urban Kink: Canadian Fiction Shakes Off Its Rural Roots," *Quill & Quire* 66:4 (April 2000).

Human Resources Development Canada. "Literacy Skills of Canadian Youth," HRDC *Bulletin* 4:1 (Winter Spring 1998).

Hussey, Valerie. "TV, Toys and Other Tie-ins," *Quill & Quire* 66:4 (April 2000).

Jack, Ian. "Chapters Investigated on Book Marketing Share," *National Post* (25 February 2000).

_____ . "Bound and Gagged: Small Fry Scared to Squeal on Chapters," *National Post* (8 March 2000).

_____ . "Ottawa Should Consider Letting U.S. Book Superstores into Canada, Liberal Says," *National Post* (14 April 2000).

Jones, Patrick. *Connecting Young Adults and Libraries: A How-to-do-it Manual*. New York: Neal-Schuman Inc., 1992.

Kerr, Don, *et al. Children and Youth: An Overview*. Ottawa: Statistics Canada/ Prentice-Hall Canada, 1994.

Ketter, William B. "Market-Driven Editorial Content—How Viable?" *Editor & Publisher* 127:42 (15 October 1994).

Kingsmill, Suzanne and Benjamin Schlesinger. *The Family Squeeze: Surviving the Sandwich Generation*. Toronto: University of Toronto Press, 1998.

Kinsella, Bridget. "Coach House Closes, Blames Government Cuts," *Publisher's Weekly* (22 July 1996).

_____ . "Publishing 2000," *Fiction Writer* (February 2000).

Kirn, Walter and William Dowell. "Rediscovering the Joy of Text," *Time Canada* 149:16 (21 April 1997).

Klein, Naomi. "Why Slacker Mags Suck: Because They're Editorially Vapid," *Ryerson Review of Journalism* (Spring 1996).

Knight, Graham. Review of Sarah Course, *Nationalism and Literature, Canadian Review of Sociology and Anthropology* 36:1 (February 1999).

"Labour Market Polarization . . . What's Going On?" HRDC *Applied Research Bulletin* 2:2 (Summer-Fall 1998).

Laver, Ross. "The 'Lost Generation'," *Maclean's* 110:22 (2 June 1997).

Lecker, Robert. *Making it Real: The Canonization of English-Canadian Literature*. Toronto: House of Anansi, 1995.

Levinson, Paul. *The Soft Edge: A Natural History and Future of the Information Revolution*. New York and London: Routledge, 1997.

Leyton, Elliott. "A Generation No Better, No Worse," *Globe and Mail* (21 April 2000).

Lincoln, Clifford, *et al. The Challenge of Change: A Consideration of the Canadian Book Industry*. Ottawa: Standing Committee on Canadian Heritage, June 2000.

Lindsay, Colin, *et al. Youth in Canada*, Second Edition. Ottawa: Statistics Canada, 1994.

List, S.K. "The Right Place To Find Children," *American Demographic* 14:2 (February 1992).

Litt, Paul. *The Muses, The Masses and The Massey Commission*. Toronto: University of Toronto Press, 1992.

Lorimer, Rowland. "Opening New Chapters in the Book Wars," *Globe and Mail* (28 February 2000).

_____ . "Book Publishing in Canada," Vancouver: Canadian Centre For Studies and Publishing, 1995 (posted at www.harbour.sfu.ca).

Lorinc, John. "Children's Bookstore Closes After 25 Years," *Quill & Quire* (February 2000).

_____ . "Internet Sales Skyrocket," *Quill & Quire* 6:2 (February 2000).

Macfarlane, David. "This Generation—My Generation—is Losing Something More Than Youth. It's Losing the Places of Summer," *Globe and Mail* (15 May 2000).

Males, Mike A. *The Scapegoat Generation: America's War on Adolescents.* Maine: Common Courage Press, 1996.

Marchand, Philip. "What I Really Think About Margaret Laurence, Michael Ondaatje, Margaret Atwood, Timothy Findley, and the Rest of the CanLit Crowd," *Saturday Night* 112:8 (October 1997).

Maynard, Rona. "A Forum For Teens," *Chatelaine* 69:4 (April 1996).

McFarlin, Diane. "Young People Don't See Themselves As Part of the Newspaper Reading 'Club'," *Bulletin of the American Society of Newspaper Editors* 757 (March 1994).

McLaren, Leah. "A Change of Scene," *Globe and Mail* (6 November 1999).

McLean, Candis. "Why Johnny's Reading is Getting Even Worse: A Hidebound Education Monopoly is Blamed for the Rising Tide of Illiteracy," *Alberta Report* 25:29 (6 July 1998).

Morris, Chris. "The Dumbing Down of Canada's Universities," *Toronto Star* (26 February 2000).

National Library of Canada. "Young Authors Add to Canada's Published Heritage," *National Library News* 29:3/4 (March/April 1997).

National Library of Canada. "Canada's Major National Literary Awards" (posted at www.nlc-bnc.ca).

Neale, John. "Betting On An E-book Future," *Quill & Quire* 66:4 (April 2000).

Niedzviecki, Hal. "Independent Minds," *Canadian Bookseller* (February 1999).

_____ . ed. *Concrete Forest: The New Fiction of Urban Canada.* Toronto: McClelland and Stewart, 1998.

_____ . *Smell It.* Toronto: Coach House Books, 1998.

Nikiforuk, Andrew and Deborrah Howes. "Why Schools Can't Teach," *Saturday Night* 110:7 (September 1995).

Olijnyk, Zena. "Digital Book to Make Debut at Chapters," *Financial Post* (17 February 2000).

_____ . "Indie Bookseller Takes on Book Chains," *Financial Post* (13 March 2000).

_____ . "This is What it Must Feel Like to be Operated On," *National Post* (7 March 2000).

Olive, David. "The Best Days of the Web are Yet to Come: And the Net Mania has Given Print a New Vitality," *Financial Post* (14 April 2000).

Perrin, Burt. *How to Engage Youth in Literacy: Lessons Learned from an Evaluation of a Cluster of Youth and Literacy Projects.* Paper presented to The Literacy and Youth Cluster Steering Committee (12 October 1998).

Picard, Andre. "B.C. Teenagers Defy Reckless Stereotype," *Globe and Mail* (28 September 1999).

Picot, Garnett. *What is Happening to Earnings Inequalities and Youth Wages in the 1990s?* Ottawa: Statistics Canada, July 1998.

Potter, Mitch and Betsy Powell. "Agonizing over Ecstasy," *Toronto Star* (20 November 1999).

Probst, Robert E. "Adolescent Literature and the English Curriculum," *English Journal* 76:26 (March 1987).

"Profile of Book Publishing and Executive Agency in Canada, 1991-2 to 1994-5 and 1996-7." Ottawa: Statistics Canada, n.d.

Raugust, Karen. "TV Tie-ins Target Teen and Preteen Girls," *Publishers Weekly* 245:3 (19 January 1998).

Reading, Bill. *The University in Ruins.* Cambridge: Harvard University Press, 1996.

Reed, Arthea J.S. *Comics to Classics: A Parent's Guide to Books for Teens and Preteens.* Delaware: International Reading Association, 1988.

Report of a Survey of Book Reading among Canadians. Montreal: Data Laboratories Research Consultants, 1978.

Reynolds, Simon. *Generation Ecstasy: Into the World of Techno and Rave Culture.* New York: Routledge, 1999.

Riggan, William. "Of Obstacles, Survival, and Identity: On Contemporary Canadian Literature," *World Literature Today* 73:2 (Spring 1999).

Ross, Val. "Canada Council Finally Tuning Into the New Media: Goodbye Gutenberg," *Globe and Mail* (2 March 1999).

Rutherford, Paul. *When Television Was Young: Prime Time Canada 1952-1967.* Toronto: University of Toronto Press, 1990.

Ruttenberg, Danya. "Taming The Paper Tiger: The Book Industry Roars Online," *E Business Magazine* (November 1998).

Said, Edward. "Opponents, Audiences, Constituencies, and Community," *Critical Inquiry* 9 (1982).

Schiller, Bill. "Extra! War Heats Up for Newspaper Readers," *Toronto Star* (23 October 1999).

Schissel, Bernard. *Blaming Children: Youth Crime, Moral Panics and the Politics of Hate*. Halifax: Fernwood, 1997.

Seay, Ellen A. "Opulence to Decadence: The Outsiders and Less Than Zero," *The English Journal* 76:69 (October 1987).

See, Lisa. "Appealing to Urban Teens," *Publishers Weekly* 230:21 (November 1986).

Shalla, Vivian and Grant Schellenberg. *The Value of Words: Literacy and Economic Security in Canada*. Ottawa: Statistics Canada, May 1998.

Simmons, Dale. "Read Up On It: Looking Forward to the Next Ten Years," *National Library News* 30:9 (September 1998).

Slopen, Beverley. "Brighter Times Ahead for Canada?" *Publishers Weekly* 245:21 (25 May 1998).

Statistics Canada. *Inequalities in Literacy Skills among Youth in Canada and the United States*. Ottawa: Statistics Canada, 22 September 1999.

Statistics Canada. *National Longitudinal Survey of Children and Youth: Transition into Adolescence*. Ottawa: Statistics Canada, 6 July 1999.

Stevenson, Mark. "Youth Unemployment Lowest in Almost 10 Years, Labour Market Survey Shows More Living at Home," *National Post* (24 December 1999).

Stoffman, Judy. "Children's Bookstore: The Final Chapter," *Toronto Star* (15 January 2000).

Survey of Young People's Reading Interests. Toronto: Toronto Public Libraries, 1976.

"Survey Reads Canadian Adults," *National Library News* 29:9 (September 1996).

Tapscott, Don. *Growing up Digital: The Rise of the Net Generation*. New York: McGraw-Hill, 1998.

Taylor, G. "The Serene Teens," *Maclean's* (15 April 1991).

"This Just In" (advertisement), *Quill & Quire* 6:2 (February 2000).

Thomas, Adele, ed. *Family Literacy in Canada: Profiles of Effective Practices*. (Welland: Editions Soleil, 1998).

Toller, Carol. "Chapters Launches Digital Delivery," *Quill & Quire* 66:4 (April 2000).

Tuck, Simon. "AutoSkills Reads Into Future of Educational Software," *Globe and Mail* (16 December 1999).

Turbide, Diane. "Increasing Their Word Power: Authors and Readers Flock to Literary Love-ins," *Maclean's* 110:44 (3 November 1997).

Vipond, Mary. *The Mass Media in Canada*. Toronto: Lorimer, 1992.

Watson, Kenneth F. *Leisure Reading Habits*. Ottawa: Infoscan, 1980.

Webber, Marlene. *Street Kids: The Tragedy of Canada's Runaways*. Toronto: University of Toronto Press, 1991.

Weiler, Derek. "An Elusive Gold Mine: Online Book Marketing Still Shows More Promise Than Return," *Quill & Quire* 66:4 (April 2000).

_____. "Pegasus Buys Children's Wholesaler," *Quill & Quire* 66:2 (February 2000).

_____. "Toy Story: In the Lucrative Licensing Business, Canadian Publishers are Mostly Stuck on the Sidelines," *Quill & Quire* 65:10 (October 1999).

Wershler-Henry, Darren. "A Manifesto for Electronic Publishing in Canada," *Quill & Quire* 66:3 (March 2000).

Willms, J. Douglas. *International Adult Literacy Survey: Inequalities in Literacy Skills Among Youth in Canada and the United States*. Ottawa: Statistics Canada, September 1999.

_____. *Literacy Skills of Canadian Youth*. Ottawa: Statistics Canada, September 1997.

Wood, Leonard A. "How Teenage Book Tastes Change," *Publishers Weekly* 230:22 (August 1986).

_____. "Teenage Book Buying Matches Adult Purchasing," *Publishers Weekly* 230:25 (July 1986).

Wright, Robert. "Dream, Comfort, Memory, Despair: Canadian Popular Musicians and the Dilemma of Nationalism, 1968-72," *Journal of Canadian Studies* 22:4 (Winter 1987-8); reprinted in Diamond and Witmer, eds., *Canadian Music: Issues and Identity* (Toronto: Canadian Scholars' Press, 1994).

_____. "Historical Underdosing: Pop Demography and the Crisis in Canadian History," *Canadian Historical Review* 81:1 (December 2000).

_____. "I'd Sell You Suicide: Pop Music and Moral Panic in the Age of Marilyn Manson," *Popular Music* 19:3 (Autumn, 2000).

_____. "Reading Canadian: Youth, Book Publishing and the National Question," (Ottawa: Department of Heritage, 2000).

INDEX

MEMBER OF THE SCABRINI GROUP

Quebec, Canada
2001